Making a Living
While Making a Difference

Making a
Living While
Making a
Difference

A Guide to
Creating Careers
with a Conscience

Melissa Everett

Bantam Books

New York   Toronto   London   Sydney   Auckland

MAKING A LIVING WHILE MAKING A DIFFERENCE

A Bantam Book/August 1995

Library of Congress Cataloging-in-Publication Data

Everett, Melissa.

Making a living while making a difference : a guide to creating
careers with a conscience / by Melissa Everett.

p.   cm.

Includes bibliographical references.

ISBN 0-553-37410-9

1. Vocational guidance.   2. Work ethic.   3. Professional
ethics.

4. Job satisfaction.   5. Social values.   I. Title.

HF5381.E853   1995

331.7′02—dc20   95-7410
                                                      CIP

ISBN 0-553-37410-9

Published simultaneously in the United States and Canada

Bantam Books are published by Bantam Books, a division of Bantam
Doubleday Dell Publishing Group, Inc. Its trademark, consisting of
the words "Bantam Books" and the portrayal of a rooster, is
Registered in U.S. Patent and Trademark Office and in other
countries. Marca Registrada. Bantam Books, 1540 Broadway, New
York, New York 10036.

Contents

Part Three: Afterthoughts / 281

Making a Living
While Making a Difference

Introduction:
An Expanded
Work Ethic

In the early 1980s, Nick Wilson was a science teacher. Now he has a profitable cottage industry recycling toner cartridges for laser printers and is able to enjoy the collaboration of his entire family in this home-based business.

Penny Barrows worked as an outplacement consultant during much of the '80s, helping hordes of angry, confused, laid-off middle managers search for options that didn't seem to exist. Now she is helping to create those options, as a business consultant, by promoting trade and sustainable economic development in Vietnam.

Jimmy Capelano served time in prison in the 1980s. Now he is a trainer in stress management and violence prevention.

This is a book about career security in a very strange era, and about people who have changed their lives to achieve it in refreshing new ways. In business, government, and nonprofits, in large organizations and cottage industries alike, people like these are making their lives work and making their work count for something in the world. They are taking a fresh look at their values and the opportunities for making a significant contribution through their work. Instead of focusing only on where the jobs are now, and second-guessing the ever-changing predictions of anonymous experts, they look for the most pressing needs and find or create work of genuine value there.

An Emerging Social Sector

In spite of all the chaos and pain, many people are doing much more than surviving. A remarkable shadow economy is emerging into the light. It is made up of people and organizations that are creatively redefining their work by taking the world they live in seriously, gaining new survival skills as a result. With disarray of epic proportions around them, they are builders. They may be bringing a stronger ethical vision into business, new ideas and openness into government, or fresh approaches to human services. They may be cleaning up the environment—a business that in 1993 included 70,000 companies with over $130 billion in sales.[1] They may be handling investments screened for social and environmental responsibility, worth more than $630 billion in the late 1980s.[2] They may be promoting holistic health care alternatives, which over half of U.S. people say they've used at one time or another.[3] They may be educators or advocates in the nonprofit sector, whose diverse institutions represent 10 percent of the economy. They may be challenging abuses of power in decaying institutions, or creating new workplaces that reflect a more hopeful view of human potential. They are doing what's needed, mending what's broken, and preserving what's precious to them.

Some of the most interesting bursts of creativity are in business. Consider Merck, the pharmaceuticals giant, which made an agreement with Costa Rica's forest ministry to hold a massive area of rain forest in trust in exchange for the exclusive right to sustainably develop medical products from it; the Sun Company and General Motors, the first large corporations to sign the CERES Principles of environmental accountability; companies like Springfield Remanufacturing and QuadGraphics, which take the principles of open information and worker self-management to new levels; Levi Strauss, which is dedicating itself to breaking the "glass ceiling" for women and minorities in corporate management and has developed a revolutionary new global sourcing code to promote environmental protection and attention to human rights; and over 2,000 growing social ventures such as Stonyfield Farm Yogurt, which buys its milk only from New England family farmers to support sustainable agriculture.

Many of these once-isolated alternatives are now growing together into a social and environmental sector with self-awareness and the beginnings of coordination. This sector encompasses business, non-profits, and government. It has organizations such as Businesses for Social Responsibility, an "alternative chamber of commerce," and its campus affiliate, Students for Responsible Business. It has a research arm of sorts, represented by groups such as the International Society for Ecological Economics and the Council on Economic Priorities. This emerging sector even has a presence in the military, as troops find an expanding role in peacekeeping and disaster relief and as the Army Corps of *Environmental* Engineers claims a role in ecological restoration.

These institutions are not utopias. But they have departed significantly from earlier ideas about what's possible. They have embraced social and environmental values, as well as personal ones, and have integrated these into a vision of what their work is about. By virtue of that strategy, not in spite of it, they have won visibility and credibility, and have preserved jobs in the process.

Today, the people who want to build their careers on a humane vision are a swelling majority. According to 1993 research by *Working Woman* magazine and the Roper organization, 86 percent of a sample of working adults agreed (59 percent strongly) that they would prefer to "make an adequate living doing work that makes the world a better place, instead of just making a lot of money."[4] People who saw themselves as most successful were characterized by a "people-centered view," with an emphasis on family, community, spirituality, and control of their time. What's more, more than half the sample (53 percent) said their definition of success had changed in the last five years. These findings do not add up to any one simple definition of good work. But they signal a strong commitment to living out the questions that matter.

Fulfillment, integrity, and contribution are the major ingredients of what I call an expanded work ethic. This ethic must rekindle trust and ensure quality, allow for quality of work life and fair compensation, and pay attention to social and environmental responsibility as a natural outgrowth of conscientious performance, not a separate realm.

This book is a manual—and a manifesto—for everyone who is attracted to an expanded work ethic. It will help you to craft your career to work with the realities of the current labor market, adding value and increasing your security in organizations worthy of your commitment. This book will not put forth any simple view of the work to be done or the ethics of work, but will encourage you to expand your contribution and minimize the harmful side effects of your activities, in your own eyes, in an open, continuous way. It will engage you in dialogue. It offers exercises that you can use by yourself or with friends, in "everyday consciousness" or as meditations. At times, it will send you out to explore the world around you for new ideas. It provides you with worksheets, some of which you might want to photocopy for multiple use. It is a workbook and a storybook, a research guide and a personal report.

A Value-Based Strategy

More powerfully than ever, our personal and collective security depends on the values that are reflected in the daily work we do. Value-driven enterprises of all kinds are taking on a critical role as human economies shift into the realm of information and services, where far-reaching value judgments underlie every choice. At the same time, humanity's relationship with the global life-support system is entering a critical phase. Not only our comfort but arguably our survival depends on realigning economic activity with shared values.

To accomplish this, many of us will have to turn a cherished assumption about work upside down. It's the assumption that there is a trade-off between security and fulfillment—that there are "dream jobs" and "realistic jobs," and that they're rarely the same. And most of us, at one time or another, have had to face up to a mismatch between the available jobs and the "real work" we would like to be doing for community, society, or the environment.

In the interest of security, many of us have settled. But we have not gained security. Quite the opposite. In the first half of 1993 alone, more than 100,000 jobs were lost in major downsizings in the most ostensibly secure, well-established, and respected companies.[5] We can respond to this trend by clinging more and more tightly to whatever we have or by rethinking our assumptions at the roots and getting back in touch with what really matters.

Values, meaning, and self-knowledge are not "extras" in life; they are the organizing principles for coordinated, effective actions. Management consultant Margaret Wheatley, who is something of a specialist in working with "crazy" organizations, reports that people who survive the best, personally and professionally, in situations of organizational chaos are those who find, or create, meaning in their situations, and who help others do the same.[6] A similar observation is made by Barbara Reinhold, head of the Smith College Career Development Office, who has observed that "people whose source of direction is internal rather than external, who pursue what's really important to them, do not seem to be falling off the career ladder in large numbers."

This quest can pay off tangibly, not just with warm feelings, but with effectiveness in the job search. Here is an illustration. A group of Texas Instruments middle managers whose jobs were being eliminated were invited to take part in a journal experiment.[7] Three groups were asked to keep a journal, each in a different way. One group wrote lists of activities involved in the job search. One group wrote whatever they pleased. The third group wrote about the feelings connected with their process of transition. That group found new jobs much faster than either of the others.

As these observations suggest, being true to your values can liberate creative energy and make you more capable of finding your way intact through a tough transition. If you're going to need to struggle anyway, you might as well struggle for something that's worth your while.

Passion, as I mean it, is not always flashy. It is deep, authentic sentiment about what's important. Passion can serve as a homing device to draw you to the most humane, interesting, and enduring work situations, and give you the will to let go of those seductive "opportunities" with hidden dark sides. It charms your strengths and talents out of hiding. When cynicism and sloppiness seem to be everywhere, passion helps you maintain high standards and hang on to hope.

In talking about values, I am addressing more than everyday courtesy and decency. Every working person is part of a society and an ecosystem. Every working person makes decisions that reverberate with broad effects on fellow employees, customers, suppliers, regulators, managers, and shareholders, as well as on communities and ecologies that may or may not be represented in decision making. I believe that widespread inattention to the social meaning of work has been a major factor in producing that strange combination of drivenness and emptiness that was taken to extremes in the 1980s but has always been a strong element in Western culture. As Robert Bellah and his research team observe in *Habits of the Heart,* their study of individualism and commitment:

> The American understanding of the autonomy of the self places the burden of one's own deepest self-definitions on one's own individual choice. . . . Most of us imagine an autonomous self existing independently, entirely outside any tradition and community, and then perhaps choosing one. . . . We may assert the right to our dream of running a company or opening up a lovely little restaurant or leaving an ambitious career in midlife to go to seminary. But we expect ourselves to make all these choices without reference to the social framework, the needs we might be serving, or the struggles we might face.[8]

Conventional wisdom among psychologists and educators is that people must first deal with basic requirements for survival and comfort before they are able to appreciate the social framework. But an alternative view is emerging: that seeing our situation in social and historic terms actually opens up new possibilities for action, cooperation, and creativity. As clinical psychologist Sarah Conn, a developer of the new field of ecopsychology, observes:

> Great potential for personal empowerment can be found in attending to our awareness of global problems and to our understanding of how they connect with each other and with our personal lives.

The process of naming the danger, saying aloud that the threats to life on earth are real, moves us from the numbness of denial to the aliveness that makes action possible.[9]

To use a simple example, suppose you are unemployed due to a downsizing. A common but paralyzing response is self-blame. The realization that your life has been altered by economic and social forces (not to mention specific management decisions) allows you to recontextualize the situation and seek new options that reflect current realities. Now suppose you are facing an uncertain economic future because the field you are involved in—say, timber or fisheries—is running up against environmental limitations as it's presently practiced. If you focus on your personal situation without examining the larger context, you are likely to fight to keep your job as it is. However, if you look at the context, you just might be more likely to direct your energies toward transforming your job into a more sustainable form and lobbying for the retraining and support you and your co-workers will need during the transition.

Personal restlessness and concern about individual security are pushing many people to ask fresh questions about their working lives, but world events are also sounding a powerful wake-up call. The end of the cold war has created new understandings of national needs in a global context, one in which security has economic, social, and environmental dimensions. This means fewer jobs in the arms industry but more in environmental protection and restoration, civilian technology transfer, and ideally even conflict resolution. There is a staggering amount of work to be done to reverse the ecological crisis, public health crises such as AIDS and breast cancer, and social crises including infant mortality, illiteracy, homelessness, violence, and persistent poverty. There is work to be done on a global scale to deal with international debt, trade, and sustainable development issues. These issues affect even the most prosperous among us. As Monty Bruell, a Chattanooga building contractor who devotes himself to minority job creation and community service, reflects, "It is no longer possible to view life as a zero-sum game. You can't build a house big enough to insulate yourself from the toxic stream nearby or the violence in the streets a few miles away. The only way any of us can be secure is if we are all secure."

A Paradoxical Lesson

Many of the strategies in this book have crystallized in my mind as a result of the twists of my own career path through computer programming, journalism, research, and career consulting. I was launched into adulthood with a paralyzing contradiction implanted in my mind about work ethics. From my father, an engineer, I had gotten the message that the act of going to work, again and again, was honorable and necessary. From my mother, a homemaker, I learned that work could be satisfying and expressive as well, not just something to get done but something to enjoy. From the stream of speakers who passed through my Long Island high school, I learned that there was work to be done in the world to help people live in tolerable balance with the natural environment and each other.

I came of age convinced of the absolutely essential place of creative labor in a civilized society. At the same time, finishing high school in the midst of the deep recession of the mid-1970s, I became convinced of the impossibility for most people of finding that creative labor. That's how I became a computer programmer for a time—and a very bad one, although I lasted three years. The storm that led to my exodus from the field took the form of a labor dispute, triggered by the sudden announcement that our company would be moving south and a factory full of outraged workers would be left behind. I did not know then that I was witnessing the early phases of one of the decisive trends of the 1980s, job migration. I only knew that the whole situation felt ghastly, and I was innocent enough to think there was a better way to do business. I resigned in protest and never looked back.

During the months that followed, I took a few courses and traveled cross-country, went to lectures and dances, wrote in my journal in truck stops and read on hillsides. I got some perspective on the cynicism I had developed in only a few years of consciously choosing work that had no meaning for me. I realized that there was a direct connection between my ineffectiveness in that job and my willingness to hide most of my values for eight hours a day. As I worked with the possibilities before me, I had the distinct sense of putting my *self* together for the first time, with work as a vehicle.

As a writer, I essentially created a "sink or swim" situation for myself. I didn't do this because I was such a great adventurer, but because the money had run out by the time the decision was clear. The fact that I swam brought me face to face with an illuminating paradox. A career in management information systems, a job field known for its security and growth potential, was utterly insecure for me. A career in writing, a field notorious for its turbulence and competitiveness, has given me a decent living and a rich life. It has led me into other, complementary fields such as research, advocacy, and career counseling—all with the purpose of helping people adapt and expand themselves to play a constructive role in the social changes that are taking place. The difference between my two lives was the degree to which I was able to bring my full self into my work.

A Ten-Step Program

Over the years, I learned what worked for me and began sharing ideas with widening peer support networks. Eventually, a set of homegrown guidelines came to life as the Ten-Step Program for Principled Career Development that is described in this book. These steps are not one-shot actions, nor are they a linear sequence. They're really a series of disciplines for continuously re-creating your working life.

Before we get to the Ten-Step Program, two introductory chapters will examine the context of work. Work Beyond Jobs: Crafting a Career lays out some principles of career development and identifies high potential fields of work. Making a Living and a Difference Internationally speaks to anyone who identifies himself as an international worker, or would like to.

Next comes the program, whose steps are these:

∾ Step 1. Wake up.

The skills of self-reflection, self-promotion, self-motivation, and self-renewal all require awareness of your state of heart and mind. Simple as it sounds, learning to pay attention to yourself and the world around you is the step that opens the door to these skills.

❧ Step 2. Stabilize your life.

Here we step back from examining work directly and look at the context of your life. What's working? What gets in the way of making the changes you want and need? How can you extricate yourself from the knots in your life—whether they're financial obligations or unsupportive relationships—in order to participate fully in the quest for meaningful work?

❧ Step 3. Create a vibrant support system.

Community creates possibilities that may be far beyond the reach of isolated individuals. This chapter explores the art of identifying, and building, the supportive community you need.

❧ Step 4. Cultivate critical research skills.

Identifying options is more than information gathering; it's the art of interpreting what you see. This chapter is about research skills, strategies, and sources. It gives you a detailed introduction to important sources of information on fields of work, labor markets, and other career information; provides worksheets and suggested questions for organizing your research on opportunities; and introduces some principles of in-depth investigation of employers when their practices cause you concern.

❧ Step 5. Take a fresh look at what you have to offer.

You are more than your skills and experience. You're a human being with values, guiding principles, personality strengths, and a complex mixture of attractions and aversions to the world around you. All these affect your working options. This chapter provides a framework for self-assessment focused on your values and the ways you see yourself developing.

❧ Step 6. Identify the essence of your work in the world.

Knowing yourself and the options doesn't necessarily mean knowing what to do. This chapter is about putting the pieces together, starting with identifying the essence of the work that sustains you.

❧ Step 7. Commit yourself to doing your work in some form.

The most controversial and challenging point of this program is to shift responsibility from *them*—the creators of jobs, the hirers of people, the shapers of economic policy—and onto *you*. This chapter presents some models of patience and purpose, and identifies important skills that are required to sustain commitment.

❧ Step 8. Let go of assumptions about doing your work.

One of the strongest elements of career success stories in the 1990s is surprise. This step is about assumption busting and about the power of opening up to the unexpected.

❧ Step 9. Mine your experience for gems.

People who excel in the art of re-careering and professional development are those who use every facet of themselves—skills, life experience, character strengths and foibles, painful history. This chapter shows the value of continuous learning and the ways your splendid uniqueness can work in your favor.

❧ Step 10. Be a co-creator of the workplace you want to see.

All this would be easy if a majority of the work situations out there were of the humane, creative, sustainable variety. They're not. This chapter explores the processes of organizational change and activism to help you nudge your workplace in a positive direction, assess the risks and benefits of your initiatives, and use your political and economic power to expand your options at work.

Finally, I have included an abundance of resources—books, articles, tapes, databases, organizations, and networks—to support you as you apply these principles to your distinct situation.

If there is one central message to the Ten-Step Program, it's this: learn the art of continuous evolution, learn to love your changes, and learn to direct your evolution in the service of your highest values. That means organizing your life around the commitment to rise to opportunities, rather than around the avoidance of risk or the reaction to injustices you have suffered. It also means playing a role in creating the viable, resilient, positive organizations you want to work for.

There is work to be done. But this only sometimes translates into jobs or business opportunities. A major emphasis of this book is on ways to plant seeds of new possibility, even if you have limited resources. A second major emphasis is on getting back to basics, seeking not to have it all but to have enough and to make your life count.

A Learning Moment

If there was ever a moment to be seized, this is it. *Work matters.* It's where we earn our livelihood and find out what we can be. It's also a major arena where we participate in something outside ourselves and have most of our impact on the world around us. What's needed on a societal scale is also what's needed for individuals: to engage in the struggle to contribute through their jobs, to develop as people who can create and set priorities and lead and preserve hope. It's not about trading in our current lives for something totally different, but about living the lives we have for all they're worth.

This can be hard. But it can also be surprisingly easy. When I need a reminder of that, I think of Howard Newman, a Los Angeles engineer.[10] A pacifist, Newman did not feel comfortable working on weapons projects. He took a direct approach, typing at the bottom of his résumé NO WAR WORK. As a result, he has had a satisfying career in industries from toys to health care. Newman has never been out of work as a result of his position. But he did struggle in the beginning, wondering what the path would be like.

During that struggle, Newman did a little interview project. He tells this story: "I figured that the real experts on life's trade-offs would be people who had lived a long time and could look back, so I started talking to all the old people I could find. I asked them what they were happy about and what they regretted in their lives. I had conversations with fifty or sixty people. And with one exception—just one—they all said what they regretted were the risks they had not taken. Mistakes, failures, struggles—all those they had made peace with. Their lasting regrets were the risks, and the opportunities, they had missed."

Part One

The

Context

Work

Beyond Jobs:

Crafting a

Career

In my twenty-five years in leadership training, I have never seen a time when principles and pragmatism pointed in the same direction the way they do today.

Steven Covey

In 1994, *Fortune* magazine declared an end to the job as we know it. Author William Bridges argued that there is not just a shift in the number and distribution of jobs, but a more fundamental change: the job, as a way of organizing work, "is vanishing like a species that has outlived its evolutionary time."

There is work aplenty. But fixed jobs are less and less common as a way to organize that work. Static job descriptions are out. Continuously evolving responsibilities are in. This is just one of many simplified yet revealing prophesies about the so-called new economy in which we must all find a livelihood and create a life. Bridges goes on to observe that

> The conditions that created jobs 200 years ago—mass production and the large organization—are disappearing. Technology enables us to automate the production line, where all those job holders used to do their repetitive tasks. Instead of long production runs where the same thing has to be done again and again, we are increasingly customizing production. Big firms, where most of the good jobs used to be, are unbundling activities and farming them out to little firms, which have created or taken over profitable niches. Public services are starting to be privatized, and government bureaucracy, the ultimate bastion of job security, is being thinned. With the disappearance of the conditions that created jobs, we are losing the need to package work in that way.[1]

Most working people can remember a time when there were hierarchies that we could follow and trust. Now we must determine our own paths and create the conditions to make them viable.

Not surprisingly, the questions many of us are asking about our livelihood cut deeper than usual. We're not just deciding what to do; we're deciding how to decide. Where are the jobs? What is happening to them? What do I want to do when I grow up? How do I handle the pressures to grow up faster than I know how to, whether I'm twenty or forty or sixty? Why, when I'm inundated with self-improvement books and job listings and people cheering me on, do I feel so deeply clueless? How much stress, abuse, contradiction, and outright craziness do I need to put up with in my work or my job search? How much should I be listening to the little voice in me that (despite "reality") is raising seductive, unheard-of possibilities: starting my own business, going to seminary, becoming an activist, running for office? Even for people who are currently working, these are restless times. Everything is up for grabs.

The much-vaunted new economy isn't all new, but it has certainly proven itself to be disconcerting for the job seeker. More global in scope, the new economy is also more integrated and interdependent than ever, challenging every sort of boundary and rigid system of control; its products and services are highly experimental, feeding on innovation and favoring people who add recognizable, marketable value. While it contains as well a wide range of new organizational structures and systems for organizing work, many aspects of this economy are, unfortunately, driven by the pace of telecommunications more than by the rhythms of the human body.

Many of these new approaches to work are still being tested and refined. That means many new uncertainties and opportunities for the enterprising worker. More than half of the Fortune 500 has made some use of self-managing work teams. Individual jobs have been changed by telecommuting, job sharing, and the use of computers. Information systems give workers more responsibility for self-management and decision making but also involve a constant scrutiny of productivity and work quality. There is more and more reliance on nontraditional structures including joint ventures; public-private partnerships; "virtual corporations," or short-term alliances that are created for specific projects and limited duration; and outsourcing for services, ranging from high-tech assembly to catering to corporate management.

At the same time, ecological and social concerns are affecting business structures and practices. As human population reaches the limit of the earth's capacity, peoples are facing up to their global interdependence. China's decisions about whether to power its industrial development by coal or by solar and wind energy affects global climate and the ozone layer. Brazil's policy decisions about whether to favor rubber tappers or loggers in the rain forest have a profound impact on the forest that acts as the planet's lungs. Individual lifestyles and economic decisions affect the rates of global resource depletion and the burden of waste disposal faced by the planet as a whole.

Today, humanity's most important challenge is to realign economic activity with the needs of the ecological life-support system on which we all depend, so that we are not forever forced into no-win choices such as "development versus environment" and "jobs versus natural resources." We must find ways to organize work, as individuals and as a society, in communities and in workplaces, that are true to a vision of sustainable development. That goal is inseparable from a vision of a more equitable global society, since the greatest drains on the planet's life-support systems come from the very wealthy and the very poor. In the words of the Dalai Lama, "There are no human rights on a dying planet."[2] By the same token, there aren't too many dream jobs in an economy that is running out of control.

This linkage of economic, ecological, and social concern is no longer a minority point of view. Swiss industrialist Stephan Schmidheiny, founder of the Business Council for Sustainable Development, wrote in 1992 that continued economic development now depends on radical improvement in the interactions between business and the environment. This can only be achieved by a break with 'business as usual' mentalities and conventional wisdom, which sideline environmental and human concerns."[3]

Vice-President Albert Gore expressed similar convictions in *Earth in the Balance:* "Modern industrial civilization," he writes, "as presently organized, is colliding violently with our planet's ecological system. . . . We must make the rescue of the environment the central organizing principle for civilization," just as, in the previous era, the defeat of communism was the central principle for much of the industrialized West.[4]

Other factors make the economy-environment link hard to ignore. There are international treaties such as the one signed at the 1992 Earth Summit in Rio de Janeiro; rising financial settlements for corporate polluters, such as the $5 billion fine levied on Exxon for the *Valdez* disaster; increased use of criminal penalties for corporate environmental violators; and rising interest, among industrial leaders, in market mechanisms such as green taxes to encourage responsible resource use. No one can predict how these forces will interact. But it is not unrealistic to agree with *The Ecology of Commerce* author Paul Hawken that "we are going to see substantial environmental improvements and initiatives on the part of business in our lifetime."[5]

In business decisions and individual career planning, the tensions of these times can push managers and working people into fragmented and short-term thinking. However, many other forces are working in favor of greater independence, ethical vision, and creativity, as the stories in these pages indicate. The new economy isn't a fait accompli; it's a starting point. Its evolution depends in part on public policy. But it also depends on the innovations of employees and small businesspeople all over the planet. We all have a part to play.

Developing Your
Postmodern Career

Above all, current realities require taking total responsibility for your own next steps. The term "freelance skill merchant" sums up that approach. In his excellent new book, *We Are All Self-Employed,* Cliff Hakim describes the critical qualities for success as a mix of independence and interdependence:[6] independence in taking initiative and following through, and interdependence in working collaboratively and building alliances. What doesn't work, he emphasizes, is dependence on other people to create your future. Taking total responsibility doesn't mean working in isolation or playing the martyr in impossible situations. It means taking the lead, defining the situation for yourself, and actively cultivating skills and possibilities.

Executive career strategist John Wareham suggests that, in this era, success will come to the "tribeless warrior" who is psychologically and technologically equipped to work independently and deal with constant change.[7] Psychologically, he is self-reliant; initiative taking; comfortable with new ideas, people, and cultures; free of inhibiting prejudices; cost conscious and highly flexible. Technologically, she carries a tool kit that includes a cellular phone, computer, fax modem, and tape recorder. Wherever the action, the tribeless warrior can function there.

Wareham's term describes executives who move from home office to remote factory to speaking engagement and back to the factory, but it has a wider relevance. It applies to anyone whose work includes home-based businesses, "mosaic" careers made up of various part-time commitments, telecommuting, job sharing, or other flexible approaches. The tribeless warrior is not just a person who travels a lot, but a person who owns and carries her basic working tools and is extremely self-managing.

The tribeless warrior's world is certainly biased in favor of people who can pay for the required conveniences. But a surprising number of people outside the ranks of the elite are beginning to see themselves this way. Itinerant chefs, language teachers, apple pickers, and untenured academics all know this life.

Writer Ray Bartkowech, from the Boston suburb of Woburn, took the leap into tribeless warrior status when he left his job as editor of a town newspaper. With computer, fax modem, and tape recorder, he transformed himself into Bartkowech Copywriting and Creative Service. He can travel to a corporate site; sit in on a meeting or act as a coach or problem solver; carry out an assignment given to him at the meeting; and leave the finished product behind before returning home.

According to Bartkowech, "People always ask you how you cope with the self-employed lifestyle. But the other side of the question is how you cope with the alternative. For many of us, the moment comes when we realize that working as an employee is costing us too much. You realize it's time to go and you have your bag of tricks packed."

The tribeless warrior, like many figures in mythology, is a blend of reality and fiction. Certainly, some of the most prized capabilities among modern workers are those of this warrior: flexibility, continuous learning, problem-solving, self-organizing, stress management, superb interpersonal skills, and technological literacy. These talents, in different forms, are sought out in production workers and general managers, platoon commanders and schoolteachers. But these capabilities are insufficient without another set of strengths, those that keep the tribeless warrior from becoming rootless and amoral. These are the subject of the Ten-Step Program: mindfulness; the ability to live in balance and in community; the ability to gather information and ask critical questions, morally as well as intellectually; clear core values and well-developed sense of identity. These principles allow us to build, and rebuild, our own "tribe" of working relationships based on shared purpose and mutual assistance. Freed of the restriction of a lifelong tribal affiliation, we can be warriors for a better world only if we choose our new loyalties consciously and carefully. There are four key factors to consider in making these choices:

Transferrable skills: what you can do

Products and services: what you apply your skills to

Markets for those products and services: your clientele

Value-added: the "you" part of your job

Making a Living:
Where the Opportunities Are

Where are the jobs and business opportunities? Where are the human and environmental needs? Where do they intersect in a way that suggests a career with a positive impact? It may be true that opportunities for work are growing dramatically more fluid and less standardized, but before anyone talks about where the work opportunities are, three facts must be recognized.

First, economic forecasts are based on so many simplifying assumptions that we can't casually refer to them for guidance.

Second, jobs are more diverse and specialized than ever, and many interesting ones are outside the major, established professions and businesses.

Third, the viability and growth of particular fields of work will be shaped by choices made by working people. Creative choices today will have a significant impact on where the work is tomorrow.

So, if a field you're interested in doesn't appear in the following discussion, do *not* abandon the idea. You don't need thousands of opportunities; you need only one.[8] Your ability to target a job and to develop useful skills and contacts is just as important as the number of opportunities to choose from.

Let's look first at several areas of high projected employment growth, which contain diverse opportunities.

Management and White-Collar Professions

Shake-out or not, the Bureau of Labor Statistics predicts growth in the numbers of management jobs. However, that growth is not expected to absorb the massive numbers of competing candidates, and people with management aspirations must deal with the fact that there are fewer opportunities for generalists. Some fields that will have the greatest demand are marketing, advertising, and public relations; tourism, travel, and hotel management; tax law; labor and employment law; intellectual property law; environmental law; legal secretaries and paralegals; and forensic accounting (to protect financial systems from white-collar crime).[9]

It's worth noting that the streamlining in many organizations is proving beneficial to administrative assistants and paraprofessionals who have inherited responsibility formerly held by middle managers. Some of these jobs can be more high powered than they appear, and in many cases the scope of an administrative job is negotiable. Conversely, there's declining demand for managers of managers, and for data-tracking jobs that can be done by computers.

Computer Systems
and Office Technologies

In spite of wave after wave of shake-outs in computer manufacturing, all those zany futurists of the 1950s seem to have been right when they said computers would come into our lives and stay there. Growth continues in manufacturing and marketing, using the machines and supporting the users, as well as in setting the standards and preventing traffic jams on the information highway. There's work to be done by computer scientists and systems analysts; programmers; technical support people who help users solve problems; operators of computer-aided manufacturing systems; computer security specialists, especially those protecting networks from hackers and viruses; and by those most-loved people in many an office, the repair technicians for personal computers, copiers, and fax machines.

At the same time, the availability of computers has decreased demand for bookkeeping, word processing (as a stand-alone job), and traditional machine operating.

Telecommunications

A related industry, huge and volatile, telecom has shown both high growth and massive shakedowns. Both reflect fast technology changes, especially the shift from analog to digital that has given rise to the new generation of wireless technologies. The fiber optics revolution has vastly expanded the commercial potential of mobile cellular phones and cable TV. Rapid innovations in areas such as broadcasting, data and text transmission, and satellite communications have created high demand in engineering, marketing, sales, and customer service.

Broadcast innovation is not limited to technological developments. The major TV networks have been challenged, globally and locally, by cable TV and by independent media production houses. Program development, and especially multimedia technologies, create opportunities for people who have a little of the artist and the technician in them.

Information service is an explosive market that covers on-line information, "900" phone numbers, and directories and guidebooks for markets made possible by on-line technology.

Health Care

The great health care debate in the U.S. has considerably inhibited short-term hiring. But it's safe to predict significant need for physicians, both general and specialized; managers of health care networks and private practices; nurses, especially those with advanced-practice specialties; home health aides; geriatric specialists; physical therapists; sports medicine practitioners; nutritionists; and public health professionals. There is new interest in a range of holistic and preventive health fields, which will be discussed below.

In declining demand are administrative personnel in hospital admissions offices, pharmacies, and laboratories.

Environmental Careers

The Environmental Business Council predicted in 1992 that more than a million new environmental jobs would be created by 1996 in private industry alone.[10] That doesn't even take into account the substantial work in government, research, or advocacy. Many of these opportunities will have an international aspect—in technology transfer, environmental management and compliance, sustainable development, education, and grassroots activism.

An environmental professional can be a planner, corporate or nonprofit manager, systems analyst, technician, researcher (in lab, field, or library), lawyer, journalist, educator or trainer, mediator, PR person, regulator, or activist. Sophistication and rapid evolution of job and field are becoming the norm in environmental work. No longer are there just "environmental planners," for example; there are wetlands and floodplain planners, municipal solid waste management planners, and so on.

Service Industries

A service is anything that isn't a product: office temping or massage, language translation or landscaping. Travel and tourism, entertainment and culture, education and human services all fall into this category. Even your eight-year-old knows that much of the industrial world is shifting to a service economy, but nobody knows yet what that means exactly, and this is where things get interesting.

There are two basic types of service: physical (serving your dinner, taking your pulse, towing your car) and informational (forecasting the weather, tracking business trends, writing ad copy). A subtle but substantial battle is going on for the soul of each of them. In the information services, the battle is about democratizing or hoarding its precious commodity, information.

In the physical services, the battle is for basic dignity. At issue are wages and working conditions, which have deteriorated as services from office cleaning to component testing to food preparation are outsourced to subcontractors. There are plenty of stereotypical thankless "McJobs" in direct service, from janitorial work to fast food, but independent providers are also standing up to be counted, with nontoxic cleaning products, natural foods catering businesses, and more.

The Nonprofit Sector

There are more than 100,000 nonprofit organizations in the U.S. alone. Nonprofits include trade associations and corporate "Washington offices" (aka lobbying arms); affluent symphonies and struggling theater troupes; churches; universities; summer camps and youth groups; old-fashioned social welfare organizations like the Red Cross and the United Way; and activist groups promoting social justice and community involvement.

With the exception of political campaigning (which is illegal for tax–exempt nonprofits), just about every skill can be put to use in a nonprofit setting. These organizations absorb vast numbers of technical specialists in fields from wildlife biology to statistics to gerontology; educators, researchers, and communicators; computer applications specialists; finance people; field staff such as organizers, canvassers, and fund-raisers; and support staff. Working conditions vary, of course, but in general, the words of the Environmental Careers Organization are applicable:

> There is always too much to do in a nonprofit organization, and for survival one must learn to leave work at the office. On the positive side, nonprofit organizations encourage, even demand, that staff members stretch their creative potential to the fullest. Usually, you work on a number of projects and it is up to you to guide them to completion. Nonprofit organizations are also known for flexibility, fair treatment of employees, and promulgation of democratic principles in the workplace. If you like to take occasional sabbaticals and are a valued worker, nonprofit organizations are likely to accommodate you.[11]

Nonprofits, too, are engaged in their share of soul-searching, facing difficult questions about strategy and management, and even about their particular missions. A 1991 study of major environmental organizations pointed to a widening gulf between national leaders and local communities, and called into question the methods of many national groups that *represent* members but do not *involve* them.[12] Another study, of the eighty-five largest nonprofit organizations in the United States, found that most of them were best at providing amenities and services to the social groups that supported them financially and worst at addressing social or economic injustice.[13] The nonprofit sector also has its mainstream and its fringes. On almost any issue, you will find a minority of organizations pushing to address problems at the roots; to reach further and blend more voices into the dialogue. These can be among the most challenging, and rewarding, places to work.

Government

Not even government has escaped the drive to reassess and redesign. The U.S. National Performance Review, in the early years of the Clinton administration, was the first systematic effort to apply the principles of total quality management to the "reinvention" of government.[14] While the Review and the Republicans' midterm landslide have given rise to downsizing and hiring freezes in some federal agencies, the jobs that remain may be more interesting. That's because the budget axe is least likely to fall on the positions with the clearest tangible impact.

Government is more than national. You can work as a local transportation planner, a state literacy program coordinator, a regional water quality engineer, or an international service provider for refugees. Interesting jobs are abundant, but competition for them is high.

Making a Difference

That's the overall view. Now for the particular, the value that you can add by integrating your work with your thinking about what's needed in the world.

In what ways can a job make a difference?

The most powerful way is directly, by matching the mission of the job or organization to your own. Basically, there are five kinds of missions that signal opportunity to contribute:

1. Service. You can make a difference in an individual's life through direct assistance, from dog walking to piano tuning to legal representation. You can also make a difference in the lives of a group. For example, you can offer dog walking for bedridden senior citizens, piano tuning in historic mansions, or legal services for Haitian refugees. These provide different kinds of satisfaction, and also establish you on different paths. For instance, walking dogs for senior citizens might be a first step into geriatric social work. Walking dogs in the wealthiest neighborhood in your town might land you a job as an executive assistant.

2. *Information.* This is also a service, but is such a vast field that it deserves special attention. In print, electronic signals, or (dare we forget?) human interaction, the availability of information affects the ease or difficulty of everything we do. In military intelligence, trade secrets, satellite tracking of forest growth, or the blood type of an infant rushed into surgery, information feeds decision making and therefore change.

3. *Advocacy.* Whether for an idea, a grassroots campaign, a law, a product, a way of doing business, or an oppressed population, advocacy means taking information and putting political, social, or economic pressure on decision makers to act. A trial lawyer is an advocate; so is the test marketer who stands in the supermarket and asks you how you like today's variety of cheese. There are entire career fields, such as sales and community organizing, in which the mission is advocacy. There are also people who find ways to be effective advocates no matter what their job description says.

4. *Innovation.* Innovation means finding new ways to do things (or new things to do). Electric cars and soy burgers are technical innovations. Car pools, potlucks, and the singles-ad section of the newspaper might be called social innovations. There are also a number of "innovations" that really come down to adapting and affirming old ways: midwifery; organic agriculture; windmills. Innovation includes devising, testing, and commercializing new ideas.

5. *Sustainable economic development.* Finally, for all but the professional malcontents among us, the purpose of all this change-promotion is to find satisfaction and to contribute. A great deal of the work of the future will consist of the same old work done in new ways. That means bringing sustainability, ethics, and justice into running the supermarkets, trolleys, schools, courts, clinics, banks, department stores, brokerage firms, lumberyards—reintegrating the work we do with a tangible purpose and values.

Fields of Change

Here are some fields of work where you can make a living and a difference. All these areas are worth considering for jobs or for business start-up opportunities. This list includes functional areas that can fit into many kinds of business and nonprofit settings, as well as promising product and service fields. These are particular niches rather than general economic sectors. But most employ tens of thousands and are growing. While some are new areas, others are conventional careers with potential to guide an industry or profession in a new direction. This list isn't intended to be complete, but to suggest the range of possibilities. Many of these fields are evolving rapidly. Consult the Resources section to find starting points for research into any of these.

Adult education, seminar production, and meeting planning. All these venues allow info-preneurs to offer teaching and training, sometimes full-time and often on a part-time basis. Some managers and marketers are also needed. Few of these businesses are secure. But many are well-run and provide, at least, a useful piece in a patchwork career.

Bioethics. Birth and death, genetic manipulation and animal research all help to keep an estimated 2,000 bioethicists busy in hospitals, universities, and research centers. Some enter the field with a background in philosophy, theology, sociology and/or psychology—but most are also well versed in the law.

Caregiving. Consider the Age Wave of babyboomers; the coming-apart of the governmental safety net for chronically ill and disabled people; massive public health challenges such as AIDS and Alzheimer's; and the mounting interest in hospice care. These factors add up to an enormous need for service providers (physicians, allied health professionals, aides, social workers and other counselors, administrators, marketers, managers, researchers, aides) and for effective new models of service delivery.

Child care. This fast-growing service field employs people in homes, free-standing centers, and corporate daycare facilities. Career paths include supervision, training, marketing, and advocacy for the field—which sorely needs it. Child care can be a high-stress, low-paying occupation. But the human rewards can compensate.

Clergy. One of the last true generalist positions, ministry is an opportunity to develop organizations and programs, speak in public, raise funds, network, counsel, intervene in crises, lead struggles for justice, fix the boiler, and make coffee. This makes it a mecca for the workaholic and a profession fraught with politics as well as opportunity.

Community access television. Thousands of cities and towns have community access television stations, modestly funded for the most part, which exist as outlets for community members' programming. Paid staff members may be producers, trainers, fundraisers, editors, camera crew, publicists, or managers.

Community organizing. Employed by advocacy groups across the spectrum, members of this profession are part marketer, part manager, part communicator extraordinaire. Known for its low pay and high demands, community organizing attracts talented people because it is one of the highest-impact fields around.

Community planning. Planners are the people who turn a community's ideas about how they want to live and work into concrete visions of streets, parks, waste management systems, housing, and public space. This profession requires an interesting mix of technical and social skills and aesthetic sensibility.

Corporate community relations. This emerging field tends to focus on achieving corporate strategic goals by sharing resources (such as philanthropic dollars and volunteers) with communities touched by the business's decisions. Community relations officers rarely influence policy directly, but they are a vital communication link.

Corporate ethics. Ethics officers in medium-to-large companies act as internal consultants for managers and employees making tough decisions. Their work integrates law, philosophy, communication, and psychology, and often commands higher than average earnings. Many of these positions are still being defined, so candidates should expect struggles as well as creative opportunities.

Cross-cultural training. Business, governments, and nonprofits all need to adapt their staff training to the needs of people who hail from outside the host culture. Generally requiring a graduate degree or relevant experience such as teaching, cross-cultural training is a skill that travels well. Salaries for training managers can reach six figures.

Demand-side management. Public utilities have begun to realize that they have painted themselves into a corner by defining themselves only as energy suppliers. "Demand side management," also known as energy conservation, is about helping consumers make smarter use of energy. The field employs program planners, technical innovators, and the utility delivery people who bring energy-efficient light bulbs to your door.

Ecological accounting. Ecological accountants can help to assess the costs and benefits of a course of action from the dual vantage points of the organization and surrounding ecosystem. As companies become committed to sustainability, accountants with ecological sophistication will play a critical (and well-compensated) role.

Employee assistance program counseling. Stress is bad for productivity. It's also bad for working people. Employee assistance programs in workplaces, which offer counseling and referral services, can therefore serve workers and the bottom line as well. In spite of occasional tensions between those two goals, psychologists, psychiatrists, social workers, and other helping professionals are attracted to EAPs as vehicles of development for organizations and the people in them.

Environmental education. As Paul Hawken points out, "That an average adult can recognize one thousand brand names and logos and fewer than ten local plant species is not a good sign. We are moving not into an information age but into a biologic age." Education of children and adults must keep pace. There's a need for teachers of adults and children; for curriculum development specialists, writers and editors, multimedia specialists, administrators, fundraisers, and more.

Environmental management. Corporate environmental managers develop and implement plans for legal compliance and positive initiatives, using a range of technical and leadership skills. Senior salaries can reach six figures.

Environmental retail and product innovation. There is weight to the argument that "green retailing" is an oxymoron. But specialty stores carrying environmentally gentler products, and others with educational or inspirational value, have sprung up in many cities, towns, and suburbs. Mail order businesses are also alive and well as an outlet for promoting more environmentally sound products and discriminating consumer behavior.

Geographic information systems. Customized mapping and data analysis make it possible to computerize such activities as selecting waste sites and redrawing political or school district lines. Geographic Information Systems professionals are in growing demand in real estate, marketing, planning, environmental protection, and politics. GIS is a well-paid profession which makes good use of both technical and social aptitudes.

Holistic/preventive health care. Whether serving as adjuncts to established western medicine (e.g., acupuncture instead of Novocaine for dentistry) or replacing specific techniques (e.g., midwifery), these methods are rapidly gaining in popularity. It is no longer uncommon for physicians or nurses to add a holistic or preventive specialization, or to work in a multidisciplinary practice with nutritionists, acupuncturists, and others. Special programs in major hospitals provide opportunities for work in direct care, research, and training.

Job training and economic development. Whether working for federal or state agencies, nongovernmental organizations, universities, or private sector businesses, professionals concerned with job training and economic development are key players in economic revitalization. They include employment counselors and interviewers, social workers, trainers, instructors, and administrators. Some are bureaucrats, but others push the envelope of innovation.

Labor organizing. The labor movement ("the people who brought you the weekend") is still alive. Union organizers build support for union representation and engage in ongoing education and advocacy. An organizer is usually, but not always, a practitioner of the trade or profession being represented. Skills in communication, administration, and consensus building are also prized.

Land preservation. Some 800 groups around the United States are dedicated to protecting land from unsustainable development, either by raising funds to purchase tracts or by counseling owners who want to create land trusts. Jobs in land preservation can use skills in administration, finance, law, media relations, community organizing, architecture and construction, resource management, real estate, and environmental restoration.

Language instruction, at home or abroad. Language skills are like oxygen for immigrants, tourists, business travelers, and the service providers who work with each of these populations. Language teaching is a skill that travels, and an opportunity to build cultural bridges. Earning power varies widely according to the population you choose to teach.

Library science. While some blessed generalists remain, many librarians are charting specialized paths, managing collections, and tracking issues for corporate, nonprofit or government clients. On-line systems have revolutionized library science. A moderate-salary, moderate-stress field.

Literacy instruction. Literacy teachers may work with homeless adults, on job sites, or in special programs run by school systems. There are also trainers of teachers, designers of programs, fundraisers, lobbyists, and administrators. Soft money makes some of these situations unstable. But literacy workers who make it through a few years tend to find ways to stay in the field.

Lobbying. Advocates at the state and federal levels must have mastery of issues, of the process of drafting legislation, and of communication and negotiation skills at a high level. Often, too, they can influence their organizations by reading the legislative writing on the wall and bringing it back to the home office with ideas for proactive responses. Compensation, and stress levels, can be high.

Mediation, negotiation, and violence prevention. Mediation and negotiation are emerging as professions, along with specialties such as divorce mediation and labor negotiation. A growing emphasis in the conflict resolution field is on violence prevention by teaching communication and coping skills, especially in populations at risk. Earnings vary widely.

Member services. Many nonprofits perform the dual functions of advocacy and service, and member services are a critical part of their strategies for growth. Professional societies, unions, and interest groups all employ professionals to develop and market member services from health plans to discount merchandise.

Multimedia production, writing, marketing. Visuals, text, and sound are coming together in ever more sophisticated ways to create computer-based packages for education and entertainment known as multimedia. Training departments, entertainment companies, and software houses are all involved in this fast-growing field, which can pay well for expertise in education, writing, and editing, as well as in developing the technologies.

Occupational health and safety. Doctors, nurses, medical technicians, researchers, issue experts, administrators, and advocates can all find a place in this specialty. With many workplace and environmental policy issues up for grabs today, this field is unstable but more necessary than ever.

On-line network administration. Requiring a blend of computer and administrative skills, network administration can involve ordering and maintaining equipment, monitoring usage, training and troubleshooting, and developing computer-based information services for users.

Philanthropic foundations. Few activities have a higher direct impact than giving away money. An enterprising grants officer in a foundation can have an impact by noticing worthy new projects, as well as by spotting trends. Communication skills and an unromantic ability to assess the feasibility of program proposals are a must. Likewise flexibility and, in many cases, willingness to travel. Support staff, administrators, accountants, and researchers are also part of the foundation world.

Public interest law. Public interest lawyers may help individual defendants who cannot pay for services, or they may advocate for the interests of an aggrieved group. They may work for law firms, regulatory agencies, labor unions, professional groups, and other nonprofits, earning less than in other legal specialties but assured of a living wage. Paralegals, research assistants, and a few marketers can also find a place in public interest law.

Recycling. "Today, the waste stream has become the raw material inventory that can be turned into resources, jobs, and profits," *In Business* magazine proclaims. Besides the labor-intensive process of collection itself, recycling also creates jobs in financing, community outreach and education, development and marketing of technologies, and matchmaking between sources and users of materials.

Renewable energy. Public utilities are building wind farms. Over 18,000 homes are powered "off the grid." Large companies such as Texas Instruments are working on new generations of solar panels. In both the private and public sectors, engineers, research scientists and technicians, building contractors, technical writers, product managers, marketers, venture capitalists, and fundraisers are riding out a bumpy road today because they know the payoff, sooner or later, will be significant.

Research on environment and sustainable development. The research agenda includes developing cleaner industrial processes, improved materials recycling, toxic waste cleanup methods, climate modeling, and sustainable techniques for meeting the world's needs for food, energy, transportation, and other resources—to say nothing of the study of human behavior. Funding is highly competitive. But niches can be found in industry as well as academia.

Senior advocacy. The senior population often falls prey to fraudulent insurance, exorbitant rents, and other economic abuses. There is a growing role for elder advocates, consumer affairs specialists in government or nonprofits concerned with preventing ripoff of senior citizens.

Socially responsible investment counseling. As the number of socially screened portfolios grows, so does the number of finance professionals (brokers and financial counselors) serving investors with this perspective. Jobs in this field are easier to create than to be hired into. There's high income potential here; high pressure is optional.

Spiritual/transpersonal psychology. Counseling psychologists and social workers are creating new blends of conventional and innovative therapies, for use in private practices, hospitals and hospices, schools, corporate training, and employee assistance programs. While the rise of managed care has put many of these practitioners on the defensive, it is still possible to make a solid living while helping people uncover their potential.

Sustainable agriculture. In the aftermath of the 1980s farm crisis, organic methods of food production have sparked the interest of farmers on every scale, not to mention agribusiness, university extension services, commodity brokers, wholesalers, and retailers. With natural food retail sales rising 20 percent a year, the field is also attracting marketers, managers, and other business pragmatists.

Sustainable architecture. In the building trades, there is rising interest in ways to use less toxic materials, more energy-efficient design, and more recyclable components. Sustainable architecture is a way to apply aesthetic, technical, and business skills to create dwellings and public spaces that harmonize with natural surroundings.

Working the Boundaries

Suppose you see a need for profound change in most of the institutions in which you could be employed. At the same time, suppose you are personally uncomfortable about promoting those changes either by influencing from within or advocating from without. Perhaps you're a gentle soul who finds confrontation distasteful or an unmanageable spirit who finds patience elusive. Or perhaps you've had a hard time finding organizations in which you're comfortable working. If you feel caught up in this conflict, this section is for you.

Some years ago, a group of science students at a major university asked me to participate in a panel on the subject of "Work Within the System?" These students wanted to mix principles and pragmatism. They thought the question had a single right answer, but the truth is there are many answers just as there are many definitions of "the system." There are individual institutions; groupings of them, such as associations; their clients and suppliers; regulators; training grounds such as universities and trade schools; and the small businesses and social services that rise up around major institutions. Around any institution, there are concentric circles of others that may be closely or distantly related, including their critics, with whom they often develop a kind of symbiotic relationship.

The concepts of "inside" and "outside" have never been less clear than they are today. If you want to see how interconnected a "system" is with its "surroundings," visit a military base that is closing, or a community where a large new business has just sunk roots. And watch the impact on local businesses that, on the surface, have nothing to do with the large institutions.

Some of the most interesting processes in any system happen at its boundaries, where information and incentives flow in and out. People, on the inside and on the outside, control that flow by their interactions. Therefore, if you want to gain influence in an industry or profession, your choices are not limited to placing yourself at the dead center of it or organizing opposition from a distance. You can work the boundaries.

There are numerous ways to do this by providing information or other services. For example, Peter Sandman of Rutgers University consults to industry, and to grassroots groups, on the psychology of "risk communication." Using this tool, he helps warring parties in a dispute sort out which of their differences have to do with substance and which have to do with style.

One perspective on these boundary positions comes from Alan F. Kay, an opinion researcher, activist, and successful founder of an information business called AutEx: "Think of all the business and professional fields there are—tens of thousands," he begins. "Then think of all the services they need. There are standard services such as marketing, research, finance, and employee training, which can be provided in virtually the same form to many clients. There are specialized services: lobbying, management consulting, workshops, publications, and computer software, for starters." Many of these services are growth areas, all the more so because of the popularity of outsourcing.

Kay's own testing ground for outsourcing, AutEx, was created in the early years of computer applications to bring state-of-the-art communications technologies to markets that could pay very well for them. The year 1969 found him operating one of the first commercial systems for electronic communication among securities traders. Later, this software was adapted to other markets—each one carefully selected according to criteria for profitability. Based on that success, he emphasizes two principles. First, research the structure and definition of your market carefully, even if it takes a lot of time. It's the targeting that can make this approach work best financially. Second, pay attention to economies of scale, and target the largest possible market you can serve with integrity. "If you can find a way to service a whole industry," he notes, "you can sometimes gain a thousandfold leverage in terms of costs."

This entrepreneurial approach to finding a niche and influencing a field can be tailored to a variety of objectives: building a financial base, helping to redefine a field or a set of issues, or serving a particular clientele. It can be used, as Kay's AutEx shows, to create wealth. The strategy, in simplest form, is to identify a market that attracts you and that has the ability to pay well for your services. Some of these services can be value-neutral, while others can help shift thinking in your chosen market. An enterprising small company can build itself a financial base by choosing a large enough market, and can also provide services that help clients exercise social or environmental responsibility. Depending on your resources and needs, you can start such a company or seek a job at one already established.

For example, Robin Alden turned her lifelong love for the Maine coast into a small business, a newsletter for the fishing industry called *Commercial Fisheries News*. The idea was born during a leave of absence from college, when she found work as a local journalist and became fascinated with the economic and environmental controversies connected to fishing. Alden remembers that moment: she was covering a meeting on fisheries policy when a screaming match erupted between a state policymaker and a working fisherman. "I can get these people communicating," she thought. After many twists in the road, she started what has become the newspaper of record for the New England fishing industry. Alden is now a respected speaker on ecologically responsible fishing and has started two other newsletters, *Fisheries Product News* and *Fish Farming News*. She also takes pride in having created "eleven good jobs on the coast of Maine."

Carol Cone started a marketing and communications firm to help companies build brand loyalty by connecting their products or services to social values. Her clients include Ryka, the women's footwear company that donates a percentage of pretax profits to the fight against domestic violence, and MTV, which airs ten thousand public-service messages promoting tolerance and diversity every year. Cone calls the theme of these projects "passion branding." In addition to getting the word out about companies' incentives, she helps them design programs that "go beyond a 'cause du jour.' "

If You're Not Independently
Wealthy or Highly Educated

Some of the work options I've been describing are highly specialized and may require advanced degrees, while others require the straightforward skill training found in a community college, trade school, adult education center, or public library. Some even capitalize on your innate communication, trading, and organizational skills rather than any schooling. Because nearly all work is evolving in more knowledge-intensive directions, it's critical not to close off educational opportunities prematurely. However, life itself is an educational opportunity, and we all know people who have used it for what it's worth without formal schooling. If you have not had the education you wish for, or if you feel that your past training has left you poorly prepared for the present realities, here are some career-development strategies:

- Performance-oriented professions such as sales, marketing, lobbying, fund-raising, or grassroots organizing, where toughness and results are valued over credentials
- Technical paths in an emerging field (installing windmills, growing organic produce, manufacturing or fixing alternative vehicles)
- Skills you can teach yourself using resources from public libraries, mail order, community colleges, and adult education centers (foreign languages, computer applications, gardening specialties)
- Small business in general, and especially service businesses (natural foods catering, mediation, bike repair, haircutting) that can be started with very little capital and marketed especially in communities you want to work with in other ways. In fact, even a simple service business can create innovative special programs. Take Bikes Not Bombs, a bike repair shop that also fixes up old donated bikes to send to developing countries. Cofounders Carl Kurtz and Mira Brown started a special project to teach bike repair to inner-city teenagers. Teachers and students volunteer their time, but kids who complete the program receive a free bike.

In a strange way, the economic shake-out of the last few years has been a great equalizer. People who thought they were most secure have had some of the rudest awakenings. People who have not found conventional success are seeing open doors to more unconventional success. The information explosion has led many of us to scramble, but it also presents enormous new possibilities for communication and self-teaching. Working people are struggling for psychological, as well as material, survival. But we are beginning to relearn the art of struggle in a way that makes a significant victory possible.

Making
a Living and
a Difference
Internationally

In the old town square in Prague a couple of summers ago, the human meaning of globalization really came home to me. Walking out of a café, I was pleasantly disoriented to hear the pipes and drums of an Andean band. I followed the sound, and came upon a circle of Japanese and Western European tourists swaying to the Latin rhythms. Billboards advertised Apple and Sony and Toshiba against the backdrop of stunning thousand-year-old towers. That moment made it clear: there is hardly anyplace left on earth that is not in touch with everyplace. Rich and poor, people take mobility for granted, whether they are global managers or migrant laborers or traveling musicians.

It was easy to feel part of one big, exuberant world, if I didn't look too closely. But neither the café nor the music nor most of the consumer products were within reach of the majority of Czechs. Most of them were too focused on making ends meet to take part in this lighthearted moment.

One of my reasons for being in Prague was to write about Western environmental consultants who were helping devise ways of reversing the country's air and water pollution crises. They, and thousands like them working all around the world on cleanup and pollution prevention efforts, represent one major theme in any discussion about making a living and a difference around the world. Before I propose others, let me say just a bit more about the ways in which the international context shapes career planning.

Globalization represents a breakdown of boundaries and a potentially explosive upsurge of interconnections. It is a constant unfolding of opportunities to create something new out of the interplay of traditions and ideas. As William Irwin Thompson, one of the most enthusiastic proponents of an emerging world culture, describes his life as a planetary citizen, "When I go into the kitchen and cook . . . I cook what you could call, using a musical metaphor, planetary fusion. Mexican nachos with Indonesian *sambal sate* mixed in with the beans, then topped off with a cheese from Switzerland. And music is the right metaphor for what I see going on with planetary culture. Traditions from all over the world are jiving and giving us everything from Moroccan rock to Parisian rap."[1]

But globalization is also a process with winners and losers—fragile cultures overrun by others more aggressive, to cite an obvious example. That is partly because some of the players bring so much more to the game than others in terms of economic and organizational resources, and partly because the unknowns are so great. Each time a boundary is broken down between people, societies, or organizations, there is a world of possibility for collaborative creativity. Or damage. Or both. The outcome depends a lot on how the relationships are negotiated, and on what each player is willing to invest and to risk.

Wendell Berry, a Kentucky farmer, poet, and essayist, has long celebrated the local and decried the global. You only take responsibility for what you love, he says, and you only love what you can know in a deep and direct way. "Properly speaking, global thinking is impossible," Berry cautions, "and those who have practiced it have tended to be tyrants."[2] In his view, environmental and social conscience only comes alive when people can see the impact of their choices, directly and emotionally: an eroded gully, a deforested hill, a population that can no longer grow food because the soil has been stripped or the water has been diverted. However, you can live in a place all your life and hide out psychologically, declining to pay attention to the land and the rivers and the cultures around you. Or you can develop this kind of passionate relationship for a place you have only visited for a month. For many of us, it is possible to travel all over, enter into a new culture, and truly believe ourselves to be emissaries of peace and fair trade and cultural cross-fertilization. With all that, we can still fail to bring our vision to life.

The stakes are raised by the emergence of multinational business organizations, which date back to the days before Columbus, but which have become economic players of unprecedented power in the modern era because of their technologies, information links, and sheer size. Deborah Leipziger, director of the Transnational Corporation's Project for the Council on Economic Priorities, reflects on the imperative of aligning this power source with a vision of humane, sustainable development:

The future of the international institution is in doubt. The United Nations, GATT, and the World Bank are increasingly seen as inadequate to address the challenges posed by the 1990's. But the large corporation is on the rise, with 37,000 companies accounting for one quarter of the combined gross national product of all the countries of the world. Transnational corporations (TNC's) have become the powerhouses of the global economic system. The $36 billion annual TNC investment in developing countries affects economic growth, employment practices, technology transfer, and the environment. Because such significant resources are at the disposal of the TNC's, there is increasing recognition that with global influence comes global responsibility.[3]

In order to weigh these factors in a particular work situation, it is necessary to be awake to the range of errors and abuses that are part of the global business scene. To list a few of the more glaring problem areas:

- grossly unsustainable logging of Central American and Malaysian rain forests and Siberian old-growth forests by international timber companies
- aggressive marketing of cigarettes to Third World teenagers
- large-scale shipment of toxic and radioactive wastes to Third World countries from the industrialized world, often with inadequate labeling and preparation for safe handling
- preventable industrial tragedies in zones of rapid economic expansion, such as the 1993 fire at a Thai toy factory that killed 118 workers because sprinkler systems were not functional and doors were locked to prevent theft
- the sexually oriented tourist industry, which targets business people in developed countries and engages "escorts" among the poorest women in such countries as Thailand and Indonesia

Are these abuses the inevitable path of transnational industry? Hardly, say another set of companies that deserves a more detailed look.

Gillette Indonesia pays workers three to four times the required local wages, offers U.S.-style retirement and benefits packages, and has built a mosque on company property for Moslem workers.

Merck, the U.S. pharmaceutical giant, has developed a long-term partnership with the Biodiversity Institute of Costa Rica (InBio) to document the plant and animal species in the rain forest. Merck donated $1 million plus $140,000 worth of equipment to the project, by far the largest of its kind in a tropical country. InBio prospects for plant and insect specimens with likely medicinal properties; Merck will have first right to screen these specimens; InBio receives royalties and technical assistance, and 50 percent of those royalties are earmarked for national park protection.

And Levi Strauss's global sourcing code has been a major wake-up call to show the textile industry what a difference can be made, within the context of global capitalism, by choosing to bring a set of previously invisible concerns into the calculation of profit and loss. The code spells out acceptable practices in workplace safety, environmental protection, and human rights; 5 percent of Levi's 700 subcontractors have been cut off for failure to adhere to this code.

For the job seeker, choosing a direction in the global economy is extra complex because the necessary information must be patched together from many sources, and because the records of even the best employers are inconsistent. As Leipziger puts it, "A company can be doing wonderful things in Malaysia and terrible things in Hong Kong."

There is a tendency to talk about the awakening of global connections as though they were an impersonal force, and the power of some of the technologies and policies to set the agenda do make it seem that way. But as these examples make clear, the globalizing of human experience is the result of personal, governmental, and corporate decisions. It may be too late to reverse a lot of these processes, even if many people were interested in doing so. But it is not too late to establish some conditions on the roles we each play.

Futurist Hazel Henderson points out six different processes of globalization, reflecting both danger and potential: globalization of[4] technology and production; work, employment, and migration; finance, information, and debt; military weapons and the arms races; the human impacts on the biosphere; and culture and consumption patterns. Each of these trends points the way to clusters of career areas in which people are already working, as well as questions that can be catalysts for brand-new areas of work. To start with an arbitrary list of fields of work that put you in the middle of these global flows, consider:

- International information services, including translation, editing, marketing of both print and on-line services;
- International law, paralegal work, and legal research;
- Global finance and information services (working for the financial giants of the developed world, or the emerging financial industries of the less developed world, or for the social investment movement, or for an information service that might help level the playing field in your particular area of interest);

- Refugee resettlement, advocacy, economic development, and social services;
- Community-scale development (building infrastructure, transferring skills, organizing cottage industries);
- Technical and process innovation to help weapons companies diversify, so that arms exporting won't be such a seductive path;
- Technology marketing, or maybe a law or policy career in regulating technology transfers in the public interest;
- Consumer marketing, hopefully of the most ecologically sound and safe products you can find, or of services that address root causes of social and environmental problems; or the marketing of new ideas. Or how about consumer advocacy, an idea that is highly developed in some countries such as the Netherlands and that begs to be transferred to countries just opening up their consumer markets?
- The export and interplay of culture, through consumer marketing or maybe cultural exchange promotion. This can take forms as varied as the world music industry and the Boston Museum of Fine Arts's opening of a sister museum in Tokyo. The global culture business, too, is ethically complex; rural and land-based cultures from Peru to Pennsylvania are endangered by global mass culture, but at the same time it has been enthusiastically embraced by many people in the developing world, and especially by the global Generation X. Wherever you stand, at least, it's worth remembering that the toxic materials you export will come home to roost just as much if they are slasher movies as if they are hazardous waste drums.

And of course, there are the universal fields that make all the rest possible: language translation and teaching; cross-cultural training; travel and tourism; government and diplomacy; conflict resolution; disaster relief; (sustainable) development and environmental restoration; and all the forms of support that are needed by people in these fields.

In all these lines of work, there are dilemmas to be faced about methods as well as mission. There are also rich examples of people who have found or created jobs for themselves working globally in ways they see as life affirming. The following cases illustrate the range of options you can seek out or re-create in your own style.

Ecotourism

Tourism is the second most important item in world trade, after oil. It is also one of the fastest growing, leading to growth in hotel and restaurant business, roads, airports, water and sewer systems, demand for food, and other major stresses on rural economies where people in the developed world go "away." According to U.N. research, 75 percent of visitors to Ecuador tramp through the Galapagos Islands. Their presence has altered the habits of native animals, and has left erosion and litter on the trails where Charles Darwin confronted the mysteries of evolution.

Concern about tourism's impact, coupled with economic opportunity, have led to a fast-growing "alternative" travel movement. This movement is illustrated by small tour companies with intercultural sensitivity, like Amazonia Expeditions of Florida, which leads tours to two Peruvian communities, arranging opportunities for the indigenous people and visitors to talk in depth about each of their traditions. It's illustrated, too, by outdoor expedition guides who encourage environmental ethics on the trail. Two travel companies, Journeys International and Wildland Adventures, have organized staff and client volunteers to clean up trails in Peru, as well as helping with reforestation and repairing monasteries in Nepal.

When it comes to hotels, resorts, roads, harbors, airports, and other chunks of infrastructure that accompany tourism, the stakes are higher. That is because the impact of these developments on land, forests, and waterways is physical and often dramatic. For people in the developed world considering work in the travel or tourism industries, the well-known hard questions boil down to "How much (restraint) is enough?" in dealing with fragile ecologies and cultures. That question will never go away. But another one is joining it in center stage: "How much positive impact can a well-designed tourism project have?"

One of the most visionary approaches to that question comes from Stanley Selengut, a New York civil engineer and developer who has found a stimulating new life running a "research resort" called Harmony in the U.S. Virgin Islands. Powered by sun and wind, off the local electric grid, the facility is advanced in aesthetics as well as engineering. The multicolored roof tiles are made of crushed glass. These, and the floorboards of recycled newspaper, are made in local workshops. Rainwater caught on the roofs is channeled into solar showers; composting toilets make septic systems unnecessary. Features like these make a sustainable resort much less expensive than a conventional one to construct, and therefore more profitable. Selengut is also researching ways these ecologically advanced construction methods can be creators of local jobs. He comments,

> There are real opportunities for win/win solutions in this business, providing you can control greed and don't leverage yourself at such a level that one mistake will bring you down. Resorts of this type, with individual units, can start small and expand. You can assess environmental impact and carrying capacity as you go.

> Most hotel management is like making cookies with a cookie cutter—it's all the same. This work is site-specific and much more interesting. Your palette is all the indigenous assets, natural and cultural. The challenge is to bring people into an environment, and into communication with each other, in a way that opens them up to new ideas.

By combining high tech and low impact, Selengut has attracted some powerful partners for assistance with materials and monitoring, including the U.S. National Park Service and Sandia National Labs. He is convinced that "there are tremendous entrepreneurial opportunities" for sustainable architecture and design, and for travel destinations where people can sample the state of this art.

Selengut shows the possibility of a fresh start for engineers, technicians, and others whose prospects in large organizations may be dimming but whose talents and vision are more needed than ever. The next example, halfway around the world, varies this theme and, like Harmony, can be emulated almost anywhere.

Capitalism, Community Style

When the Soviet army left Eastern Europe, it left military bases behind in every country. One of these sites now houses one of Hungary's first business incubators. With a laundromat, French bakery, auto shop, denture manufacturer, electronic and metal shops, computer consulting service, and other small businesses, the incubator shows a living alternative to central planning. Not only this, but it is linked to a national network of small business incubators, formed by Hungarian nongovernmental organizations and international agencies collaboratively.

The former Soviet empire has been described by one business executive as "a company, eleven time zones wide, in the middle of Chapter 11."[5] The material and human needs throughout the region are staggering. Social conditions, and a desperate environmental situation, magnify those needs. This adds up to staggering opportunities to serve or to exploit, to clarify or to confuse.

The twenty-five-year-old nonprofit that help establish the Hungarian incubator project, SPEDD Incorporated, is an experiment in what might be called partnership economics. It acts as a catalyst for community economic development, bringing in technical assistance, funding, and models from other successful experiments. This allows other international companies and agencies to bring in more targeted forms of technical assistance, and to build trade relationships. It also creates a structure in which Hungarian resourcefulness and energy can be brought alive.

Bradley T. Shaw, the U.S.-based coordinator of the program, started out with a perfectly normal engineering career. Feeling stale after a few years, however, he returned to school, encouraged by opportunities that seemed to open up when people found out that he was "an engineer who knew how to write." Working in the declining machine tool industry near Pittsburgh, Shaw developed a natural interest in economic development and got himself a master's degree that turned out to be a collector's item. It was one of twelve awarded in Science, Technology and Values at Rensselaer Polytechnic Institute, before the school changed the name to fend off chuckles from employers.

For the most part, "economies don't really collapse," Shaw observes. "They just go underground. Under the surface of what looks like inactivity, you have people running catering services out of their kitchens, people running landscaping businesses."

Shaw now divides his time between Pittsburgh and Eastern Europe. At home, he supports similar incubators that have helped bring new life to the Monongahela valley after the demise of the steel industry. He also hosts international visitors attracted by Pittsburgh's reputation as a turnaround city, including a steady flow of Russians and Eastern Europeans. Abroad, he acts as an information source and broker to create interest in undervalued local resources.

In this work, Shaw finds his technical background valuable but relies more on the skill of "reflective listening." He convenes groups of local people who think they might like to start a business, then keeps a conversation flowing among them until they figure out for themselves who has the resources and the most viable ideas. "There's a lot of hard work involved in putting together funding packages for these projects," he admits, "but the biggest mistake you can make is to 'overthink' the process."

As an outside agency, SPEDD avoids prescribing the kinds of businesses that will work, but keeps an eye on situations that might affect the viability of a project. "In most industrial cities," Shaw notes, "the 'best' real estate is often tainted with some kind of industrial waste. It becomes very important to know the technical aspects of cleanup as well as the financial resources available for environmental initiatives." In the United States, some states have loan funds for the cleanup of polluted properties, business ventures that use recycled materials, and other ways to integrate sustainability into development. Internationally, lending agencies and foundations can always be tried. One of the greatest challenges for people from the developed world who are working to promote development is to balance the needs of the earth with the visions and wishes of the communities they are serving.

Economic
Development with a Vision

Sustainability isn't a major part of the development picture yet in South Africa, where the relationships of human rights, economic development, and the environment are visible in every mined-out rock face, overgrazed field and polluted factory town. "It hits you from the moment you arrive," admits Gail Leftwich, a business consultant who has visited the country regularly since the lifting of economic sanctions. While most of the emerging black-owned businesses in the country have been too preoccupied with basic questions of survival, marketing, technical and management development to bring sustainability onto center stage, Leftwich recognizes the question as critical in the long run because "you can't separate business activity from the overall development context."

One of the ten largest external markets identified by the U.S. Department of Commerce, South Africa has emerged as an area where economic development and social justice can richly complement each other. A spirit of rebuilding and expansiveness has drawn many South African exiles home. More than 200 U.S. companies disinvested in the late 1980s, but many are now finding their way back, with the blessing and guidance of the new government. Companies represented in a 1993 trade mission, led by Commerce Secretary Ron Brown, included Apple Computer, ARCO Chemical, Pratt & Whitney, IBM, Time Warner, and Lehman Brothers.[6]

Work with South Africa has been especially attractive to African-American professionals like Leftwich who want to be of service but feel more comfortable as entrepreneurs than advocates. "The poor understand that you need economic development," she says.

A lawyer with a background in real estate, she spent two years at Harvard's John F. Kennedy School of Government laying the groundwork for a program on South Africa, then started her own business in order to rely on venture capital rather than grant funding. She reflects, "As a lawyer, I know about starting companies. I also know about gathering and using large amounts of information. Those are the primary strengths I use in my work—those, plus a lack of political or ideological baggage, since I wasn't involved in the issue when I was practicing law during the apartheid years."

Although the rush of aid, relationship building, and investment over the last few years has been largely well intended, Leftwich points out that good intentions alone do not answer all the questions about the kinds of economic involvement that genuinely help. Even people with a strong commitment to the social vision of the majority government have lessons to learn about local needs and cultural factors. She explains, "There is a lot of common cause between African-Americans and black South Africans, but there are also differences which outsiders don't always grasp. South Africa today is a majority-ruled society. That means that South African blacks don't struggle a lot with their identity or the legitimacy of their power. People who come in and try to help them take charge are kind of irrelevant. Every grandmother in that country has a memory of the land she once owned and has lived through the apartheid years knowing that, if she didn't live to reclaim it, her children or grandchildren would."

Because South Africa is a huge market in which black-owned businesses from around the world enjoy a long-overdue advantage, tensions can arise between the political and economic agendas of South African and foreign business people. International funding agencies debate about whether to support only minority-run companies or to award aid based on the merit of a project. Activists in the labor, religious, and socially responsible business communities who have been focused on keeping business out must now realign themselves and find new ways to bring business, responsibly, in. Most disturbingly, Leftwich notes, "In the early days after the economic sanctions were lifted, some business deals were being cut in which outside investors were reaping much faster profits than the South Africans, and that is the opposite of the steady commitment that's needed."

Of course, it isn't necessary to go halfway around the globe to promote economic development and social justice. Leftwich admits, "I could be doing something similar in my own country, but that isn't what caught my attention. I don't know why. I just know that I feel a tremendous attraction to helping my buddies in South Africa, and that's what I'm going with."

Following your own attraction has to be the starting point in creating an international career. The path you choose must be exciting and uplifting enough to hold your attention. At the same time, there is nothing like an international career to remind you that you are not just working for personal gain in isolation; you are working in an interdependent world for some sort of enlightened, long-term self-interest, which is meaningless without more secure, sustainable relationships between peoples and with the planet. In the Caribbean or Eastern Europe or South Africa, there are perennial questions. What do we mean by development? What are sustainable practices? Who decides? Who pays? How do we keep ourselves honest?

One of the most interesting of these questions has to do with the scale of a global enterprise. Many of the best-known corporate and governmental players are the giants: the transnational corporations; the relief and development agencies operated by governments, churches, and other nonprofits; the U.N. and other international institutions such as the World Bank and the bureaucracies set up to enforce trade agreements. However, it is far from clear that economies of scale always favor large-scale efforts. Small, nimble operations, and innovative structures, can offer an extra measure of economic advantage in the global context. Thinking small also makes it easier for global enterprises to maximize benefit and minimize social and environmental costs. In fact, some of the most exciting multinational corporations and nonprofits these days are the smallest:

- Catherine Boyle of Winchester, Massachusetts, returned from a tour of duty with the U.S. Information Agency in Africa, where she had been appalled at the shortage of resources for scientists and policymakers working to reverse the continent's environmental problems. She started Environmental Briefs, a scientific news service providing the latest resources electronically to contacts around the continent. Her slogan: "Just because you're saving the world, you shouldn't have to reinvent the wheel."
- Ultimo Decene Compera and Elihu Petnov, Caribbean natives living in the U.S., founded a visionary nonprofit called Professional Equipment for the Needy. Since 1982, they have recycled $1.6 million worth of ambulances, fire engines, and emergency supplies to developing countries where these basics are in short supply.
- Satellife, a nonprofit based in Cambridge, Massachusetts, installs systems for electronic communication in dozens of developing countries in order to help health care professionals in isolated locations tap into on-line systems for information and support.
- Kenneth Leavitt, a foot surgeon in Wilmington, Massachusetts, is opening up a branch office in Vilnius, the capital of Lithuania. He has set up the business, with about thirty consulting partners, so that he and others can spend six to eight weeks per year providing an alternative to the deteriorating state-run health care system.
- The International Council for Energy Conservation, with offices in London, Washington, and Bangkok, brings technical and policy consulting on appropriate technologies to developing countries.
- Green China, a Boston nonprofit, maintains a network of environmental reporters around Asia and publishes a magazine, in Chinese, on environmental problems and solutions.

Carrying an expanded work ethic into a global career requires making your own assessments of each new situation. As Sabrina Birner, an energy conservation consultant working in Thailand, reflects, "You can't automatically apply the same standards in Bangkok that you would in Harvard Square. But you can make a serious assessment of both current realities and the potential for change." That means listening to the strongest players in each new place and the most vulnerable ones as well, getting excited about your potential contribution but being vigilant about the potential downside. It means following as well as leading. It means constant questioning. And so this section ends with an extra measure of questions for you to tape to the wall, near the place where you keep your passport and guidebooks.

Questions to Ask Yourself About Any International Opportunity

1. Where are you going, literally and symbolically?

2. What are you leaving behind?

3. Who will be affected by the work you do in this situation?

4. Will the outcome of your work involve winners and losers?

5. Who will lose if you win? (Try to get beyond the abstract to consider real people and other living beings.)

6. Are there actions or attitudes you could take on the job that would make it more of a win/win situation?

7. How certain are you of your power to produce a fair outcome?

8. What do you know about the people and cultures of the place where you're considering working?

9. How have you chosen your sources of information about them?

10. Are there others you should consult for a balanced view?

11. What technologies and tools will you use in your work?

12. How will they affect the quality of life and the balance of power you and your co-workers have with the local population?

13. What do you want to believe about this place?

14. What attracts you most?

15. What scares you?

16. What do you know about the ecology and natural history of this place?

17. What can you do while you're there to help protect or restore a healthy ecology, including taking responsibility for the impact of your style of living?

18. What peoples have held this place sacred?

19. How will your actions affect their lives, communities, and cultures?

20. What can you do to learn more about indigenous people and bring their message, whatever it is, back to your home community?

21. Will you displace or compete with local people who could otherwise be doing "your" work?

22. What local social or political groups will you be most closely allied with in this place?

23. Could this put you into conflict with any others?

24. Are there ways you might realistically serve as a peacemaker in the community where you'll be?

25. Are there ways you could do the good things mentioned above without actually transplanting yourself to this place?

26. What kinds of power will you bring to this situation?

27. How will it compare to the power of the people you'll be working with, supervising, and reporting to?

28. Are there ways you can make this power balance fairer?

29. Is this trip or move a rite of passage for you in any way?

30. How has it come to have this meaning?

31. Are there ways you could achieve the same symbolic goal with accomplishments or adventures closer to home?

32. How do you define your commitment to your home community?

33. Whatever choice you make, how can you maximize the positive impact of your international work and minimize the negative?

Part Two

The Ten-Step
Program for
Principled
Career
Development

Step 1:

Wake Up

*The real voyage of discovery consists not in seeking new
landscapes, but in having new eyes.*

Marcel Proust

*The signs of hope are not necessarily coming from the business
organizations but, I think, from the personal growth movement—
more and more people seeking power from within themselves.*[1]

Dr. Deborah Bloch,
Baruch College

If you doubt that there's a connection between performance and psychological state, ask your local athletic coach or a good teacher, social worker, nurse, corporate manager, even a prison guard. Ask anyone who gets to watch the differences in people's performances over time in the same outward circumstances. Human capabilities are powerfully tied to expectations and attitudes.[2]

There is a state of mind, body, and spirit in which people have peak performances. When they're in that "flow state," things click.[3] They know what to do and do it effortlessly. At the workbench or on the dance floor, they are fully present and in tune.

People who love their work and excel at it show a particular set of attitudes toward themselves and their vocation. Management consultant Sharon Connelly summed these up with the term "workspirit," and set out to study it through in-depth interviews with twenty people who loved their work.[4] Connelly's sample fit no mold in terms of political views, age, socioeconomic class, or job description. The group was equally divided between entrepreneurs and managers in bureaucratic organizations. Many of their jobs were very difficult: starting up organizations, marketing new ideas, traveling in war zones, resolving tough conflicts. What stood out was their sense of engagement with work, as revealed by their language: "zeal," "the flow state," "walking into an energy field," "glowing," "the presence of sexual energy," and "magical chemistry."

These spirited workers stood out in seven ways: high energy; a positive, open state of mind; a sense of purpose or vision; a full sense of self; a belief that they were participating in important creative or nurturing activity; common experience of an inspired "risking/sensing/living moment"; and an understanding of themselves as part of a higher order. Those qualities were woven together in a sense of purpose and a sense of themselves as able to rise to the challenge of that purpose.

When have you come closest to expressing your full potential in a work situation?

What did it look like?

What aspects of the workplace were most supportive?

What aspects of the work itself were most satisfying?

What did you learn from that experience that could be applied to your present situation? If the answer to this question isn't obvious, stay with the question.

◆

Wake Up to the Arts
of Listening and Questioning

One powerful way to focus your attention and quiet the inner noises that interfere is through listening: to people, to music, to the sounds of the ocean or the city or the ballpark. Listening is not the same as waiting for another person to finish talking so you can have your turn. Listening means opening up to new information without letting your expectations screen it out.

One of the most powerful illustrations of the potential of listening is a highly effective nonprofit called the Piedmont Peace Project. This multiracial community organization in rural North Carolina has registered more than 15,000 African-American voters since the mid-1980s, and produced a major shift in the voting record of the region's representative in Congress. The project uses teams who make door-to-door visits in low-income neighborhoods, meeting people who are not already jaded by salespeople or pollsters. These teams gather people's opinions about how their tax dollars are being spent and how well their voices have been heard in the Congress. Then activists write campaign materials using the language they've heard directly from their neighbors. Not surprisingly, it works.

Imagine listening, really listening, to people you work with and for, and to people you hope will help you in your job search.

Connected to the art of listening is the art of asking questions. Skillful questioning gets you more than answers. It gets you a relationship of creative exploration with another human being. Career strategists Sam Deep and Lyle Sussman promote the art of questioning as a tool for gaining organizational power in their book, *What to Ask When You Don't Know What to Say: Seven Hundred Powerful Questions to Use for Getting Your Way at Work* (e.g., "How will we determine whether or not my performance merits a raise?").[5]

But questioning does not just benefit the questioner. It can help the "questionee" focus on an issue and break out of mental boxes. Social change consultant Fran Peavey teaches a process called "strategic questioning"—asking questions systematically in order to uncover a higher order of possibilities in a situation.[6] Strategic questions are those that move you beyond obvious information, beyond yes and no and multiple choice. They invite you to imagine new possibilities and explore the ways to remove barriers. "Look for the long-lever question," she advises— that is, the question with the most leverage to get things moving. For instance, "What would it take for this change to be possible?"

~

When have you felt really listened to, in your private life and on the job?

At work, how often do you listen deeply to other people?

What could you do to promote more attentive, thoughtful communication?

What are you waiting for?

~

Wake Up to Your Own Assumptions

Questioning is a big-time test of how awake you are. Questions help you wake up. People's answers will only rarely match your assumptions. What comes out of your own mouth may also contain a surprise or two. So the process is a doorway to another valuable awakening: to the assumptions we all carry about what's happening and what's possible.

"All jobs are the same."

"Nobody is going to help me if I take an initiative."

"I'm too old to make a career change."

Psychologist Martin Seligman studied people who suffered from depression to see how they developed "learned helplessness," which led them incorrectly to conclude that they could not change their lives, even when other people in very similar situations could change.[7] Seligman saw that depression came not only from experience but from what he calls "explanatory style," the way a person draws meaning from what's going on. This style has everything to do with people's ability to perceive options. Seligman focused on three major aspects of explanatory style:

Permanence. People who resist depression and function with high effectiveness tend to believe that the causes of bad events are temporary.

Pervasiveness. People who function effectively and resist depression tend to make specific explanations about events, rather than generalizing from one experience to other areas of their lives.

Personalization. People who resist difficulties tend not to take them personally, but understand them as part of the wider pattern of events to be faced and overcome.

This pattern was borne out in research with 104 sales agents from the Metropolitan Life Insurance Company who were tested for optimism at hiring and secretly classified as "eagles" or "turkeys." The eagles greatly outsold the turkeys from the start, and the differences between the groups multiplied as the years went by.

This is one of countless ways that assumptions and interpretations can open or close the gate to action. Some of the most limiting assumptions are the ones we make about our own capabilities and untapped resources.

Recall a time when you've felt stuck. How did you explain the situation?

Did you make any assumptions that might have limited your sense of possibility?

Recall a time when you accomplished something exciting, large or small.

Have you made any assumptions about that experience that might limit your ability to build on it?

Wake Up to a New Story About Work

When the world was created, according to Navajo myth, the Great Spirit wanted a place to hide the secret of the universe.[8] It had to be a place where the secret would be invisible and protected, no matter how the world evolved. The Spirit considered hiding it in the sky. But there were birds in abundance soaring everywhere. The spirit wondered about the treetops as a safe place. But squirrels and monkeys and owls lived there. Caves were a possibility. But they were home to bats and other creatures. Finally, the Great Spirit hit upon the answer: "I will hide the secret in the hearts of the two-legged ones. That is the one place they will never look."

The human capacity for cluelessness is older than the Industrial Age, older than technology, older than all the other factors it's so easy to blame. But there are signs of awakening and new models, new stories emerging around the world. Theologian Thomas Berry writes:

> It's all a question of story. We are in trouble just now because we do not have a good story. We are in between stories. The old story, the account of how the world came to be and how we fit into it, is no longer effective. Yet we have not learned a new story. Our traditional story of the universe sustained us for a long period of time. It shaped our emotional attitudes, provided us with life purposes, and energized action. It consecrated suffering and integrated knowledge. We awoke in the morning and knew where we were. We could answer the questions of our children. We could identify crime, punish transgressors. Everything was taken care of because the story was there. It did not necessarily make people good, nor did it take away the pains and stupidities of life or make for unfailing warmth in human association. It did provide a context in which life could function in a meaningful manner.[9]

To claim our place in this new story, we must each become fully awake to our part in the old, what keeps us attached to it, our potential for contribution, and the environments we need to create to help us fulfill that potential. What's necessary to rebuild the economy and society, to live in harmony with the environment and ourselves, is the ability to make choices with greater self-awareness, a process of learning to learn and to infuse work with a sense of liberation.

❧

Start telling stories about your work history. Just do it, whenever the social occasion arises (in small doses, of course, and paying special attention to the interest shown by your listener).

Alternatively, you can write your stories, talk into a tape recorder, or barter listening time with a friend who might find the same process useful.

Write your career history. Notice repeated patterns or events. How did you interpret them then? How would you interpret them now?

Pace yourself with ministories—vignettes that have special significance as triumphs, defeats, turning points, or revealing episodes.

Celebrate the strength and resourcefulness of the person who lived through all this and is now on the threshold of something exciting.

❧

Wake Up to the
Interconnectedness of Everything

As John Muir pointed out a hundred years ago, "When you look at any one thing you find that it is inextricably hitched to everything else." A blip on the Tokyo Stock Exchange can disrupt home mortgage lending rates in Kansas City. North Americans' dependence on beef contributes to keeping people in the developing world away from land and water they need for subsistence farming. Whether or not butterfly wings whirring in China can really cause storms in the Gulf of Mexico, as the chaos theorists have suggested, every action we take is part of an intricate web of causes and effects among human communities and the natural environment.

The skill of seeing these connections and appreciating their significance is sometimes called systems thinking. Peter Senge's management best-seller, *The Fifth Discipline,* demonstrates that systems thinking is a major characteristic of organizations that are able to learn, and thus to transform themselves rather than stagnating when conditions change.[10]

The same is true for people as they do their work and build their careers. You are a system of thoughts, feelings, information, unconscious imagery, memory, and more, all interwoven and interdependent. You are also part of a complex social and ecological system. You have a choice: you can view these relations as sources of complexity to be avoided, or as resources to be tapped.

This recognition gives rise to a new understanding of well-being and human potential that has been articulated by many developmental psychologists and by the emerging field of ecopsychology. In this view, a human being is much more than what Western mystic Alan Watts called the "skin encapsulated ego." A human being only develops in relationships with others and with the natural world.

Systems theorist and religious scholar Joanna Macy points out that the systems view "implies a new understanding of personal power— quite different from the power of force, or hierarchy. Power can also come from interaction, openness, even vulnerability. According to the new notion of power, systems relate like nerve cells in a neural net, constantly interacting and interdependent.... Systems thinkers call this synergy—when cooperation produces results that are not only greater in magnitude than the sum of their components but also qualitatively greater in scope."[11]

Relationships are wellsprings of ideas for creative work. Keep an eye on unexpected success stories in business, and you will often see friends, dorm-mates, spouses, and lovers who decided to put their chemistry to the test by working together. Newbury Comics, a profitable retail chain in New England, was started in a low rent Boston apartment by two MIT friends who shared an aversion to studying. Karen Fenske and Jeff Lubbers, of Michigan, met at the local landfill while doing their respective jobs—hers in materials recovery at her family's landfill, and his in waste hauling. They got together to form Lubbers Resource Systems, a waste pickup and recycling company, and ended up marrying as well.[12]

Enlightened self-interest has a lot to do with recognizing opportunities for creative work that are also opportunities to deepen powerful relationships and benefit from them. This is very different from seeing yourself as a lone, vulnerable contender, competing with droves of others for a limited range of identical spots. When you take interdependence seriously, competition for its own sake loses its attractiveness, while negotiation and collaboration are revealed as the path of enduring strength.

Who do you work for (or, if you're out of work, who do you imagine yourself working for)?

Did you naturally leap to one answer? How many other ways can you answer it?

Do you work for an organization? A boss? Customers? Shareholders? The people who rely on your paycheck? A social movement? An innovation you dream about? Future generations? All life on earth?

What are your agreements, spoken and unspoken, with each of these groups?

When there's a conflict among these loyalties, as there's bound to be, how is it resolved?

Interconnectedness Exercise

Consider the range of effects you want your work to have. Take a piece of paper and pen. If you have a blackboard or big piece of newsprint, that's even better. Think of examples of personal, community, or global, political, economic, or ecological problems that concern you. Whatever pops up, write it down in brief phrases—but not in a list. Scatter your words all over the paper as your imagination dictates. When you have run out of ideas or filled up the paper, draw lines to indicate any connections you see between problems. They may be cause-and-effect connections. They may have a similar source. They may affect similar people. They may trigger the same responses in you.

According to psychologist Sarah Conn, who designed this exercise, "Many people have a little 'aha!' moment when they do this; they realize that, wherever they choose to take action or make change, the effects will resonate through the web of connection in ways they never dreamed. What's more, taking action in any area connects you to others in a way that opens up new possibility."

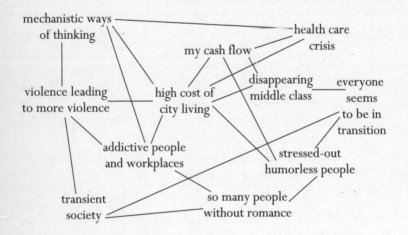

Wake Up to the Beauty
and Pain of the World

The same qualities of attentiveness and receptivity that help people excel—whether as athletes, artists, cooks, managers, teachers, or factory workers—can also increase compassion and response-ability in the wider world. Those qualities are essential if we want to integrate our working lives into a more coherent vision of what it means to labor on earth at the end of the twentieth century. "Shoulds" are just not strong enough motivators, as you have probably discovered. Fear can be effective in the short run, but it leads to burnout and cynicism. Compassionate identification with the larger world—and openness to the information, feelings, and imagery we receive from it—leads us to understand that cleaning up our messes and caring for each other is enlightened self-interest, not an extra-credit activity to be deferred until things are in order close to home.

Openness requires overcoming denial of the dangers, from local to global, that touch our lives and the lives of all we love—breaking out of what the *New York Times* behavioral science writer Daniel Goleman calls "the social trance."[13] This is not altogether pleasant news. Waking up to our potential and our opportunities for contribution means taking in the vastness of the disarray and danger around us—not in a spirit of blame, guilt, or victimhood, but as participants capable of focusing our attention in a way that liberates power.

Part of this wake-up call is about the present realities of our working lives. In some ways, it's easier to acknowledge the pain of the Kurds in Iraq or Cuban refugees than it is to face the sense of compromise, frustration, and failure many of us feel in our own jobs or job searches. For most people, work is demanding and at times cruel, an observation borne out not only by seething tensions but by overt workplace violence—an epidemic that cost American employers $2.4 billion in 1992.[14]

Grief, confusion, and rage are all possible responses. But on the other side of them, new creativity is possible. Activists in the movements for nuclear arms control and environmental protection have used this principle by developing educational methods to help people uncover and express their emotions and images about the global situation. Breaking out of numbness means tapping hidden resources of response. And when the focus of the nervous system is no longer on avoiding emotional pain, the ability to appreciate the beauty and sacredness of life is enhanced.

Psychologist James Hillman believes that the modern global crisis is rooted in the fact that people are anesthetized—literally, cut off from the ability to respond to beauty in a vigorous enough way to fight for its preservation.[15] To the extent that this is true, the effort to uncover new work opportunities leads to such questions as:

When and where have I been moved by beauty lately?
Where can I create beauty? Or preserve it, or make it more
democratically available?
Where can I ease suffering or help to eliminate its root causes?

❧

Seeing, caring, and connecting to the planetary drama in all its forms is also a path to seeing ways out of conflict, stepping out of limiting frames of reference, and finding unexpected solutions to problems. It is anything but a soft skill. This attentiveness helps keep life's tasks and projects on track (and worth doing), a fact recognized by more and more businesspeople. James Autry writes in *Love and Profit:*[16]

Listen.
In every office,
you hear the threads
of love and joy and fear and guilt,
the cries for celebration and reassurance,
and somehow you know that connecting those threads
is what you are supposed to do
and business takes care of itself.

❧

*Do you "cocoon," or hide out in the coziest possible domestic nest
    every moment you can?*
*When you socialize, do you seek out a diverse crowd or stick with
    people who think and dress and play the ways you do?*
*If you tend to isolate, or to hang out with people who don't
    challenge you, why?*
What are your images and feelings about the state of the world?
*Do you read the papers or watch the news? When you do, notice
    how it makes you feel. (This is not as easy as it may sound.)*
*When you come upon stories that are especially moving—maybe
    inspiring, maybe painful—get in the habit of talking about
    them with someone. Ask yourself: If I were fearless and
    had unlimited resources, what action would this story inspire
    in me?*[17]

❧

Wake Up to Yourself

The capacity for self-reflection is essential to long-term change. But it's one of the hardest skills to cultivate and to integrate into a demanding life. A New York architect I met a few years ago spoke for many people when he said, "Sure, I have time to reflect on my life— sometimes five minutes at a stretch, if I'm alone in a cab." Without this capacity for self-reflection and the time to exercise it, changing your life for the better is almost impossible. This is why people often try on new behavior patterns, but can't fit them into an integrated sense of self and therefore can't keep them going reliably. According to educational psychologist Nevitt Sanford, "No amount of situation or behavior changing will lead to personality development in adults unless accompanied by self-reflection."[18]

Self-reflection requires initiative, commitment, and the courage to step out of habitual ways of seeing. As Duane Elgin writes in *Voluntary Simplicity:*

> The crucial importance of penetrating behind our continuous stream of thought (as largely unconscious and lightning-fast flows of inner fantasy-dialogue) is stressed by every major consciousness tradition in the world: Buddhist, Taoist, Hindu, Sufi, Zen, etc. Western cultures, however, have fostered the understanding that a state of continual mental distraction is in the natural order of things. Consequently, by virtue of a largely unconscious social agreement about the nature of our inner thought processes, we live individually and collectively almost totally embedded within our mental con- structed reality.[19]

Self-reflection does not mean self-obsession. In my experience, the people who strike the best balance between introspection and action are those who spend most of their time focusing outward and functioning without undue complexity, but "check in with themselves" with some regularity.

Columnist Colman McCarthy links a widespread hunger for self- reflection, and for the time and freedom it requires, to the rising popularity of monasteries and other religious retreat centers among people of every conceivable background, who come for weekends or longer spells of quiet, meditation, walking, and reading.[20] McCarthy, who spent some years in a spiritual community "to get some traction before lurching into adulthood," has put his ear to the ground to learn more about this phenomenon. He quotes professional golfer Tom Stewart, who checks himself into Gethsemane monastery in Kentucky every fall for a decompression period that is the opposite of a retreat. In Stewart's mind, it's "an advance—because you go forward" more effectively when you stop to get oriented.

Going to a special place for this purpose screens outside stimulation and distraction, but it also segregates the process of reflection from the rest of your life, and it adds financial costs that can turn this spiritual necessity into a luxury. Many people prefer to identify places and times for quiet that can fit into their everyday lives. One useful approach comes from Danaan Parry, a former Atomic Energy Commission scientist who now heads the Earthstewards Network and runs workshops internationally on spiritual, earth-centered living.[21] Following the traditions of many Native American nations, Parry recommends identifying your "power spot" in nature, a place "where you can relatively easily tap back into your Aloneness. It's a natural setting that holds for you the qualities of calm, quiet, wild, earthy, grounded, centered. It is for you only." That power spot should be close enough for easy access, yet self-contained and far enough away from human settlement to welcome your whole being, not just the civilized parts. A park or rooftop garden, a meadow on the edge of town—any of these will suffice if they ease you out of habitual ways of seeing and into a fresh perspective.

What's important is that you find time to reflect, no matter what commitments and complexities you may be tangled up in. This, in turn, requires paying new attention to the balance of your life.

❧

What does it take for you to find "downtime" for reflection and renewal?

What opportunities for self-reflection exist in your everyday life—morning quiet time, for example?

How could these be expanded or better protected, even in little ways?

❧

Step 2:

Stabilize Your

Life

W ith so much to choose from, no wonder many of us think we can
keep doing a little bit of everything, and somehow the important stuff
will take care of itself. And small wonder our powers of concentration
are so faint we need written instructions to remember to feed the cat.[1]

Deborah Baldwin

Some of the biggest barriers to getting a grip on our working lives aren't found in the workplace, the job market, or the economy. They're in the totality of work and play, home life and social relationships, memories and hopes that help to determine our sense of possibility.

A computer systems analyst I know was looking to leave a corporate job and find a place in an environmental organization. "What gets in the way?" I asked.

"I have one foot in a bad marriage and one foot out," he replied. "I'm spending all my free time in couples counseling, not to mention all my emotional energy. There's nothing left of me for a job hunt."

Interconnectedness isn't just a buzzword. It's a reality of our lives, for good and for ill; it's a power source. It means small actions can have unexpected ripple effects. It means we can draw support from surprising sources. But the downside is gridlock. If you're stuck in any one area, it's a struggle to keep that stuckness from spreading throughout your life.

The quality of interconnectedness becomes obvious when you start to engineer changes in your life. Start anywhere. Change anything. And watch everything else shift. Switch jobs, and watch the changes in your social life that result from the new rhythms of your schedule and your new associations. Start or stop a romance, and notice the impact on your motivation to job hunt. Break out of a limiting self-image, and watch some of your friendships grow stronger while others fizzle or blow apart because your so-called friends had an investment in seeing you as you were.

This step is about unsnarling the tangled connections in your life and creating the conditions for long-term change in the gentlest, most coherent way possible. It's about making sure there's enough balance in your life for you to consider long-range choices without uncontrollable laughing or sobbing. Don't worry, we're not going to try to solve all the rest of life's problems before proceeding on the work front. The goal here is simply to see that the steps ahead will not backfire by having an unexpected impact on any other aspect of your life, and that the process of career change will not send you into a tailspin.

Stabilization means increasing the chances that the structures you choose to build in your life will stay built, rather than toppling in the next crisis. It also creates conditions that let you make decisions calmly and with the greatest possible awareness of the alternatives. Mark Levine, a psychologist and coordinator of community service projects at the University of Massachusetts, makes this point about idealistic students who become paralyzed by the terror of infinite possibilities: "The first thing you have to do is become confident that you will survive. Do whatever it takes to gain that experience and perspective. Then you will be able to look out at the options in a more expansive way."

This step is my response to the question "How can you talk about making a difference in an exciting way when so many people are struggling just to maintain what they've got?" Certainly, it is very difficult to think about long-term possibilities when just getting through the day is a battle. Vision and adventurousness do not come from some special gene or magic potion. Often, they come from a secure foundation, psychologically and materially.

If you aren't one of the privileged few who were born with such a foundation and you feel the lack, you have two choices now: feeling like a victim and focusing on your limitations, or building a more solid foundation for yourself at whatever pace you can.

If you are a wild and restless sort, you may be tempted to ignore this chapter and keep thriving on chaos. If that works for you and doesn't drive your loved ones and co-workers mad, fine. But please note that bringing more balance into your life does not mean giving up all adventure and risk. It simply means changing the ratio of risk to pain.

Balancing may just be a matter of fine-tuning for you, although, many people who are in transition in their working lives are in outright crisis. If this applies to you, you aren't alone.

Maybe you've just lost your job. If so, get your librarian to rush-order Kathleen Riehle's *What Smart People Do When Losing Their Jobs.*[2] This informative, compassionate manual covers everything from financial planning to interim health insurance to unemployment benefits to family coping.

You may be in some kind of acute trouble that keeps you pinned in an undesirable work situation (or keeps you from finding work). You may be stuck in a violent relationship, an addiction, psychological struggles, or even a job situation so dangerous or demeaning that it leaves very little left of you with which to create a future. If this is the case, let me say again, you aren't alone. Please do all you can to break free, and do it soon. Let the attractive force of more interesting work give you the courage to draw new boundaries in your life. Consult the resource list in the final chapter of this book for a lifeline or two.

However, if you're in "just" the usual disarray experienced by a person whose work situation is uncertain, read on. Stabilizing your life involves a number of issues:

Surveying the terrain—looking at what's working and what needs attention, what personal and material resources you have and what's missing, which struggles are inevitable and which ones are the result of bad planning;

Plugging major leaks in the structure—stemming any uncontrolled flows of time, money, or attention that keep you from effectively making the changes you desire;

Removing toxic influences—looking at current relationships (on the job, social, or intimate) that may be holding you back, and at scars from past experiences that may be unconsciously limiting your sense of possibility;

Strengthening the foundation—reinforcing your life-support system in every sense, from education to financial self-sufficiency to the availability of tools you need to make your chosen changes.

This is obviously too much to do all at once. But it is a process to begin now and continue as you move through the steps ahead. A gentle, steady approach is recommended here. Campaigns based on brute force tend to disrupt more than they smooth out. Look carefully for what's stuck, and at what it's sticking to, as if you were untangling a knot of necklaces that has been lying in the dresser drawer for years. That calls for three qualities: attention to detail, the ability to look at a situation from many different angles, and high levels of frustration tolerance.

Two particular unblocking techniques have saved my life many times. The first technique is to respond to any project that seems overwhelming by breaking it down into smaller and smaller components until you identify a bit that's manageable, even if you have to get down to a really tiny level. Then, when you've identified absolutely do-able steps, act on them immediately in whatever order is possible for you. As you take action, keep looking back at your list of actions and see whether some that looked impossible have begun to seem possible.

The second technique is to identify a trusted friend or family member who will serve as your "buddy," accompanying you through your resistance to the project or issue with which you're dealing. Your buddy might call you at intervals to see how you're doing, or be available for you to call when you're feeling blocked. Your buddy might even sit with you while you do the task or burst into tears trying. Often just knowing there's someone available to look over your shoulder can be enough to make you leap into action.

A few years ago, I was finally forced to take my own advice about stabilizing my life. A dozen years into a highly self-directed and satisfying career as a freelance advocate for social change, I was drowning in paper, terrorized by my computer, maxing out my credit cards to fund business travel, entertaining clients on rickety furniture, and exhausted from constant scrambling. I created for myself a half-time job, for an entire summer, called "getting organized." It really took that much time.

I found the time by doing some extra projects for income and by taking a deep breath and borrowing money—not always a good idea, but an investment in this case. I pitched old files, scoured yard sales in the better neighborhoods for a classier style of cheap furniture, bought in baskets and out baskets and color-coded files. I earmarked the income from a couple of writing projects to pay off parking tickets and buy new equipment. As the crowning delight, I bought an inexpensive picnic table that has become my "outdoor office" in the summer. Those things gave me the breathing space and the enhanced work environment I needed.

Sometimes even changes that seem minor can have a major effect in lessening stress. A lawyer I know cut his stress and got in physical shape with one simple policy. Whenever anyone wanted to meet with him, he suggested that the meeting be held outside—walking briskly. It worked for him, and didn't do his meeting partners any harm either.

The Life/Work Wheel

One tool for surveying the terrain of your life is the Life/Work Wheel (below). Points on the wheel represent major elements of a healthy, satisfying, response-able life: paid labor, self-employment, volunteer activity, rest, play, social relationships, creativity, a relationship of some sort with the natural environment, education, psychological and spiritual development, and citizenship.

Some of these will play a more prominent role in your life than others. Take a look at the wheel and see whether there are elements you'd like to add or delete (but don't wield that strikeout pen too impulsively). See also if renaming any of these categories would make them work better for you. Feel free to adapt to your life the questions that follow the wheel. You might want to photocopy this figure before beginning to write on it, since you will want to return to it on a continuing basis.

There is, of course, no one right balance among these elements. But they are deeply related. Your vision, stamina, needs, and desires in any one area are dependent on what's going on in all the others. The task is to integrate and balance them in a way that gives you the most room to move and the sturdiest foundation, that helps you define both your comfort zone and the ways you are choosing to challenge yourself.

The wheel can show you balances and imbalances in your life. "All work and no play" is one of the most common imbalances, with such variations as "all personal growth and no play" or "all job hunting and no play." One woman, in the throes of a job search, was led by this exercise to make a commitment: "Every week I pledge to spend at least one hour not obsessing on finding work."

Other signs of imbalance can provide clues about directions for stabilizing your life and guiding your work. If you look at the "natural environment" category and draw a blank, it might be a sign that the city or the office park has too much of a grip on you. (Professional environmentalists are the *worst* in this respect.)

The wheel is not just about quantitative balance, but about ways that strengths used and lessons learned in different dimensions of your life can be useful in other dimensions. Maybe you are stuck in an utterly crazy job that makes you feel ineffectual and confused, but you do weekly volunteer work that makes you feel effective and clear. What's the difference between the situations? Maybe there are things you do in the volunteer situation—say, spend a little extra time getting to know the people, or take initiative in resolving conflicts—that would be useful in the job. Maybe you need to look for workplaces where those behaviors are encouraged, or to explore the possibilities of using them in your present situation.

The Life/Work Wheel

Questions to consider for each category in turn:

1. What are some visual images, feelings, and words that arise in your mind when you consider this aspect of your life?

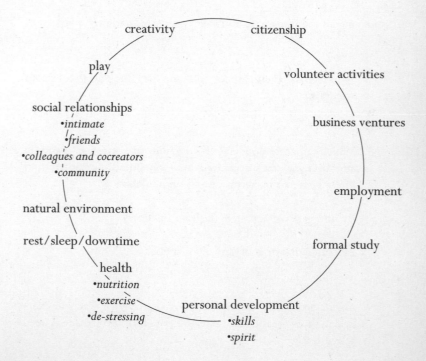

2. How is this category "working" for you?

3. What's strongest about this aspect of your life?

4. What's most shaky about it?

5. What would it take to make this area of your life really satisfying?

6. In this area, what is one step (however modest) that you could take right away to stabilize your life?

Considering all the categories and the relationships among them:

7. To which of these aspects do you pay the most conscious attention?

8. Which of these aspects of your life are most in need of attention and change? How could you simplify or adapt your life in order to make this attention available:

   By letting go of activities (at least for now)

   By combining or reorganizing activities

9. Which areas are working best? What strengths that you exercise in those areas could be transferred into the areas that need attention?

10. How could the elements of the wheel be better integrated in your life?

11. Now, focusing on your plans or hopes for your working life—however specific or general they may be at this point—in what ways can your awareness and choices in each of these areas of your life make a difference in the process of career change?

Now that you have a more concrete and current idea about the kinds of stabilization that would benefit you, don't panic if they all seem unattainable. Each step you take toward balance will make future steps easier. Give yourself at least six months to rein it in, starting now. That's not a long time, especially if you are seeing some progress every week. Consider what you could do with a six-month stabilization plan in the following realms:

1. Material. Where are the toxic dumps in your home? Your office? What would it take to get just one of them well organized and keep it that way? How about tackling one every month? This could include returning borrowed items (and renewing lapsed friendships in the process); finding, bartering, or buying the hardware and software that will help you if there's a job search ahead (résumé, briefcase, business cards, fancy clothing; not to mention mailing list, database, and desktop publishing software); and putting your filing systems into an order that's harmonious with your style and the way you retrieve information.

2. Workplace. If you're working, but feel that a change is not far ahead, it's important not to give up on your present job situation but to put that house in the best possible order before moving on. This also includes creating space for job hunting by clearing up any backlog you have control over, keeping track of vacation and sick days that may be useful in the search, and even negotiating a flexible schedule or slightly reduced hours, if at all possible. Dennis Jaffe and Cynthia Scott's book, *Take This Job and Love It,*[3] offers guidance in grappling with an important question: Do I really need a new job, or do I need a new set of attitudes and supports in my present situation?

Career strategist Marilyn Moats Kennedy suggests thirty steps for getting your career on more solid footing and positioning yourself for a possible move, including:[4]

- getting out to meetings to jump-start your network
- inviting a handful of friends to read a book that would do you all good professionally, then meeting for dinner and sharing capsule summaries
- finding a way to get some new and positive items into your employee files
- thanking your boss for something you genuinely appreciate

3. Relationships. Do you have time and emotional energy for friends? Are there important relationships in your life that need attention and care, whether it's clearing up misunderstandings or just spending time together? Do you have dependents—kids, parents, or others—whose requirements significantly limit your ability to focus on the job front? These are tough situations, but it's worth looking for even the littlest bit of flexibility. Do you have a friend who would barter caregiving help one evening a week in exchange for some equally significant kind of support after you've made your transition? Are there expanded day-care options available for a while? Can you engage the people who depend on you in some discussion and brainstorming about how to meet their needs while giving you more flexibility for a job search? Unless you're dealing with infants or others with limited ability to understand, just bringing those you care for into the information loop and involving them in planning can lighten your burden.

One of the most important small steps you can take is to update people close to you about the winds of change in your life, and ask for their advice and support. This reassures kids and other dependents, prepares friends to be helpful in more concrete ways, and opens a door for discussion with any loved ones about how your changes might make them uncomfortable. You may or may not be keen on the advice, but requesting it and listening as well as you can is a good step in enlisting support. Diverse perspectives may be more useful than they seem, whether or not you take every piece of advice you're given.

4. Finance. There are financial planners galore to help you stabilize your life in this area. And they cover an incredible range, from counselors with degrees in psychology to securities salespeople working on straight commission. Interview potential helpers before choosing one. Or get your hands on a very powerful book called *Your Money or Your Life* by Joe Dominguez and Vicki Robin.[5] It presents a structured and tested program for people who are, in any sense, crazy about money—either addicted to accumulation or addicted to a scarcity mentality. It will help you bring income and expenses into the same order of magnitude, separate needs from wants, develop more resourcefulness in meeting your needs, and free yourself from the psychological hold of money in order to reclaim an even more valuable resource, your time.

For most people in career transition, the most immediate work of financial stabilization is finding alternate ways to meet real needs when the income stream grows less reliable. In my workshops, we often brainstorm about things you can do to earn income on an interim basis. These can be activities learned through living or easily self-taught, such as child care, gourmet cooking, landscaping and lawn work. They can be technical skills that are learned in a simple course or from a knowledgeable friend (e.g., tax preparation, tutoring for aptitude tests, being a notary, desktop publishing, and other kinds of computer temping). They can be jobs that use and even sharpen basic communication skills (telemarketing, door-to-door canvassing for a citizen group you support). And they can take advantage of resources you may live with but not recognize (e.g., turning your home into a bed-and-breakfast; hosting foreign students—many for-profit language schools pay congenial hosts who will offer meals and an opportunity for guests to practice their English).

If your financial empire is wobbly, consider devoting a day or even half a day each week to earning extra income. Try to pick a method that takes you out of your usual patterns and habits. If you've been working in an office, consider waiting tables. And before you gravitate to the most depressing fluorescent eateries, see whether there's a lovely (and high-tipping) new place in town that's staffing up. Or, if your usual line of work is physical, try an income-supplementer that uses your language skills—maybe you'll even tolerate a few months of telemarketing to develop sales experience for a move in that direction.

An alternative is to slow down your ideal path enough to phase in a higher-paying moonlighting job. One author subsidizes her writing by freelancing as a church organist. Another shoes horses on the side.

The hallmark of a survival job is that it will not, and cannot, take over your time or distract your attention from your authentic work. It will probably have its stresses. But it can't exhaust you or demoralize you so much that you lose your creative commitment. Ideally, it's a situation you can punch out of and forget.[6]

When you've stabilized your finances, don't jump to quit your survival job. Consider hanging on another month or two, and use some of this extra income to establish a special fund, earmarked for moving you forward on the path of your longer-term working goals. If necessary, this fund could help you buy letterhead, business cards, briefcase, and the rest of the trappings of job hunting. It could enable you to take some trips to investigate possible employers, job fields, or schools. It could subsidize a course or two. It could, by its very existence, help you feel less powerless.

When job insecurity triggers financial insecurity, there is also an opportunity to look at the ways you use money in your life and the ways it may have the upper hand. Frugality is not a sign of weakness, as observed by one of its most inspiring advocates. Maine farmer Amy Dacyczyn, publisher of the *Tightwad Gazette* newsletter, notes that:

> A tightwad tends to be fearless in an uncertain economy. He knows that as long as there is enough money for basic needs, he can live quite happily without luxuries. He knows that there will always be Christmas because he can create it from nothing. He knows he can wring more miles from his old car. He knows he can feed his family well from his extensive repertoire of hamburger recipes. Most importantly, he doesn't feel like a victim of economic circumstances beyond his control. While he might dip into savings for a period of time, his lifestyle need not change. He is in control.[7]

5. Health and stress levels. Aaagh! You know what's out of balance, right? What kinds of food are you putting into your body? Do you meditate when you're stressed out, or only when things are going smoothly? How much exercise are you really getting? (As one of my clients, a labor organizer and long-distance runner, put it, "A good sweat on a daily basis is what kept me alive through unemployment. And it's free.")

A frightening number of people these days are functioning on the edge of burnout. This is not a joke. Burnout is a chronic, decreased capacity of body and mind with symptoms such as fatigue, irritability, lack of enjoyment, difficulty in focusing and decision making, and a sense of hopelessness. One of the most important hedges against burnout is setting limits. As my friend Sally Crocker reminds me, " 'No' is a complete sentence." But if you've been inconsistent about saying no and are suffering the consequences, these standard stress management recommendations might help:[8]

- live one day at a time
- prioritize activities and focus on quality rather than quantity
- let go of the need to control everything
- claim time for renewal
- celebrate yourself for the values and commitments you hold
- exercise, rest, play, laugh, touch, breathe deeply, have time alone

Many of these remedies are more accessible to people at higher income levels. But resourcefulness seems to increase as income decreases, so I will not insult low-income people by suggesting that they are not up to this challenge. All of us who still live stressful lives might do well to look at the ways in which we are saying yes to them. Whatever objective pressures you might face to perform, produce, and juggle, ask yourself what subjective pressures—from within yourself— you feel in addition.

I am growing skeptical of the whole idea of stress management. The illusion that the mysteries of experience can be managed is one of the fundamental sources of stress. Like all signals from the body to the soul, stress is to be faced, respected, and treated as a teacher. Less management is called for, and more vulnerability, to restore a sense of equilibrium. One of the primary ways to face and reduce stress is to keep your body awake and healthy.

Besides celebrating and caring for your body, a second strategy for resisting stress is surrounding yourself with beauty. Another brainstorming exercise we do in my support groups is to identify things you can do to take exquisite care of yourself, even when money is tight. For example:

1. take out new kinds of musical records and tapes at the library

2. walk in new neighborhoods

3. go to the museum on "free days"

4. trade massages with a friend

5. stretch and exercise regularly

6. go for a hike or a boat ride

7. hang out with people of many generations

8. call friends on the phone and pay attention to how *they're* doing

9. dance around your living room

10. take bubble baths

11. notice sunsets

12. spend time in the natural environment

13. keep a journal

14. read things you don't normally read, and get plenty of fiction and poetry in your literary diet

15. draw or make up stories with your kids

16. sketch, paint, or make collages

17. introduce yourself to neighbors

18. look for free concerts, lectures, and performances

19. plant trees and edible flora, or do local environmental restoration projects, with family members

20. get interesting cookbooks from the library and make new treats

21. sing

22. meditate

23. make love

6. *Balance with the earth.* There is one more form of stabilization that might not be as obvious as the others. I am referring to the

relationship of your life with the long-term capacity of the planet. This is an integral part of your personal economics in the long term. If you're like me, you're inconsistent. I recycle and refuse excess packaging. I resist using air-conditioning if the temperature is under 100. But I remain hooked on tooling around in the car to save the planet.

What do you consume that's nonrenewable? What do you pass on as waste that's nonbiodegradable and nonrecyclable? What values do you promote with your purchasing? How sustainable is your working life? Do you accept a long commute in the car without exploring alternatives? Are you hooked on paper? Tiny though each one is, these daily activities reveal our assumptions about the reality of the situation and our ability to make a difference. Learning to clean up our own messes is part of coming of age as guests, not owners, of the earth.[9]

It's worth saying again and again. An ethic of service and social responsibility is not about martyrdom. It's about contributing in order to develop, and developing in order to contribute. Self-respect and self-care are not luxuries bought at a high price by attending workshops or taking pricey vacations; they're essentials that working people with modest incomes need to reclaim.

Stabilizing your life starts with defusing crises that paralyze you. This frees you to create an environment for asking the most interesting possible questions, and following the answers where they lead. That supportive environment is inseparable from the quest for nourishing work. Both are aspects of the same process of self-realization. That is the path of integration—of work and play, satisfaction and contribution, private and public life, long-range planning and immediate action.

Step 3:

Create a Vibrant

Support System

Build community. It will help you out a whole lot more than
money when things start to fall apart.

Fran Peavey,
author and activist

Why Community Is Not a Luxury:
Steve's Story

Steve Kropper, a small business owner in Boston, divides his working life into two phases. For most of the late 1970s and early 1980s, he was out on some kind of a limb or other, running a variety of energy-conservation businesses and projects that demonstrated new technologies as well as new ways to enjoy work. In the second phase, which is still going on, he deals in information and does good work. But he is far more cautious.

Graduating from college during the energy crisis of the 1970s, Steve opened up shop to perform energy audits of public buildings and recommend energy-saving measures. At the time, public funds supported those audits, as well as tax credits for conservation and renewable energy projects. Steve's work fit an ecological niche. As a result, it was possible to make a living, make a difference, and attract customers with only a moderate amount of superhuman effort.

I was one of his three employees for a while, and I didn't realize until later just what a job from heaven it was. We worked as a team almost constantly. We shared skills and information. We laughed a lot. Three seasons out of four, we held our meetings in the park.

All of us in that little company knew we were part of something larger, a movement of community activists who were dealing with the city's infrastructure as a way to promote environmental sustainability and self-reliance. Because the work was such an extension of our lives, we could throw ourselves into it and still feel as though we were playing.

The early '80s were tough years for Steve and others like him. Oil prices bottomed out, and federal support for conservation disappeared. He went through a divorce, returned to school for an MBA, and became a telecommunications consultant. The new Steve tried a few corporate niches, including one where "it was just the four-star generals and me in the meetings." Eventually he started another small business, this time selling information for home buyers.

Steve reflects, "I'm giving people something they want. I'm not doing any harm. But these days, I content myself with more modest contributions. I go out of my way to give responsibility to people who might be discriminated against in other workplaces. I love taking my Boy

Scout troop out kayaking, or doing environmental restoration projects. I'm certainly not taking the kind of risks I used to, or feeling the kind of excitement."

I asked him why his life had changed that way. "In those days," Steve replied, "I was surrounded by people with similar values. They cheered me on, and they offered me concrete support in a thousand ways. With that kind of community, I felt much less need for more conventional kinds of security like money and a stable job. I felt confident that things would work out. But we've all gone separate ways. Without that backup, I've grown much less brave."

Something powerful happens to people when they see themselves as part of a community. They learn to value themselves. They learn to trust. They are able to see their struggles and complaints as part of a pattern, shared by others, and with causes that the community can address much more effectively than the individual. This chapter goes into detail about assessing the support systems you have and creating the kinds you need. The rest of the steps in this program will work far better for you if you are functioning in a dynamic community rather than in isolation.

Human beings may be too adaptable for our own good in many respects, and a prime example is our ability to function for extended periods as though we were encased in Plexiglas. The ability to work independently and motivate oneself is a strength, of course. But mature autonomy doesn't imply an absence of healthy relationships. Yet many of us go for days or weeks or longer without telling another human being what is really going on in our hearts. This is not self-reliance, it's self-deprivation.

Isolation doesn't only affect the lab technicians and number crunchers who spend much of the day working solo, and the telecommuters whose major bridge to customers and colleagues is electronic. It is also an occupational hazard for the salesperson who's on the road constantly and meets lots of people, but sees each one only a few times a year; for the military or industrial professional bound by a commitment of secrecy; and for anyone operating in a workplace culture that is short on trust. Where there is little trust, where stresses are high, where people are too busy or fearful even to maintain the humanizing little rituals of workplace camaraderie, people suffer and so do the organizations where they work.

Emotional isolation is a great equalizer, affecting people at the top of an organization as much as everyone else. As a (revealingly) anonymous former CEO wrote after sinking into depression and losing his job,

> Executives and managers, especially those high on the organizational chart, are particularly vulnerable to depression; higher equates with lonelier. Self-protection dictates one can't unburden one's emotional weakness with subordinates or competitive peers—or anyone else for that matter. The ultimate in emotional isolation is the chief executive. He can display no weakness, admit to no doubt or fear, and few, if any, subordinates would dare broach the subject of his mental well-being with him. [1]

Many readers of this book fall into another prime category of people who are at a special risk for isolating work situations—those whose values are in flux, and may be changing in ways that are frightening to co-workers and managers. The more you struggle with "outsider" feelings, the more attention you need to pay to building a community where you feel at home.

If "community" is about being, then "support" is about doing. Your support system is the network of people with whom you exchange aid and comfort on an ongoing basis. A support system isn't just a bunch of people, but a set of relationships and rhythms of interaction. You might have the most generous, caring, and talented group of friends in the world. But if you're not taking care of those connections, making use of them, and giving back in kind, you don't have a support system. Obviously, support is not the same as uncritical agreement. It's help in maintaining perspective and clarity. It's also practical collaboration to achieve your goals. If you create a social web that's held together by shared values, then, when you take a risk or a new action on behalf of those values, that community *will* tend to give you the support you ask for.

Some of these relationships can be developed quite purposefully. There's nothing wrong with looking around for mentors, contacts, and friends who share your professional interests and want to exchange active support. But a supportive community only hangs together if most of the relationships, on balance, are not burdened with too heavy an agenda.

I first witnessed the power of a support system in the hardest class of my college years, physical chemistry. Known as "the bone-crusher course" for chemistry majors, it required a tough problem set each

Monday morning. After struggling in isolation with the homework for many weeks, I took myself for a walk one frustrating Sunday night and saw a light on in the chemistry building.

This was a surprise, since the building was theoretically open only on weekdays. In the library, 85 percent of my classmates were assembled around tables. Several who had part-time jobs in the lab had opened the building with their keys. Pizza crusts and a guitar were strewn around, and a dog slept in the corner. The group was hard at work on the homework—collaboratively. Each table of students had taken on a cluster of problems.

This gathering was a weekly ritual, I learned. It had arisen almost spontaneously in the first weeks of the semester. By dawn, the problems would be done and the answers would be shared. Everyone in the room would have a decent understanding of where those answers came from. Those who found the subject easy stayed awake until dawn with those who were having a harder time. That's the part that has remained in my memory all these years. Rebelling against the rules, this group of students did not fall into an exploitive mentality, but a collaborative one.

That's one reason why asking for support is anything but an act of weakness. It's courageous, because it removes a major barrier to taking responsibility. A healthy support system is critical to turning ideas into tangible results and weathering the inevitable conflicts that arise when we step off the path of least resistance. Isolation provides a ready-made rationale for saying, "I can't." Community changes the message to "I can, with a little assist."[2]

Louise, a pioneering female carpenter I met some years ago, learned this lesson on the job. "I started out thinking I had to know everything by myself," she recalls. "On the rare occasions when I would ask a question, I'd start with an apologetic phrase like 'I'm sure I could figure this out on my own, but...' Then one day, up on a roof, I heard one of my male colleagues holler out to another, 'Hey, get over here and show me how to do this!' I was cured."

Louise had slipped into a set of limiting assumptions, even though things were going fairly well for her. When things aren't going so well—say, when you're embattled at work or looking for a job—reaching out for support can be even harder. The people around you may not understand the changes you're going through and may even oppose them. Or you may just feel too fragile to ask. As one of my most high-powered friends said after more than a year of unemployment, "I had such an investment in looking like everything was under control. My professional persona had depended on it. So, the more I needed someone to talk to, the more I hid out psychologically."

Even if you're good at asking for support, deciding where to look may require a little thought. This is especially true if your values and worldview are changing. Friends and loved ones who like you as you are may be disoriented by your questioning. New people you meet may be enthusiastic about your changes, but may not be able to offer the same level of understanding as old friends. Or they may pull you too enthusiastically in their own particular direction.

Still, the resources are often more available than they seem, if you focus your attention on what you need and communicate it clearly. People like to be useful. Often, friends understand that it's in their enlightened self-interest to help you move through your confusion so that you'll be more available and useful to them when it's their turn.

Support Systems at Work

In spite of the sorry state of so many workplaces, more and more people are reclaiming community and creating support on the job. At times, they receive unexpected encouragement from their colleagues and managers. Carolyn Shaffer and Kristin Anundsen's *Creating Community Anywhere* reports a number of important experiments in redesigning workplaces in this spirit.[3] For example, at the Quaker Oats plant in Topeka, Kansas, workers with problems affecting the performance of their jobs can receive peer counseling from co-workers. Initiatives like this have much power to transform work, and at the same time much potential for backfiring.

The potential for community in a particular workplace lies below the generalities. ("Oh, yes, we have quality circles and volleyball and we all love it here.") The authors of *Creating Community Anywhere* point to eight qualities of vibrant workplace community.

1. Alignment of values (among workers at all levels and the organization as a whole)

2. Employee-based structure, reflected in ownership or open-ended responsibility

3. Teamwork whenever possible

4. Open communication (for example, face-to-face dealing, two-way performance reviews, open financial books)

5. Mutual support

6. Respect for individuality, reflected in diversity of people and flexibility of policies

7. Permeable boundaries within and around the organization—for example, between union and management roles, between work and social life, and between the organization and the outside world

8. Group renewal

Certainly, finding a workplace that reflects these principles is one of the premier strategies for keeping your overall support system healthy. If that's not the reality for you right now, look for the handful of kindred spirits on the job. Even one makes a difference. For example, a group of seven Harvard employees meets monthly for coffee and brainstorming help toward their shared goal of becoming former Harvard employees. Two women who are employed by different branches of the same workaholic nonprofit organization stay in touch by phone for support in maintaining balance in their lives and refusing work that goes beyond their negotiated schedule.

Whatever the potential and limitations of your work situation, here are some other strategies for bringing a robust support system to life.

Assessing Your Needs for Support and the Barriers to Meeting Them

Start by assessing what you've got and what you need. Then survey the obvious barriers to the support system you would like, and set about removing them at whatever pace you can handle. Your "stuckness" might have to do with lack of time. But can't you reserve even an hour a week for coffee with someone who inspires you, or for phone chats with people you'd like to know better?

Your "stuckness" might also have to do with the ways you value yourself, or the health of your relationships. This includes the ways they value you, and the ways you value them. If you're feeling inexplicably stuck in reaching out for aid and comfort, start with two questions: How's your self-esteem? And how are you feeling overall about the people in your life? These questions may give you a clear wake-up call about your overall state of being. They can be followed with a more detailed look at your present and potential support system.

Exercise: Taking Stock of Your Support System

First, just make a list of the people in each of these categories:

1. The people you see at least once a week, on the job or socially

2. The people you see at least once a month, on the job or socially

3. All the people you feel you can call on in a crisis

4. All the people you could use as professional references

5. The members of your network who are the strongest positive role models in terms of character (i.e., the people you really admire, not necessarily the ones you think you should admire)

6. The members of your network whom you consider the most truly successful in their work (not necessarily by external measures, but in ways that are important to you)

7. The members of your network who work in fields related to yours (your current work or the work you're considering). Start with people you know best, then keep going until you get tired; consider especially people you like but haven't seen in a while.

8. People you can go to for an honest, informed appraisal of your strengths and limitations as they relate to your career

9. The people you can talk to when you feel as if you might fall apart

10. People in your network whom you have a special interest in helping along the way (maybe someone younger, maybe someone who is following a nontraditional path or working against a disadvantage, maybe someone who stands to make an unusual contribution)

Now review these relationships in your mind. Which ones are most harmonious with your values as they are evolving? Which ones are more reflective of past values and ways of living? Are there any relationships that need some attention in order to be healthy, clear, and really supportive? Whether it's just a how's-it-going phone call, or clearing up an ancient misconception, breathing life into your relationships is a great way to move your life forward.

Many of the skills involved in cultivating and maintaining a healthy support system are valuable in and of themselves, such as meeting people, asking questions, listening, and organizing information. Building support involves a quest for clarity about the kinds of relationships that will really help you grow; learning to give and take, talk and listen appropriately in a variety of situations; thinking creatively about the help you need and the best sources of it. For example, some of us find that the hardest part is admitting our needs and asking for help. For others, the challenge is making time or breaking out of self-absorption to give assistance back to others.

The basic philosophy of networking to build your support system may be well known to you. But, if you want a walk-through on the details, there are many good sources. For example, in *The Whole Career Sourcebook,* Robbie Miller Kaplan suggests starting by realizing how wide your present network already is, even if you haven't actively cultivated it.[4] It consists of family, friends, present and former school associates, present and former work associates, present and former professional colleagues such as members of societies and boards, professionals and tradespeople whose services you use such as dentists and plumbers, your librarian, public officials in your community, local merchants, and people who share your recreational or volunteer interests. Kaplan offers all sorts of tips for expanding your network and keeping it active including joining organizations, attending functions where you'll meet kindred spirits, corresponding with experts and the authors of articles in your field, authoring articles yourself, even in a newsletter of a group to which you belong, and sending copies to interested colleagues to stimulate dialogue.

These techniques all have value, to be sure. But what many experts in what I call the "upbeat" school of career development fail to explore is how to integrate all this activity into a viable life, how to prevent misuse of other people's time and your own, and how, finally, to say, "Enough," and get down to work. Indiscriminate networking—especially in times of panic—can rapidly lead to shoe boxes full of names, out-of-control lunch bills, and no time left to get your work done. Worse, it can lead to shallow relationships in those transition times when depth of knowledge and trust are extra important. As Jeff Reid writes in "Networking Overtime,"

> You can always use a friend. Unfortunately, some people take this idea a bit too literally. Maybe you can blame it on the '80's, when brute commerce seemed to muscle into every private sphere. Friendship—a traditional value if there ever was one—has increasingly been eroded by that scourge of the go-go era: networking.
>
> Networking, of course, derives from the ancient Anglo-Saxon words "netw" and "orking," which translate to mean "not working." Indeed, the old meaning still rings true: Today's networker most often covets a gig. . . .
>
> Who among us, in our search for meaningful human contact and meaningless fun, hasn't been detoured by those craving only business contacts? There are few things more annoying than thinking you've found a new pal when you've really just found another amiable hustler on the make, calculating a career move.[5]

During a job search, networking has to be pursued with zeal as well as integrity. The rest of the time, however, the most important consideration is that it fit into your working life in a way that is sustaining rather than draining. This homes in on the difference between networking and community building. Networking is utilitarian, and rises and falls with your needs; community building is ongoing. If you are part of a healthy community, it will come through for you when you need to network. In fact, the shared values of your community will greatly contribute to transform networking from a chore into a pleasure. The best networking occurs not when you are merely looking for a job, but when you are looking for a way to accomplish work that matters to you and your contacts as well. In that spirit, then, let me suggest two approaches for identifying and maintaining the support system you need.

Exercise: The Guiding Metaphor for Your Support System

Mentally review the support system that has worked most comfortably for you. Give yourself time to reflect on positive relationships and experiences. Now visualize an image that in some way describes or evokes the quality of that support system. It might be a team, an orchestra, a grassroots group, or a business office. It might be a more metaphorical image. The one that works for me is that of a tribe: although my friends and contacts are all over the place geographically, they have a way of identifying intuitively with each other; they share a fairly far-out language; and they stay connected through common rituals and customs, be they café meetings or annual visits or even sending photocopied journal fragments to their mailing lists.

You might have an entirely different metaphor for your support system. A church or gospel choir, for example, composed of people who treasure highly rehearsed, harmonious transactions in an agreed-upon key. Or a Mafia, in which people are tightly bound by loyalty born of high-risk activities and a fascination with power.

Whatever your image of the group, when you get it, use it as the basis of further questioning and visioning:

"Who else fits in this category?"

"How do members recognize and accept each other?"

"What steps will I have to take to find and recruit the rest of the members of my team / orchestra / tribe / family?

Exercise: Categories of Support

The second approach to maintaining a healthy support system is to identify important relationships according to their purpose. Three kinds to consider:

1. Your core personal and professional support system. These are the people you can call for emergency help, moral support, and brutally honest feedback. How many? A living-room-ful. How to choose them? Based on trust, clear thinking, and true "kindred spirithood." How to keep this network healthy? Frequent get-togethers, phone calls, giving as well as receiving support.

2. Your key mentors in your organization or profession. How many? One or two, no more. How to choose them? To some extent, they'll choose you. Cultivate and accept them based on their credibility, expertise, clear thinking, and interest in your career. How to keep this network healthy? Periodic meetings, lunches, workouts, walks, social invitations (don't overburden, follow their signals). Send "for your information" updates on your progress without expecting response. Call for help with specific problems. Whenever you can, offer help/ resources, too.

3. Your "access network" into specific sectors (e.g., vendors, customers, regulators, collaborators, areas in which you need to keep expanding your knowledge and fields into which you are contemplating a career move). How many? One or two for each purpose you identify. Choose them based on their respected and reasonably stable position in their fields (as much as anyone can ever tell); breadth of knowledge and contacts. How to keep this network healthy? Invite them to attend events of mutual interest; send them clippings and otherwise seek opportunities to be helpful; make a quick "hello" call if you've been out of touch for more than a few months. Seek out opportunities to collaborate.

Formal Structures for Support

Sometimes you need a more formal approach to support in order to handle a serious decision or a major transition, or to protect yourself from big-time stress. You may need understanding and fresh ideas, or practical help, such as review of a proposal or maybe child care while you job-hunt. Your needs may be served by a single infusion of creativity and perspective, as offered by the personal focus group described below. Or you may require the ongoing help of a group. You may even benefit from finding a structure in the community—from skill-barter networks to business incubators to revolving loan funds— that can offer material as well as social resources. The rest of this chapter will examine each of these tools.

Personal Focus Groups

From native tribal councils to corporations, groups of nearly every description have used the council or brainstorm session as a place to ripen ideas and strengthen commitments. But few individuals have realized how well this model can be put to use in their own working lives. What I call the personal focus group is a form for soliciting input for getting clear in any major life decision.[6] I have used it in working with professionals who are in career transition. Basically, it's a slightly formalized "kitchen cabinet" for thinking out loud and seeing a problem from varied perspectives. It is meant to be tailored creatively to your needs in a given situation.

The basic ingredients of the personal focus group are these:

1. A "brain trust" of reliable friends and colleagues—three to eight people who care for you and know you pretty well (your strengths and your blind spots), and who have some knowledge of the field in which you want to work. In considering candidates for this group, think about people whom you admire and who seem to have their own lives reasonably together. You may also want to include one person you like and respect but aren't very close to, in order to benefit from a fresh perspective.

2. A focusing question or series of questions, developed by the person in transition and presented to the participants in advance for their reflection. For example: "Here is a list of fields I can see myself working in. Which ones seem the best match based on your knowledge of me? Are there other possibilities I'm not considering?" Or, "I know I want to make a transition from field A to field B, and often changing fields means a leap backward in terms of responsibility. How can I minimize lost ground and make the process as interesting as possible? What

will the transition be like, and how much of it is within my control?"

3. A dining room table or the equivalent, which can be laden with bagels and coffee or pizza and beer or whatever. On this table, people can place Rolodexes, notebooks, and other tools for a real working meeting.

4. A purposeful yet open attitude. In setting up the session, explain the purpose well and encourage people who are even a little bit uncomfortable to say no. Then realize that the people who choose to be part of the group really want to be there and really want to be helpful.

Some people use personal focus groups when they're in a major transition. Others plan them at intervals. Several friends of mine hold sessions something like this—sometimes in lovely outdoor places—as part of their celebrations of significant birthdays.

By letting you think out loud and receive instant, well-informed feedback, personal focus groups offer a major jump-start for any area that's stuck. They can generate options or flesh out vague images of the possible. They can point to benefits and costs not yet considered in a decision-making process. They can function as a reality check for a plan. They can suggest strategies for networking into new areas, and even make concrete referrals. They can identify patterns in your pursuit of goals, including ways you might be shooting yourself in the foot.

For example, Molly, the director of communications for a struggling small business, was laid off after a period in which she had worked hard for the organization. Her anger about the terms of her severance, coupled with her fatigue, made planning and job hunting difficult. She developed a pattern of hiding her struggle from her friends and making grandiose plans, but spending many days in front of the television. When she sent out résumés, they often had typographical errors—guaranteed self-sabotage for a communications professional. Her personal focus group of friends and colleagues helped her shape a gentler, steadier plan to get back on her feet. As a group, they proofread her résumé and sent her back to the computer to correct all the typos, then gave her a round of applause when it was perfect. Finally, they divided the responsibility of serving as her "phone buddies" for ongoing support, with each designated buddy calling her once or twice a week to check on her momentum. She was reemployed the next month.

All this sounds highly structured. But it is minimal effort for any one person, and maximum benefit for the person at the center of attention. Every time I've seen this done, it has resulted in a radical unblocking, without undue imposition on friends—most of whom would rather contribute a little time that's used well, rather than a lot of unproductive "obsessing time" with a stuck person.

Personal Focus Groups: How to Make Them Work

If you aren't used to receiving and accepting attention, you may have to push yourself a bit to get the most out of a personal focus group. But if you're going to do it, put some care into making it effective.

To clarify your own goals and help the group know how to help you, it's useful to create an agenda in advance, while realizing that it may be thrown out the window if the session takes an unexpected, productive turn.

It's a good idea to designate a facilitator who can move the agenda along, ask useful questions, keep anyone from monopolizing or derailing the meeting, and make sure you're getting what you need. That person can also help with phone calls to confirm attendance, make fresh pots of coffee, and so on. Someone else should be designated to take notes (or, better, a tape recorder should be running). Delegating these roles frees you to pay full attention to the question at hand.

The morning after your personal focus group, you might benefit by spending some time with the notes or tape and with your recollections about what you learned. What new possibilities were opened up? What follow-up on your part would help bring these closer to reality? What questions were raised, and how can you get further clarity on them? What hopes for the session were not met, and how can you keep going in pursuit of them? Finally, what kinds of ongoing support will members of the group provide, and how can you use it well? Remember thank-you notes, and ask yourself how you might pay back each person's help in kind in the coming months.

Ongoing Support Structures

Some kinds of support are most useful in times of transition. Others become part of the fabric of your life. By keeping you steady and helping your vision remain broad, they prevent the transitions from being quite so turbulent.

Professional societies and caucuses, unions, business incubators, and networks of all kinds are, in effect, support groups. And, on a more personal level, there are as many forms of support groups as there are people forming them. Some are highly structured. Others evolve continuously. Some pride themselves in dealing with tough issues directly. Others provide an environment for growth and change simply by their presence. Some of these structures are called support groups or networks. Others just as effective are called basketball teams, bridge groups, or monthly discussion circles.

Starting a support group is easy, since there's no wrong way to do it. But there are also a number of organizations willing to offer you guidelines and contacts. On the job, one adaptable model is the Occupational Stress Group designed by Michael Lerner and his colleagues at the Institute for Labor and Mental Health.[7] These are twelve-week groups (with an ongoing commitment possible thereafter), facilitated by a counselor. They begin with simple sharing about experiences and sources of stress on the job, offer a variety of techniques for relaxation and stress management, and move on to explore root causes of stress and strategies for creating a more humane workplace. The principles developed in these groups are intended to help people move away from isolation and self-blame—rooted in the view that they alone aren't handling the stress—into an ability to see workplacewide patterns and to take stands as workers, union members, and citizens to remove the conditions that produce stress on the job.

Outside the work environment, *Utne Reader,* the alternative news digest, promotes "neighborhood salons" to discuss issues of shared interest and rekindle the art of conversation.[8] Groups like this are primarily intended to help people reenter civic life in a way that has personal meaning, but people who gather together to talk about what's important can hardly help but become resources for one another in times of transition.

The mailing list is another form of support group. Some people use theirs as a sounding board by means of a personal newsletter. Chris Halaska, a Seattle graduate student, started a newsletter called *Lean on Me* as a personal forum, as well as a way to stay in touch with friends in his old San Francisco home. He shares updates, poetry, quotes and excerpts from reading, and contributions from a widening network of readers on themes such as travel and art.

The direct power of this kind of network is shown by a 1993 appeal by Halaska's friend Dane Keehn, a teacher, mediator, and postal worker. Keehn used the newsletter to rally support for a campaign he had launched. He had taken on the role of recycling coordinator in his job at the post office in Bainbridge Island, Washington, only to be stymied by a high-level order saying it was no longer appropriate to recycle the paper thrown away in post office lobbies. Noting that post office lobby garbage, nationwide, adds up to some 500 tons per day, Keehn appealed to the newsletter's 150 subscribers and their networks to support his campaign for post office recycling at a local and national level. The effort succeeded.

As this example illustrates, support isn't only emotional. Many of the barriers we face in moving our lives forward have to do with gritty material limitations, from child care to computer access to skills and resources. Skill-barter networks have been springing up to help people exchange services from accounting to massage to bicycle repair. By this means, people can trade what they have in abundance—which is usually more than they think—for things they can't afford in the "money economy."

For example, New York City's Womanshare is a membership group of more than 100 women who gather for monthly potluck dinners and have organized a database of their skills and interests that serves as the basis for a barter system. An accountant may contribute an hour's tax advice in exchange for pet sitting or a massage; a job seeker might put out a call for leads in a field of interest, and offer gourmet cooking in return. Another example is Ithaca Hours, one small community's voucher system. You provide a service to a member (individual or group) at the price you set—in the currency of Ithaca Bucks vouchers. This is similar to the Womanshare system, but allows for more complex exchanges. An hour's massage or a tutoring session in computer graphics might be redeemable for ten Ithaca Bucks, which can then be redeemed for an hour of folk dance instruction or auto repair consultation from another participant in the system.

In this category, also, are material sources of support such as technical assistance programs; grants, fellowships, and revolving loan funds; retreat centers for creative activity; internship programs and even halfway houses for people in transition. One of the most visionary examples of a support system is a halfway house in Cartersville, Georgia, for southern Baptist ministers who have been fired, many for opposing racism within their congregations. So delicate is the political balance in the church on this issue, and so high are the passions, that people of the cloth are being sacked at the rate of one per week in Georgia alone. The house is named for Thomas Holmes, an Atlanta pastor in the early 1960s who welcomed the first black parishioner into his church—a Nigerian exchange student—over the protest of his all-white congregation. Modest but welcoming, Holmes House provides a haven for others who have taken similar risks.

Many powerful new ideas have been born in the climate of an incubator, a setting that contains the support and focused discipline to bring these ideas to life. It is no accident that business incubators are springing up in depressed areas in the 1990s. Conventional business incubators offer conventional forms of support for new enterprises: shared clerical services, computers, economical office space, and sometimes technical assistance. But a handful of unconventional incubators are cropping up around the country; these are quite proudly "social incubators" for new value systems and ways of working. National Service is a powerful incubator for young people.

Incubators can "grow" people, or enterprises, or both. Focusing on businesses with a potential to empower people and create jobs, Jim Robbins, a former trial lawyer and U.S. Supreme Court employee, is launching "green start-ups" in Silicon Valley.[9] Robbins' consulting firm, Business Cluster Development, helps create synergies among established businesses and newer enterprises in a way that grows businesses and jobs to meet emerging social needs.

In San Jose and Los Angeles, Robbins has brought together defense companies with excess capacity, environmental firms seeking to grow and cross-fertilize, and nonprofit organizations willing to take on administrative responsibilities such as office rental and payroll. The incubator adds value by bringing elements together wisely: small businesses that aren't in direct competition and can share ideas and resources, corporate surplus such as furniture and equipment, and compensation packages earmarked for laid-off managers and technical specialists, which can be turned into loans for new business ventures.

A similar strategy can be seen in the not-for-profit sector, for example in a low-key but visionary project called Ashoka Innovators for the Public. Named for an ancient Indian king who helped to spread spiritual values in rural India, Ashoka is a model "project incubator" that supports innovations for social and environmental renewal. Founder William Drayton, a former corporate consultant and EPA official, travels the world identifying people and projects likely to make a difference—like Clovis Ricardo Borges, a Brazilian veterinarian and zoologist who founded the nonprofit Wildlife Research and Environmental Education Society; and Didit Adidananta, an Indonesian who has created a shelter and educational institution that helps street children reclaim their lives. Drayton and his small staff match each of these "fellows" with a network of supportive groups who raise funds, gather and transmit information, and generally do what's needed to help the project establish itself. That support lasts an agreed-upon period of one to four years. Ashoka focuses on helping a new generation of grassroots leaders and innovators come of age, primarily in the developing world.

Structures like these give your support system form, coherence, and continuity. This is a useful strategy for withstanding chaos. But there is also value in the more informal approach to support discussed earlier, for these can be adapted to meet your evolving needs. Combining these elements is an art whose power most of us underestimate. In the words of psychologist Tova Green, co-author of the guidebook *Insight and Action*, "effective support means getting so close to someone that the only way they can move is forward." That's a vision powerful enough to transform work, and to renew human community.

Step 4:

Cultivate Critical

Research Skills

Most of us are growing apprehensive about our seeming inability to deal with, understand, manipulate the epidemic of data that increasingly dominates our lives. Where once, during the age of industry, the world was ruled by natural resources, it is now run on information, and while resources are finite, information seems to be infinite.[1]

Richard Saul Wurman,
Information Anxiety

I have an ex-boyfriend who is tops in his field, computer science. One day, facing a looming deadline, I tried to cajole him into going to the library and gathering some information for me. In spite of my promise to return the favor with back rubs, he turned pale at the request. "You don't understand," he said. "I got my master's degree in computer science because it was the only field I could go into without having to write a single paper. Libraries give me hives. I am one of the permanently research-impaired."

He's not alone. This chapter is about cultivating the research skills needed to go after work that has value to you. This includes defining the necessary information, gathering that information, and—the hardest part even for people who do it for a living—interpreting it realistically. We will talk about ways to identify job and career goals exciting enough to fight for, to uncover strategies for achieving those goals, and to conduct an in-depth investigation, in those rare but significant job situations when there's evidence of abuses or illegalities.

The Need for Critical Perspective

The easy part is saying you want to choose a line of work that makes a positive difference. The hard part is identifying one. That includes finding candidates from which to choose, as well as deciding which ones to trust by evaluating the claims of potential employers and the counterclaims made by critics and competitors.

For instance, would you like to work for the Stride Rite Corporation, one of Boston's most respected charitable givers? Stride Rite has endowed a major scholarship program at Harvard for students entering social service careers, and has lobbied state and federal officials for enlightened family leave policies. But it also recently closed down its inner-city plant in the shell-shocked neighborhood of Roxbury, laying off 160 employees who could least afford it.[2]

Or McDonald's, which has made leaps with lower-bulk packaging, recycling, and smoke-free stores, but which would not exist without the car culture and which helps keep that culture alive?

Or Ben & Jerry's Homemade, which has been accused by smaller ice cream makers of using the same overaggressive marketing tactics that caused B&J's screams of protest when dished out by Häagen-Dazs?[3]

Or the Commonwealth of Massachusetts Department of Environmental Protection, which has been forced by the E.P.A. to acknowledge that many of the state's worst environmental violators have been state agencies?[4]

For that matter, what about working for an idealistic nonprofit such as Greenpeace, which has been plagued by internal discord and poor labor relations?[5]

Trade-offs are inevitable in any working situation. But there's a difference between consciously choosing an imperfect situation and falling into one because you didn't do the necessary homework. Very shortly, we will be looking at ways to do that homework. But first, a brief discussion of the difficulties to prepare for, and the attitudes that will help you handle them with grace.

Difficulty number one is information overload. The quantity of numbers, lists, research reports, news clippings that flow through the life of a print-oriented person is just mind-boggling. A few years ago, people laughed nervously when describing the piles of paper sitting in their offices or on their kitchen tables. Now I'm hearing more sounds of despair. Most of the information we are called upon to digest is abstract, packaged, and removed from the heart of daily life. Yet it speaks important messages and we do our best to pack them into our minds and act on them when we're able. But this mental exertion takes a toll. As sociologist Orrin Klapp points out, "While we tend to think of boredom as arising from a deficit of stimuli (information underload), it also (and, in fact, more commonly) arises from excessive stimulation (information overload). Information, like energy, tends to degrade into entropy—into noise, redundancy, and banality—as the fast horse of information outstrips the slow horse of meaning."[6] Information is not meaningful until it is interpreted and that takes time, will, care, and a rested mind.

Side by side with that overload, however, is information underload—the problem of missing pieces, gaps in the available data. The abundance of information floating around out there doesn't translate into abundance of the right information to meet a particular need.

One of the major information gatherers and brokers in almost any country is the government. Most governments have very few laws limiting their own ability to control the flow of information they gather. In the U.S., the groundbreaking Freedom of Information Act—which (in theory) codifies the citizenry's right to know—has fallen on hard times in recent years. Government is charged by the people with keeping on top of information that has bearing on the public interest, through agencies from the Securities and Exchange Commission to the Department of Labor to the Occupational Safety and Health Administration. But the actual flow of information to the people themselves was dammed by bureaucratic means in the 1980s, and it could easily be again.

Between 1980 and 1992, vast amounts of data held by the federal government were reclassified, and many of the functions of information handling were subcontracted to private companies with limited public accountability. Price tags became attached to government documents that were once freely available. Documents whose shelf lives had been measured in years were discontinued after weeks or months.

This problem became so dire in the late 1980s that the American Library Association—not a hotbed of radicalism—began to issue a report called *Less Access to Less Information for and about the U.S. Government.*[7] Since 1992, some federal agencies have made admirable moves toward openness by declassifying many archives and by involving the scientific community in deciding what information really needs to be secret. The Department of Energy, which oversees many weapons programs as well as research and development on the energy front, is a prime example, having put teams of scientists to work full-time just to declassify documents. But budgetary limits, and the slow pace of the necessary evaluations, leave the situation still unsatisfactory.

Even when enough information is available, few among us are really adept at drawing meanings from it. The overeducated and the undereducated may be equally cursed. In the U.S., large numbers of students are still being graduated from the public schools without knowing where their own country is on a world map, without knowing the names of their representatives in Congress, and even without distinguishing very well between reality and creations of the media. This does not bode well for modern workers' ability to think clearly, to put work and career choices in context, even if they are highly knowledgeable about their own jobs and opportunities.

A truly well-informed vocational choice doesn't just require researching job categories, employers, and business opportunities; it also requires awareness about the issues that affect one's life, and a sufficient sense of history to be able to put those job opportunities into context. This doesn't mean getting a Ph.D. in history before making your next job move, but it does mean taking stock of your knowledge and its limits; it means finding new ways to stay informed and involved. Without asking questions, we are doomed to be casualties of the information wars raging around us. As Greenpeace's Bill Walker observed at a "green marketing" conference in the early 1990s:

> Green garbage bags. Green gasoline. Computers, hamburgers, compact discs; all here, all green, already. In California, where I live, supermarket chains that refuse to stop selling pesticide-dusted grapes are trying to promote themselves as environmentally correct because their pickle jars are reusable (you know, you can stick flowers in them). They're getting away with it. The chairman of Du Pont has the *New York Times* practically comparing him to John Muir. An oil company is forced by federal regulations to put a few bucks into preserving wildlife habitat, so it spends ten times that much to buy newspaper ads patting itself on the back for obeying the law. Do people buy it? People do.[8]

If that gullibility is a handicap for consumers, it is many times worse for the job seeker. Overcoming it requires becoming and staying informed and developing a skill for asking questions and integrating the answers. This skill can only be cultivated through lots of conversations—with employees of a company you're considering, and with people, representing a range of views, who have reason to pay attention to the company's practices (for example, union representatives, community activists, colleagues in professional and trade associations, local government, and Better Business Bureau people).

There isn't one right way to ask questions. As you experiment, you will find an approach that works for you. You may be formal or informal. You may want to write down specific questions, or more general lines of questioning, or you may want to think in advance about your goal and then "wing it" on the details. Edwin Nevis, an organizational consultant, points to two completely opposite styles that can produce breakthroughs:[9] Sherlock Holmes— deliberate, systematic, deductive, and smooth; and the TV detective Columbo, who intuitively muddles and mumbles his way into solutions for baffling crimes. Whatever your style, and whatever your questions, the important thing is to ask them and listen thoroughly to the answers. Where's the information? What are the underlying assumptions? Who says it's true? How recently? What did they have to gain or lose?

Critical perspective means cutting through simple formulas and generalizations—the green marketing and the anticorporate rhetoric alike—and drawing your own conclusions about the kinds of situations that will best allow you to flourish, develop, earn a living wage, and make a contribution. If you're a novice at this, or are feeling rusty, it's a good idea to talk through your research plans with someone who can provide critical feedback. A friend will do. So will a friendly reference librarian.

As an alternative, here's a truly wicked way to develop your critical questioning skills. It's an exercise called "Talking Back to Tele-marketers." I'm embarrassed to admit that I have actually done this. When "Brad" from "Opinion Dynamics Corporation" calls you at dinnertime, sounding like he's reading from a script designed by highly paid psychologists, pretend that he is a long-lost friend and is actually interested in meaningful dialogue. Take your time in answering the questions. Add juicy tidbits. When you're given multiple choices, consider options that aren't on the menu. Toss some questions back and ask Brad how he feels about them. Probe the assumptions underlying other questions. Give the poor guy some usable answers, but make him work for them. The game here is twofold: to face down a totally scripted conversation and get comfortable setting your own agenda, and to become aware of your "hot buttons" that may be pushed in your mind when you are confronting confusing or distorted information.

Research Methods and Sources

Unless you are one of the few people who truly thrive on chaos (rather than just rationalizing it), do yourself a favor by setting up a system for organizing your information. There's nothing like a trip to the office supply warehouse to create a sense of mission. Do this on day one, removing any chance that the fruits of your labor can turn into uncatalogued piles you're afraid to touch.

Computers, of course, are revolutionizing the research process for those who own and can deal with them. The on-line information explosion could be a force for democracy or the opposite, depending on who gets access and how the tools are used. Major resources on job and business opportunities include:

- on-line databases through services such as Prodigy, CompuServe, and America Online. These are maintained and made accessible by private companies, usually for some combination of a subscription fee and pay-per-use arrangement.
- bulletin boards—computerized blank slates where people can ask questions and engage in dialogues with fellow subscribers around the world.
- specific job search and career counseling resources such as Online Career Center, Inc., a nonprofit venture backed by 40 major companies, including Procter & Gamble, Kraft General Foods, and Aluminum Company of America. The center, which opened in June of 1993, maintains an average of 8,000 job postings, none more than a few weeks old.

All these resources, and many more, are described in Joyce Lain Kennedy's *Electronic Job Search Revolution.*[10] These services are developing rapidly. They are easy to get your hands on (for a price) if your home office is already wired in, or if you're employed or have been recently outplaced by a company with access. If none of these approaches works for you, consider the resources in your community: public libraries, job centers, community colleges, and even churches, more and more of which are going on-line. If you're broke but stubborn, see if you have friends with computers who would barter some access for favors they may need such as child care, errands, or maybe research on job possibilities that interest them.

Sources and Strategy

How you make use of the information resources around you is partly a matter of personal style and skill. Some people can pick up a telephone and make cold calls without blinking, but avoid the library as they would a medieval prison (and may sweat visibly when the conversation turns to on-line research). Others lean in the opposite direction. Still, every information source has some inherent strengths and limitations. For example, consider the differences between hard-copy sources (print and on-line) and direct human contact.

Hard-copy sources offer a wider scope, but give you fewer of the subtle signals you can get from a face-to-face conversation.

Hard-copy sources are updated at intervals, which may or may not be known. Human sources are updated continuously; that is, people keep learning (some more than others).

Hard-copy sources can be used for hours on end without fatigue; humans get tired and stressed out, and the most valuable human sources tend to be the busiest people.

Therefore do as much information gathering as you can through hard-copy sources. Use the meetings with people when they benefit you the most: for orientation, to save time in gaining an overview; and in the final stages of research, to answer questions you haven't been able to address.

Identifying Fields of Work

The Department of Labor recognizes some 15,000 job categories, and has just, for the first time in a generation, updated them. Writers of occupational literature are scrambling to keep up with changes in job descriptions, workplaces, and the organization of work. One major difference between job hunting now and a generation ago is the exploding number of job types and the diminishing amount of information that's available about each of them without digging. But the digging doesn't have to be an ordeal.

Here are some ways to learn more about fields of work in which you're interested:

1. Career directories, several of which are identified in the Resources section at the back of this book.

2. Professional and trade associations often publish specific career information, as well as other resources that can aid you in networking. They may have speakers' bureaus, local programs on career opportunities, national job listings or referral services for members, and many more services. They may also have local or regional chapters through which you can meet real people who do the work in question.

   Consult the *Encyclopedia of Associations,*[11] a standard reference series available in most libraries, for associations connected to your field of interest. These books are fascinating and fairly user-friendly. Just by browsing through the *E of A,* you can find resources on the career niche you're contemplating. For example:

   • The National Association of Black Women Attorneys has a job placement resource for members.
   • The National Center for Mediation Education publishes a workbook and training tapes on "Starting Your Own Mediation Practice."
   • The Council for Excellence in Government publishes *The Prune Book: The 100 Toughest Management and Policymaking Jobs in Washington* and *A Survivor's Guide for Government Executives.*

3. Schools that train people in professions often have alumni networks and magazines that describe career paths and accomplishments of graduates. Alumni and career offices are used to answering phone calls asking where their graduates most often work. In these conversations, it can help if you sound like a prospective student, or the parent of one, or a reporter.

4. Adult education courses, lectures, and magazine articles can introduce you to a career field, and so can calls or letters to teachers, speakers, and authors of same.

5. Your public library catalog, especially if it's hooked up on-line to a regional network of libraries. Often you can search on a

keyword in very specific ways ("holistic health, careers in" or "biotechnology, societies and meetings"). Lists and articles you find that way will lead you, in turn, to the payoff: real live people who are doing the work that interests you.

All the roads listed above eventually lead to human sources. Nothing except personal contacts can give you the detail and candor you need to learn about a job or business opportunity. But, ironic as it may seem, many people who are drawn to exciting fields of work may get hung up at precisely this step: making the right human contact in order to learn the realities of the work and the ways to get into it. Kevin Doyle, national program director of the Environmental Careers Organization, who has advised hundreds of career changers, shares this story: "I ask people to come up with an image of someone who's doing work they're passionate about. Maybe they point to Jacques Cousteau. Then I ask, 'Okay, how would you learn more about the way Jacques Cousteau got his start?' They say, 'I'd go to the marine biology department of a university,' or 'I'd read about oceanography in the encyclopedia.' I keep pushing them. Eventually, they say, 'Oh, yeah, I could go talk to the people on the *Calypso*.' But the direct approach is always the last possibility they think of."

Networking and Informational Interviewing

In gathering information and insight from people, you will likely want to use two techniques that are universally recommended but poorly understood: networking, and interviewing for information. According to Dawn-Marie Driscoll and Carol Goldberg's study, *Members of the Club,* networking was described by one rising female executive as "hanging out with people you don't like."[12] With equal cynicism, informational interviewing could be defined as interrogating those same people about their jobs and cajoling them into opening their address files to you. Needless to say, if you regard these activities in that spirit, it's time to refine your approach.

A better definition of networking might be the cultivation of mutually beneficial working relationships. It's the development of connections that can open the door to others.

Networking is the ultimate form of democratic association. Nothing forces people in a network to stay in touch with each other—except trust, mutual benefit, and excitement.

Through networking, people can help each other with:

1. Information about career fields, jobs, and trends

2. Feedback on ideas and ways of presenting themselves

3. Finding role models and mentors

4. Support, both practical and emotional

5. Access to people and organizations, through referrals and direct introductions

6. Idea generating, through informal conversation or focused brainstorming

7. Weighing points of view

Networking leads you to people who know about organizations, fields of work, and issues you're interested in. Informational interviewing is the way you find out what they know. Your ability to focus the conversation (without forcing an agenda) makes an enormous difference. Seek out people who are strong positive role models, who have been involved in a line of work long enough to have thoughts about its evolution. Help them by summarizing what you already know and letting them know what you most need from the conversation with them.

A warning: Career counselors have been sending their clients out to conduct informational interviews for a long time, and many hardworking people who have been the object of such interviews are getting saturated. There is still tremendous goodwill out there, but it isn't infinite. The benefits of meetings of this kind will come to people who use other people's time and resources wisely. This leads to some guidelines:

1. Learn all you can before an informational interview by reading, direct observation, and enlisting the help of people who are paid to assist you, such as reference librarians and public information

specialists at professional and trade associations and unions, not to mention the organization you're interested in.

2. Focus on questions that the interviewee is uniquely qualified to answer, and that will make a major difference in a decision you're facing.

3. Offer information in return (from your research using publicly available sources, making sure you don't share any materials given to you confidentially).

4. Think ahead about your questions. If you can, ask for a specific piece of information or a contact. If you can't do that, state your ultimate goal and ask, "What information do you have that might be useful to me, and who else can you suggest that I might talk to on this topic?"

5. Take no longer than half an hour, unless the conversation is taking off like wildfire and your source begs you to stay.

Through a combination of library research, on-line research, networking, and informational interviewing, you will soon discover that there are lists, directories, newsletters, and clearinghouses for practically any category of potential employer. The resource list at the end of this book contains enough to keep you going for quite a while.

Another important aspect of job and employer research is geographic. Anyone who has lived out of a suitcase, or stretched the bonds of relationships in pursuit of a job, knows the downside of globalization firsthand. The places where we feel affinity, where we know the people and culture and land, are the places where we can work with the greatest satisfaction. The next chapter will go into more detail on this topic. For learning about an area and determining if it's right for you, chambers of commerce and local chapters of professional organizations are good starting points for contacts and for information. They are most useful when you can ask focused questions, including asking for leads for more specific research. Keep an eye on newsmagazines for features on regional economies. And consult the final resource list for more help in exploring geographic concerns as they affect the next phase of your life and work.

Potential Employers:
A Basic Portrait

Here are some information sources for answering basic questions about corporate employers you're considering. If a company is publicly held, statements to stockholders are generally on file for public viewing in your state attorney general's office. The better-appointed campus career centers also have annual reports and 10K statements on file, as do some public libraries. Annual reports can also be ordered directly from the company.

If you want to know:	Consult:
products, services, stock value	10K statement to shareholders
business locations	10K statement
number of employees	10K statement
major decisions upcoming	proxy statements to shareholders
executive salaries	proxy statements
"who owns whom" (subsidiaries)	*Dun's Corporate Affiliations*
career opportunities, training programs	*Dun & Bradstreet's Employment Opportunities Directory*
recent management shakeups	8K statement to shareholders
some toxic pollution releases	EPA Toxics Release Inventory

Researching Government
and Nonprofit Jobs

If your potential employer is not a business—if it's a government agency, university, hospital, church, or activist group with nonprofit status—many of the same questions will apply. But the information sources will be different, often less adequate. See Part III, Resources, for more leads.

- In exploring federal jobs, the Office of Personnel Management is the gatekeeper. Directories and periodicals published by *Congressional Quarterly* and *National Journal* are valuable.
- For learning about state jobs, you will be challenged a different way in each of fifty information empires. Sometimes university political science faculty with specialization in state government can be helpful guides to the ways information is organized.
- When it comes to local government, the diversity of sources is greatest but so is the likelihood that you'll find a knowledgeable friend to help you get oriented. Municipal employees and the reporters who cover city hall are among your best allies.
- Trade associations are profiled in the *Encyclopedia of Associations*.
- Many nonprofit organizations are described in *Public Interest Profiles*.[13]

It's useful to ask a consistent set of questions about a variety of employers so that you aren't forced to compare apples and oranges when it's finally time to choose the ones worth pursuing. The following worksheets are organized to help you do this, and add other points that you turn up as well.

Potential Employer Datasheet

Name of organization

Address

Phone/fax/email
Position(s) of interest

Contact person, address, phone, and title

What does the organization do? (What's the mission? And what are the methods for accomplishing that mission?)

Form of organization (e.g., nonprofit, family business, government agency)

Number of employees

Location(s)
How big is the organization's impact?
    sales volume (if business)
    budget (if government agency or nonprofit)
    number of clients served

Who owns the organization? (If a business, who are shareholders? If nonprofit, who is on the board of directors?)

Stock trends (if business) and other indications of health

Strategic plans

Significant historic events (e.g., changes in products/services, reorganizations, controversies)

Some questions to ask about
job satisfaction and work environment:

1. What's the fit between the job description and your goals/hopes?

2. What's the pace on the job? Are people around you considered hyper? Is it typical to work nights and/or weekends?

3. How about the attractiveness and comfort of physical setting? (Consider lights, noise, cleanliness, smoke, organization of workstation or office and your freedom to adapt it to your needs, occupational/environmental hazards, including potential for injury from computers and other equipment.)

4. Will you have access to the tools (including information) needed to work effectively?

5. What's your budget and support system on the job?

6. Why did the last person in the job leave it?

7. How are decisions typically made by your potential colleagues and supervisors?

8. How much flexibility is there in scheduling? (Consider formal programs such as flextime, job sharing, telecommuting, and family care leaves of absence. Consider also the informal attitudes toward them. How much are they used? Are the patterns of use fairly democratic? Are they associated with lack of ambition or commitment?)

9. What is the ratio of salaries allowed in the organization, from the highest paid executive to the lowest paid gofer? Are there formal guidelines to promote pay equity?

10. Is there an Employee Assistance Program or similar source of support?

11. Is there support for child care and other kinds of dependent care? How does the degree of support compare with that of other employers of similar size in the same field?

12. Are there programs for quality management, skill sharing, teambuilding, etc.? Are they loved, hated, ignored, or some of each?

13. Are there opportunities for community service with co-workers, whether it's a little bit on a regular basis or a sabbaticals program for long-time employees?

14. What's the organization's record on occupational health and safety? This is important not only in factory situations but for

professionals who use many kinds of lab or office technology. Consult regional offices of the federal Occupational Safety and Health Administration and the Coalitions on Occupational Safety and Health that exist in many states.

Some questions to ask about your access to future opportunities in this work environment:

1. In general, how much mobility is available—to move up or around the organization?

2. Does the culture encourage lateral moves?

3. Are there multiple career tracks with increased recognition (e.g., scientific/technical, managerial)?

4. What training and development opportunities are there to help you expand your responsibility if you want to?

5. Do educational benefits such as tuition reimbursement apply to all employees or just selected classifications?

6. How will your performance be evaluated?

7. Where does this position stand on the organizational chart (and what can you determine about the informal power available to you in the job)?

8. Where did the previous holder of the position go?

Some questions to ask about social performance:

1. What's the mission? What does this enterprise aim to do in the world?

2. Who are the "stakeholders" affected by the success of the enterprise? How is each stakeholder affected?

3. How have decisions been made about physical siting of the

offices, plants, etc.? What was here before the organization was here? What's the story behind their departure?

4. What specific programs does the organization have to contribute to the well-being of the surrounding community, financially or with service? What kinds of reviews do they get in the communities affected?

5. What local and federal taxes has the organization paid in the last few years? How does this compare to revenues?

6. Does this organization publish a social audit (as, for example, member companies of the Social Venture Network do)?

7. Would you give the product or service of this organization to someone you love as a gift?

Some questions to ask about environmental performance:

1. How carefully are resources used in the company's operations and in siting of its facilities? Are endangered species or resources affected by the company's practices?

2. What is the organization's record on waste handling? If it's a manufacturing company, is the basic approach one of pollution prevention, or cleanup?

3. How are products packaged? What efforts have been made to minimize solid waste, use recycled packaging materials, etc.? Is there an office recycling program in effect, and is it taken seriously?

4. How are waste management policies different in the organization's U.S. and foreign operations?

5. Are products or processes tested on animals? If so, are alternatives being developed?

6. What efforts has the organization made to improve its environmental performance? For example:

- Have performance goals been set (as Monsanto did with toxic releases, and AT&T with ozone-depleting chemicals)?
- Does the organization subscribe to a formal code of conduct such as the CERES Principles?
- Are there incentive systems for environmental excellence for individual workers (e.g., awards, bonuses)? How about for the organization (e.g., a "green tax" on pollution, resource use, etc.)?
- Is there a commitment to regular eco-auditing, with public reporting of the results?

The following table contains some additional places to look for these answers.

Sources of Information on Potential Employers[14]

I. From the organization
   A. Official materials
      1. Annual report
      2. 10K, 8K, and proxy statements to stockholders
      3. Marketing materials (often available from public relations)
      4. Internal newsletters and magazines
      5. Orientation materials given to recently hired employees
      6. Publications on specific areas of controversy, including press releases and reports
      7. Filings affirming compliance with minority-and-women contracting regulations
      8. Published social and environmental audits
   B. Answers to your questions (through formal meetings, correspondence, coffee meetings, or arranged social coincidences):
      1. Recruiter/interviewer
      2. Management
      3. Other employees
         a) past holders of your job
         b) co-workers
         c) former employees
         d) union stewards
         e) public information office

II. Advocacy organizations
    A. Printed materials
    B. In-house issue specialists
    C. References to groups' activities in the press (e.g., you can cast a wide net for possible environmental violators by looking up articles on environmental groups and issues)

III. Independent sources
    A. Career counselors, counseling centers, placement agencies
    B. Newspapers, magazines, journals, and newsletters (especially trade journals) and their reporters, who may be helpful on the phone
    C. Books
    D. Official documents filed with government agencies (e.g., pollution reports filed with EPA)
    E. Transcripts of or reports on government hearings and audits, such as those of the Office of Technology Assessment and General Accounting Office
    F. Staff members to committees in local government or state legislatures, who often have years' experience on a particular issue
    G. Nonadvocacy organizations (e.g., United Nations; also theoretically neutral groups such as Better Business Bureaus, which vary widely in their independence from the business communities they serve)
    H. On-line databases
    I. Information requests you put out on computer bulletin boards
    J. Friends, acquaintances, and colleagues

Potential Employer Evaluation Sheet

Use this form to list positive aspects of a potential job (+); aspects about which you're neutral or need more information (?), and drawbacks (−).

1. Job satisfaction factors

   +   ?   −

2. Work environment factors

   +   ?   −

3. Social performance factors

   +   ?   −

4. Environmental performance factors

   +   ?   −

Interpreting and
Fact Checking Your Information

Use a variety of sources in your investigation of possibilities, and be skeptical of each one. Ask the vintage of any information you get. Put most trust in the facts you get from more than one source. And do your best to verify, especially, the critical pieces of information on which you are basing an actual job decision. The two kinds of information that are most suspect are information put out by an organization about itself, and information put out about an organization by a critic or opponent.

You can't ever be sure who's cooking which information how much. All you can do is evaluate a particular claim by asking obvious questions and reality-checking the answers. Other questions to ask in evaluating claims made about an organization, its practices, or its products:

- Is there a precise definition for the terms being used? "Natural," "Earth friendly," and "green" are in the eyes of the user. Environmental certification procedures for consumer products, mentioned above, are still being developed. "Organic"—once applied shamelessly to shampoos and soda pop—is becoming a more meaningful term, thanks to state-level certification battles fought by creative alliances of producers, consumers, wholesalers, retailers, and regulators.
- Is the achievement that's being touted required by law, as many waste cleanup and pollution-reduction measures are, or is it a truly free-will initiative?
- Is the issue being brought to your attention the most important one, or did you just let your local chemical company distract you from its toxic emissions by sponsoring a TV special on the rain forest?

One way to assess the depth of an employer's commitment to community or environment is to find out, through advance research or carefully phrased job interview questions, the extent to which that commitment is reflected in formal programs. For example, you might investigate:

1. What kinds of research, development, and planning are under way to move the company toward greater environmental sustainability?

2. What kinds of training programs are in place to help employees comply with environmental regulations and occupational health and safety laws?

3. What is the company's overall educational strategy for its workforce?

4. What efforts have been made to recruit community residents for higher-paying, higher-potential jobs?

5. What efforts is the organization making to preserve jobs in this area and retrain the workforce as products and services change, especially if it is in an endangered field?

Staying Current

Do not fail to check any information that is crucial to a decision you are making. The fact that you read it in a directory published three years ago does not mean it is still true today. And the fact that you got a piece of information from an on-line database or dialogue on a bulletin board is absolutely no assurance of its correctness.

To think ahead, and research ahead, about the direction in which an organization you're interested in is moving, read trade publications and annual reports, which showcase the projects that have the most backing and which may reveal research and development budgets. In looking for signs about where the jobs will be and which ones will be most desirable for you, pay attention to the variety of economic and policy factors that have something to do with job creation. For example:

1. Where are the markets?

2. Where is the investment capital from private sources?

3. Where is the government investing, through research and development funding, procurement, and aid programs?

4. What is the effect of regulations on jobs? (For example, the Clean Air Act created a demand for thousands of air quality chemists. The Superfund program similarly created demand for geologists.)

5. How is public sentiment shaping the regulatory climate, and hence the jobs, of tomorrow? (Consider the sea change in attitudes toward tobacco in recent years.)

The Socially Responsible
Job Interview

I have been encouraging you to ask a lot of questions. Not every one is necessary in every situation, but you do need a wide range of questions in order to assess a situation. Besides eliciting answers, the questions also increase self-confidence for the questioner. The more you take your curiosity seriously and act on the idea that you deserve to know what's going on, the more you will draw information and cooperation out of at least some of the people you talk with.

Now I want to push the boundaries of questioning even further, by suggesting that there are times when it's even a good idea to ask hard questions in that most terrifying ritual situation, the job interview.

Think of it. The job interview is a marvelous focusing situation, a time when questioning becomes a high art. Can't this do you some good? It can, if you are strategic and clear in your purposes.

Granted, nothing (except nuclear war and public speaking) scares many people as much as a perfectly normal job interview, never mind the special features. But that's keep-your-head-down thinking. If you see no alternative but to go into a job interview with part of your agenda hidden, what makes you think the actual job will be any better? Be warned: It is not currently a common practice to ask potential employers too many hard questions, and especially not questions that might be perceived as exposing dirty linen. As John Hanshus of Polaroid's human resources department puts it, "People on both sides of the table are very good at avoiding these issues." But there is no better way to assess how serious you are about holding on to your values, and how clear you are in your strategies for doing this, than to let yourself explore the possibilities for dialogue with a potential employer.

For the purposes of this discussion, there are two kinds of work situations: those where you think there's a strong match between your values and the workplace's mission and culture, and those where you know there's a significant mismatch, but for some reason you have decided you need to be there anyhow. Situations of the second kind obviously call for circumspection. One reason why it's so important to do substantial research about an employer before entering into a dialogue is so that you can set your trust meter accordingly. But situations of the first kind contain possibility, and there can be benefits from selling yourself on the basis of the contribution you can make in helping an organization accomplish desired improvements. Consider the variety of employers that would like to be counted among the forces of good, if only they knew how. Some of them may have even paid a price in the past for cutting corners on ethics, environment, health and safety, or worker rights. Some of them might be delighted to see a potential employee who has a commitment to addressing a problem with which they've been wrestling. Consider the risks, but also consider the value you can add by presenting yourself as part of the solution.

There are several reasons to ask questions in a job interview: to gather information (if you were absolutely unable to unearth it in your preinterview research) or to fact check it; to gather political insight about the decision-making processes, pressures, and other interpersonal factors that will shape your work experience; and to initiate dialogue.

If you are a job seeker, it's easy to feel that this is a hirer's market. But, at the same time, there is also a talent shortage, and a large-scale mismatch between the emerging jobs and the skills of many working people. Hiring well is one of the toughest challenges confronting managers, a fact driven home by the recent tidal wave of restructuring. The availability of talent is an important factor in corporate decisions about entering or staying in a market. When 15,000 scientists, engineers, and technicians signed a petition saying they would not work on the Strategic Defense Initiative, that statement was heard at the highest levels of the military and the Congress. The concerns that hiring managers hear expressed by desirable employees are concerns that will stay alive in their minds.

There are two kinds of job interviews, screening and hiring. A screening interview is often with a human resources spokesperson, sometimes even on the phone. Any questions you ask at this stage will often be answered with a fairly standard response. However, you can use a screening interview for your own purposes, by asking the select question or two that you identify as key in determining whether the situation would be acceptable for you.

The hiring interview, by contrast, is the now-let's-get-serious conversation with a hiring manager and other decision makers. That means you can get more thoughtful and subtle answers to your questions if you take care to create good rapport and get the rest of the business over with first. This is the place to discuss the more complex questions, for example, to go beyond inquiring about a formal policy to examine the way that policy would be interpreted in day-to-day situations. Hanshus offers this advice from the perspective of a corporate employer: "When people have personal concerns or agendas that might keep them from functioning as effective members of a team, that makes a potential employer edgy. Your communication skill and ability to get a dialogue going are crucial. Actually, the best guideline is probably one of Steven Covey's principles from his *Seven Habits of Highly Effective People:*[15] "Seek first to understand, then to be understood."

If you decide to test the potential of a job interview for raising tough questions, here are some guidelines:

1. First establish good rapport and get the major business done.

2. Ask open-ended questions in a spirit of respect and curiosity; draw the interviewer(s) out.

3. When raising a difficult question, try hard to show how your concerns are compatible with the employer's mission and can contribute positively to the organization's success.

4. Draw on your knowledge of industry standards and best practices.

5. If you open a discussion topic, prepare to follow it up in a way that shows your knowledge and mature judgment. Be prepared

for success as well as challenge. (For example, what if the interviewer says, "So how would you go about cutting pollution in this plant?")

6. Continually test the waters and have a safe change of subject ready.

In figuring out what it will really be like to function in a particular workplace, learning about specific policies and practices is necessary but not sufficient. It is at least as important to learn how the culture handles decision making, communication, conflict, and change. Factors like these determine whether trying to do something about the inevitable downsides of a given work situation will be easy, or hard, or not even worth considering.

Questions like these can uncover a great deal about cultural factors:

Tell me a story about a tough internal conflict in this organization and how it was resolved.

What have been the most significant recent changes, in terms of day-to-day effects on people's ability to get their work done?

How would you characterize the most common decision-making style in this department?

You can learn a great deal about these issues through talking to present and former employees and their friends. These are some of the most ambiguous questions you'll face, and they can make a difference between tolerable and intolerable situations, so get plenty of opinions and pay attention to the spin each source may put on theirs.

In-Depth Investigation—When It
Makes Sense and How to Get Started

This final section contains information you will only need in a few situations.[16] But when you need it, you often need it fast. In doing your job or in looking for one, a question may pop up, which is not answered in print or electronic media, that may suggest a less favorable picture than the one you've believed. That question may matter to you quite a bit, especially if it applies to an organization where you are already working. Is this company as lacking in cultural diversity as it looks? Why was this policy on chemical waste handling just changed?

What is that bland-sounding political action committee the company has been supporting? Why have these lawyers been coming around? Critical research skills are not just important in identifying suitable kinds of jobs and getting hired in them; they're strong assets in doing your job with integrity.

Especially if the enterprise you're concerned about is privately owned, and therefore does a minimum of reporting to public agencies about its doings, you might have to dig for large amounts of the information you need just to make a well-informed employment decision. Independent investigation might also be called for if the enterprise you're concerned with is a major employer whose practices have a wide impact, if the misdeeds you're concerned about are actually abusive to people or the planet, or if the truth or falsehood of your worst fears would make a major difference in your own choices about where to work and why.

Digging deeper is always an option, although it's one to be used judiciously. It's a matter of balancing investment and impact. On one hand, many secrets are poorly kept, and the act of unearthing them can be exhilarating. On the other hand, after you've done so, you have to live with the knowledge and so do other people. The choice to investigate your employer can be a watershed in your life, so consider it carefully. But consider, too, the potential for unpleasant surprises if your worst fears are confirmed when you least expect it.

Even if you are confident in your ability to gather information, it's wise to strengthen your support system for this project. An investigative reporter for the local paper, a consumer affairs specialist in local or state government, your state attorney general's office, or a well-respected labor lawyer can be invaluable sources of strategic advice and reality checking. Do your best to get high-quality advice. Resist being rushed through the process. And, as you gather potentially controversial information about the behavior of others, make sure your own behavior is impeccable.

There are two very different realms of information to consider: what's publicly available and what's privately held. Digging into the public record is within your rights and can often yield valuable information. A trip to the library to learn about your company's toxic releases or campaign contributions is a low-risk activity. However, in many situations, from industrial safety to funding fraud, the tough questions can only be answered by referring to privately held (and closely guarded) records. The moment you see a need for information that is not legally accessible to you is the moment you need to be working with a skilled and highly ethical lawyer.

Some generally useful questions for evaluating the performance and the ethics of an organization include these:

- Who's in charge? What's that person's background? Strengths and limitations? Ideology? Possible conflicts of interest? What's that person's primary (probably unwritten) agenda on the job?
- What's the organization's mission, as expressed in its corporate charter or other founding documents? What have been the major controversies when continued authorization and funding have been debated?
- Who are the organization's major critics (individuals and watch-dog groups)? What pressures do they exert?

Charles Nicodemus, an award-winning investigative reporter for the *Chicago Sun-Times*, offers the following advice about gathering information and making sense of it.

First, find out how the system is supposed to work, when it works. This applies to a company, a government agency, or a process within an organization. When you see a specific disparity between the way things are supposed to function and the way they do, start asking why.

It's usually the "little people"—who keep the files, do the typing, transcribe the memos and keep the calendars and appointment books—who know what's going on. Cultivate people who have direct access to documents and may be able to share them for a good cause. But be very, very careful to protect these people.

Finally, successful investigations often hinge on the temperament of the investigator. Be imaginative, resourceful, judicious, determined, skeptical. In dealing with important information, always get a second opinion. Be careful whom you trust, if you trust anyone at all. Don't let your wishes influence your judgment.

There are many laws covering your rights to information held by government agencies or private companies. Your judicious reference to them can sometimes help convince a source to cooperate with you. Laws covering access to government information include the Freedom of Information Act, national security classification guidelines, trade secrets laws, and federal right-to-know legislation.

Corporate information with public significance is regulated by federal and state laws. Court rulings have set strict limits on the situations in which companies can withhold information that is relevant to public health and safety by calling it a trade secret. For example, the federal right-to-know law on chemical hazards provides that no information covered by the law can be considered a company's trade secret if it has been disclosed to any person without binding them through a confidentiality agreement; if it would be required to be disclosed under another law or requirement; if its disclosure of the information would not hurt the firm's competitive position; or if the identity of the chemical could be readily discovered by an engineer working in reverse, starting from the product (reverse engineering).

Finally, if your investigation uncovers serious abuses, you will be faced with a bigger quandary than whether to accept or keep a job. You will have to decide whether or not to go public with the information you have gleaned. This can be a life-changing decision. If you are considering going public about a major abuse you have discovered through investigation, refer to Step 10 for a discussion of the realities of whistle-blowing and some sources of support for doing it wisely.

Like any power source, information can be liberating or overwhelming, depending on the user, the context, and the voltage of any controversies you open yourself up to. The more knowledgeable you are, the less likely you are to blunder into a situation of abuse such as corruption, incompetence, harassment, or social or environmental irresponsibility requiring a tough decision on your part in real time. Whether you're contemplating a new line of work, or deciding how much you want to know about a present employer's practices, it pays to consider more than your immediate convenience. It pays to remember the power of information, and the costs of ignorance.

Charles Nicodemus adds this encouragement: "It is becoming increasingly fashionable to be ethical, and that's a change in substance as well as appearance. Someone has to stand up first, but that act makes it easier for others to stand up in the future. One person can make a difference. If you find problems with an organization, tell somebody. Your disclosure will make it much easier for others. It does work that way."

Step 5:

Take a Fresh

Look at What You

Have to Offer

Where shall we begin? Begin with the heart, for the spring of life arises from the heart, and from there it runs in a circular manner.

Meister Eckhart

There is no experience from which you can't learn something.... And the purpose of life, after all, is to live it, to taste experience to the utmost, to reach out eagerly and without fear for newer and richer experience.

You can do that only if you have curiosity, an unquenchable spirit of adventure. The experience can have meaning only if you understand it. You can understand it only if you have arrived at some knowledge of yourself, a knowledge based on a deliberately and usually painfully acquired self-discipline, which teaches you to cast out fear and frees you for the fullest experience of the adventure of life.[1]

Eleanor Roosevelt

Reinvention Reconsidered

A recent business school graduate found his way into my office and said, "Something's not working in my job search. Maybe it's my résumé. I've just finished reinventing myself, but people don't seem to recognize the change. I just don't get it." He wore tweed, a button-down collar, round wire glasses. He looked earnest.

"What do you mean by reinventing?" I probed.

"Well, almost all my career has been in banking. But I just invested two whole years getting an MBA and specializing in financial analysis. I'm all charged up to work as a financial analyst, but everybody sees me as a banker."

That MBA had retrained—an honorable and appropriate thing to do—but he had hardly scratched the surface of reinvention. Now, there is nothing wrong with this kind of evolution. What's problematic, if not downright scary, is when people think that's the degree of change that's possible in our lives. You are so, so much more than your skills.

In this chapter, I'll ask you to focus on the questions:

1. What are the resources you have to work with, including those you haven't yet considered? This includes conventional notions of your resources, such as your history of accomplishments and your transferable skills; it also includes the values you hold, and the values you can therefore add in a working situation.

2. What are the limits you need to set and the conditions you need to establish in order for your work to have integrity and coherence?

3. What do these two answers tell you about a path for making use of your resources while setting healthy limits?

As discussed in Step 1, our psychological stance has a tremendous impact on what we are capable of accomplishing. What we cherish and pay attention to is what we are most likely to hold on to. Skills and experience are the focus of most career planning processes. But skills can be developed, and experiences can even be created, if you have powerful enough motivation. The source of that motivation is what you hold sacred, what you're willing to take risks for. Sometimes that's obvious, sometimes it's hidden by layers of habit or expectation. But commitment is what distinguishes people who "naturally" rise to challenges.

One of my favorite illustrations of this principle is a controversial figure, but an undeniable risk taker and a leader who grew while in office. In an interview soon after he became president of Nicaragua, Daniel Ortega was asked, "What have you learned since you came into office?" He answered, "Almost everything."

To bolster the case that you can learn what you need if the passion is there, I conducted a highly unscientific survey on self-teaching in the workplace by asking a dozen friends, "What have you taught yourself in order to be able to do the work you care about?" Some of the answers included: manufacturing, networking, welding, public speaking, fundraising, sales, video, Spanish.

When I asked this question, I happened to be thinking about skills. But many people, without my prompting, told me about existential lessons as well: "I taught myself to overcome anger and keep a sense of balance." "I learned to build community, and I realized that one of the best indicators of the useful work to be done is what people around me need in their lives."

This brings us to an important paradox. Ambitious goals may be easier to achieve than modest ones because they get your attention and force you to reorganize your systems of looking at the world. If a goal captures your imagination and truly fits your sense of your highest potential, it will have a wondrous focusing effect. When you're considering a career move that represents a "should," that makes logical sense in terms of your background but completely fails to excite you, it's no surprise if your motivation is weak. But when you're considering a line of work that represents liberation and self-expression, then, if you can only say yes to it, your ability to learn and adapt will expand in unimaginable ways.

No matter how clear we may be on the theory, the practice is a constant challenge. Environmental scientist Donella Meadows tells a sobering story about how hard it can be to step out of present reality and see truly new possibilities. Meadows, who coauthored *The Limits to*

Growth and its sequel, *Beyond the Limits,* has spent much of the last twenty years talking with people about what a sustainable future would actually look like in human, economic, and ecological terms. While we're constrained in the material realm by the availability of resources and places to put wastes, she emphasizes that there is no limit to what we can do with what we have. This message inspires some people and pushes a lot of buttons for others. Meadows especially remembers one man who stared at her unblinkingly throughout a lecture. As soon as she finished, his hand shot up and he said sadly: "I can only see one thing wrong with your sustainable future. I'm a nuclear engineer, and try as I might, I can't imagine a place for myself in it."[2]

There are two parts to that challenge. There is the external part. Who is hiring middle-aged nuclear engineers these days? Public utilities? Research labs? Medical facilities? Waste cleanup efforts? Nonprofits working on health and safety issues regarding radioactive materials? And, for that matter, how secure is the job market in nuclear power itself?

That's one set of questions. Another set of questions shifts the focus from the job market to the engineer. Where can he imagine himself working? Industry, government, nonprofits? At what salary, working on what kind of problems, defining job security in what terms? From the standpoint of pure enlightened self-interest, he is called upon to examine his habits of thinking about what he does, what he can do, who he is. He is called upon to apply the creativity and determination that have been focused on technical challenges, in the very different but no less worthy area of self-discovery.

The hardest part of this process can be the beginning, the step out of history and habit. Work is, after all, a powerful socializing force. We do spend an awful lot of time at it. And our success there does have powerful connection to both survival and self-valuation. For a century or two, successful men have defined themselves substantially through their work. For a couple of generations, many successful women have joined them on this path. This approach has many seductive features, such as the illusion that you can change your life by changing your job. But, when the options narrow, it may seem as though we're not only losing alternatives for earning a livelihood, we're losing our identity as well. This is what's going on at those times when you try to imagine a different future and can only see a black hole. Of course it's terrifying.

Apparent walls, like the ones encountered by our banker and nuclear engineer, are sending many people into despair, while others are seeing writing on those walls, and finding new understanding of themselves and their abilities. To stay with the energy example, physicist Ted Taylor is a famous scientist who reinvented himself, not once, but several times.[3] A weapons designer for years, Taylor found himself haunted by images of the destruction that could result from his handiwork. He made a career change and began working on commercial nuclear power.

But Taylor did not stop asking new questions about his life, just as he did about physics. He eventually grew uncomfortable with the entire nuclear fuel cycle and took an early retirement from industry. He reinvented himself as a consultant and designer working on safer, renewable sources of energy such as hydrogen fuels. Each of these shifts involved reeducation and new strategies. Yet each phase was a logical outgrowth of the last. Today, a generation of engineers and scientists and technicians stands poised to learn new lessons about reinventing themselves, with help from models such as Taylor.

Not everyone faces such a dramatic range of possibilities. The military-industrial example will occur from time to time in the following chapters, because it is an arena of such potentially creative tension. But whatever your field, a career transition can be the ultimate opportunity to make peace with your history. The questions it's useful to ask are among life's juiciest. They're about your inner resources, purpose, self-image, attractions and aversions, relationships, and the conditions in which you flourish. They're about the influences that have shaped you in family, school, work history, and culture, the ones you're comfortable with and the others you're ready to reject. Facing them fully, even if the investment of time and energy is considerable, means you ultimately land on your feet in a more stable place than the one from which you leaped.

That's why choosing the work you will do next involves so much more than building on your work so far. As futurist Charles Handy notes, continuous change is comfortable change, but discontinuous change, in leaps and lurches, is an ever more common reality.[4] Whatever your field, the process of recognizing new opportunities will draw on your entire life story, the reasons for your past choices, the situations you gravitated to and the others you may have traversed the planet to avoid. It's a constant examination of your life from new angles. It requires acceptance of choices that may seem unenlightened in hindsight, and realization that, while past choices may limit certain options, they do not lock out future possibilities.

The rest of this chapter presents a process of self-assessment that starts with the basics as I see them: values, skills, experience, and other resources. You will be encouraged to look at your current reality as a foundation, but not as a limiting factor, and then to explore your potential and ways you would like to grow in your work.

But growing requires healing. So the basics are followed by a section on making peace with your work history and understanding, in your own terms, the relationship between work choices and your overall development. This effort, over time, will greatly expand your options and capacity to act.

Finally, this step and the next will lead to one of life's most potent questions, "So what?" What do you want to do with all this potential? How might you make a difference in the world? What events and issues, people and other creatures, turn on your compassion and draw you to work on their behalf? And how do these impulses fit in with your more personal images of a satisfying working life?

This step contains a good deal of work. So take your time, and realize that it isn't an all-or-nothing situation. My intention is to offer tools for people in a wide range of situations, and to invite you to work with whatever intrigues you. This step will be most useful if you follow three guidelines. Do what you can. Use what you learn. And stay with it. As Joseph Campbell once said to a student who complained about the reading load in his class, "You have your whole life to finish it, you know." [5]

The Basics

Naming Your Values

We all believe in peace and harmony, honesty and freedom, love and work, and a host of other universal goods. But we act on them in different ways, to different degrees. The tricky, and powerful, part of exploring values involves getting beyond the universal and the abstract into exploring the absolutely unique way each one of us defines and understands a given value. That includes the way values arise out of our life experience, the circumstances in which we apply them, and the depth of feeling we have about risk and sustaining action in their service.

What's a value, anyway? There is no single, easy, agreed-upon definition. According to Sidney Simon, author of *In Search of Values: 31 Strategies for Finding Out What Really Matters Most to You,*[6] true values are chosen freely, among alternatives. That is, values can't be programmed. They're chosen after due reflection, which might mean months of wrestling or just a few minutes of quietly paying attention. They're prized and cherished by the individual who holds them, and publicly affirmed in a community. They're acted upon, and not just randomly, but repeatedly. Finally, values you truly hold are consistent with your other values.

Most of us hold values that are not so well articulated and are hardly consistent. We may also carry around a lot of values that are not so freely chosen, but that have been burned into us by hard times. If you find yourself feeling unsure or uncomfortable with many of the questions below, or if you feel that your answers are not taking you as deep as you'd like, try to articulate these feelings. Or go with your gut.

Meanwhile, we are going to start with some questions to uncover your values, in language that works for you. Think of these as ice-breakers.[7]

1. Your dream job: Do you ever daydream about an ideal job? It doesn't have to be related at all to what you've done or consider possible. If you have any images of a real dream job—the more extravagant, the better—spend some time visualizing them, writing them down, or talking about them.

2. The job from hell: Now for the opposite. What is a job from hell? Think of situations you've been in or imagined or seen other people suffer through.

3. What have you fought for in your work? Elsewhere in your life?

4. Who are your heroes and role models? How have they managed their working lives?

5. How are you different from when you started to work for a living (assuming that's more than a month ago)? What values have become clearer or stronger? More ambiguous?

6. Consider people you've been meeting lately, especially those with whom you've "clicked." What do they seem to have in common? Do you notice any differences between new people in your life and your longer-standing relationships? What does this suggest about your emerging values and sensibilities?

7. If you won an all-expenses-paid educational experience—from a field trip to a degree program—anywhere on the planet, what would you study, and in what ways? What would you be attracted to in that experience?

8. What volunteer activities have meant the most to you in recent years—from service projects to citizen activism, anything you've been involved in? What volunteer activities have looked attractive, but haven't quite drawn you in? What does each of these answers reveal about your values?

Interpreting and Applying Your Values

In the preceding section, you came up with language for some values that are important in your life. This is a tough and important piece of work. What's next is to reflect on what you really mean by those words, and how you want the values to be applied more generally in your life. Here are a handful of questions to move that process along. For each value you singled out, take a stab at defining the term, not necessarily in a way that will please everyone, but as you see it.[8] Where have you experienced this value in the clearest form? How is this value related to decisions you're facing right now? Be as specific as possible, and keep exploring details.

You may consider some of the values you identified to apply unconditionally in your life. Regardless of the situation, it's hard to imagine a satisfying existence if these are violated. However, other values can rise and fall in importance depending on the situation. For example, for years "independence" was near the top of my list of the values I thought I required to work effectively. I was my own boss, my own collaborator, my own support system, and I loved it that way. The few times I tried to collaborate with anyone on a writing project or program design, it didn't work so well. But over the years, I started meeting more and more interesting people—better writers, and people with more highly developed skills of negotiation and organization. I also strengthened my skills and got more secure in my ability to negotiate. I realized that my fierce valuation of independence arose to protect me from unwise, ill-conceived collaborations. I found my way into team research projects, and eventually into consulting for large institutions. I realized that I could work in team situations just fine—as long as my boundaries were clear and my self-esteem healthy.

Consider the values listed below. Add any that came up in addressing the questions above, and that aren't on the list. Now, which of these values do you consider too important to compromise (I); fairly important, depending on the situation (S); and generally less important (L)?

accountability

achievement

advancement opportunities

approval and recognition

autonomy

contribution to organization

contribution to general knowledge

contribution to people in need

contribution to social change

cultural opportunities

democratic workplaces

cultural diversity

educational opportunities

emotional expression

environmental sustainability

excitement

flexible policies such as scheduling

high ethical standards

holistic ways of thinking

honesty

intellectual challenge

justice

leadership opportunities

living where I want to live

money

nonviolence

organization's health

pace and rhythm of work

physical challenge

power

security

social contacts

spiritual development

spontaneity

stature (social/professional)

time for life outside work

variety

vigorous competition

Other values not on list:

When you've gone through this list, let it sit for a day or so, and then review it. Pay special attention to the balance among the categories. For example, if you indicated that just about everything is very important without compromise, consider the ways in which you would and wouldn't be flexible. If you see just about everything as dependent on situation, ask yourself what your core values are. And if most of these values seem unimportant, try to find some better language for your real values—or ask yourself whether you've been feeling cynical or burned out lately.

At this point, you have named some values that are primary for you in your work. You have paid attention to your own unique ways of understanding those values. You have identified the ways they can vary with context or time.

This is great work, but you're not done yet. You have now reached the point at which 99.9 percent of working people get hung up: crossing the bridge between the abstract and the specific. Ask yourself, "How does all this translate into practice?" One way to cross this bridge is to ask, "How do I apply these values with respect to different people and communities my actions affect?" This is the purpose of the following exercise.

Exercise: Values in Context

Choose a small cluster of values you consider important to you in your working life. Now explore, by talking or writing, how each value guides your action with respect to:

Your overall career development

Your family and other close relationships

Your community

Cultural and ethnic groups you're a part of

Cultural and ethnic groups you're not a part of

Co-workers

Competitors

Bosses

Customers

Investors/funders

The local ecology

The ecology of your bioregion

The planet as a whole

Future generations

Be as specific as possible. This is hard, but keep at it. If you can, think of actual situations in which you've faced decisions affecting each of these stakeholders, and the ways your values have come into play.

In what kinds of situations have you been most able to act on your values?

In what kinds of situations has it been most difficult to keep your values in mind?

A second way to cross the bridge between values and their application is to explore the ways a given value looks in a specific work situation. Ask, "What specific signs will I see—in the policies or the people or the public record of a potential employer—that the values I have identified are shared, to the extent I want to see them, in this workplace?"

Again, select a small cluster of values you have identified as important. For each, begin thinking of observable signs that would indicate to you that a workplace is sufficiently in harmony with that value. This is not obvious, and it's where most people drop the ball. We know our values in the abstract, but we are in kindergarten when it comes to examining the way they are reflected, or bypassed, in day-to-day situations.

For example, suppose you selected "high ethical standards." That's an easy value to affirm, and a vexingly hard one to define. How do you talk about ethics? As minimizing harm? Obeying rules? Respecting rights? Honoring tradition?

Suppose you come up with a kind of satisfying definition. How can you connect it to documentable evidence that can be researched in a potential work situation? Some people might be perfectly comfortable with the ethical standards of any company that hadn't been implicated in a scandal. How could you find that out? By checking databases such as Lexis (which keeps track of who's involved in legal battles) and Nexis (which keeps track of who's in the news for any reason), you could screen out heavy offenders in your field of interest and feel free to pursue opportunities in companies whose records showed no major controversies. There might be very significant reasons for doing that— for example, joining a clean-enough organization with great opportunities to learn or to contribute. Conversations with employees, and the other research techniques suggested in Step 4, are essential in making this kind of determination.

However, other people might really want to push the boundaries when it comes to ethics. They might approach a job search by targeting businesses that have received awards from watchdog organizations or otherwise distinguished themselves in the last few years. With sufficient fanaticism and a long-range perspective, it would be possible to take the resulting list of a few dozen employers and build a strategy around getting a foot in the door of one of them, even if it took a while.

The previous chapter tells more about investigating some of the values represented in an organization. You might want to use it to do some research on concrete alternatives while working with these questions of value. But the focus here is personal. How much commitment to a particular value is enough for you, given your situation, right now? And what signs do you consider to be reliable indicators of that commitment? This requires thought, and reality checking as well.

To take another example, you might identify "health" as a value. What does that look like to you? Now, how might a workplace reflect a commitment to health that mirrors yours? By paying for preventive health care in its medical coverage? By being squeaky clean in terms of occupational health and safety? By offering a smoke-free environment? By offering a product or service that enhances health? By not stressing out its own workforce? Which of these manifestations of the value of "health" are essential to you, and which are merely desirable? Where do you draw the lines when it comes to an employer's commitment to health? How will you handle an opportunity to work in an organization that's exemplary on some fronts and deeply flawed on others?

Obviously, this is not an inquiry to rush through. If it feels overwhelming, pace yourself. This is potent stuff because it brings about a shift from the abstract to the particular—from vague aspirations to conditions that can be checked out, and accepted or rejected. That doesn't automatically mean applying the most demanding standards to every situation. It means becoming more and more aware of your present circumstances and their degree of fit with your values, and paying attention to each little opportunity to say yes or no in ways that can increase the harmony. This is a supremely empowering experience. In the words of career consultant Cliff Hakim, "Clarity is gold."[9]

When Values Conflict: Your Situational Selves

In the discussion so far, we have been making an assumption that you can identify a consistent set of values that are at the core of your being. For most mortals, this is far from the truth. You may be highly aggressive at work and supremely gentle at home. You may be resourceful on your own, but fairly passive when working in a large group setting. Many of us have different personas that may vary according to the social setting in which we find ourselves (e.g., boardroom personality versus locker room personality; Saturday night self versus Sunday morning self). These may consist of different internal representations of ourselves, (subpersonalities) and the different ways we behave in different settings (social roles). That makes it hard to address the question "What are your values?" It depends on the "you" that's in charge at the time.[10]

First, just learn to discern these various personas. Notice whether, and how, you "shift gears" when changing environments. For a week or more, do some reflection and journal writing daily on those subpersonalities. You might even play with listening to the voice each of these personas uses.

Psychologist Mary Watkins, who has extensively studied the development of "imaginal dialogues" and their role in creativity, notes that open-minded engagement in these conversations "can be a means . . . of creating worlds, developing imaginative sympathy through which we go beyond the limits of our own corporeality and range of life experiences by embodying in imagination the perspectives of others, actual and imaginal."

Psychologically, the quest for greater consistency and integration of social roles, and the inner voices that speak for them, is a strong force for growth. Sane and functional people through the ages have found that listening to inner voices is not a sign of madness, but of openness to new self-definition. In times of transition, an internal conversation may be especially valuable. Donald Marrs, an advertising executive who fell off the career track in a prestigious national agency and eventually opened a smaller, more value-driven business, tells this story about a critical turning point in his book, *Executive in Passage*:

As my contact with the outside world lessened, I received an increased flow of communication from within. It was as though some inner spirit had taken over my internal photocopy room and had begun sending me memos all day long. Some came from the finance department, some from personnel, and some were from the creative department or research, and each one had its own style and its own interests in mind.

But some came from deeper sources, and instead of addressing mundane matters, they carried messages about the meaning of things—of my values, of inspiration, and of goals larger than financial ones.

Soon I began to expect this flow of communications and gradually turned to it to help guide my actions. If I needed an answer that didn't come on its own, I'd ask, and answers would arrive in many different forms. So in the course of time, as the dialogue continued, I was having board meetings inside myself.

As this inner communication developed, there were two clear voices who spoke for the rest. One was cautious and saw problems in their most familiar, material context, and the other was more optimistic and suggested new visions of what could be. The first I called the "chairman of the board," because he always spoke in a pragmatic and slightly preemptive way. The chairman was having a field day with my new life. . . .

My inspiration came from the other clear voice, who was the visionary on the board. Some of his ideas sounded outrageous at first, and were usually met with silence from the chairman, but he mostly got his way. It was his idea to come out here, and he was the source of most of my optimism. Even when things were roughest, I could depend on his vision to convince me that everything was going perfectly according to plan. He was also the source of my creative inspiration, and I always thought of him as "my little voice."

"Don't listen to the chairman," my little voice would say. "You're not a corporation and your life need not be conducted according to a rational strategy the way a business is. You started writing, but you're discovering the hidden nature of yourself, and that's just as important. . . . Just stay attuned to what's inside and your new life will unfold beautifully."

I always learned a great deal from these meetings and began to look forward to their guidance when things weren't going well.[11]

Exercise:
Your Inner Board of Directors

Here is one approach to setting up an internal dialogue (or maybe a "multilogue"). Find or make a time and space where you will not be interrupted and can feel relaxed and safe. Do some stretching and take some deep breaths to relax your body. Open your attention to any voices that arise within your awareness. Let them come into you without rushing to name or categorize them. They may have very well developed "personalities," and their quirks may be a gold mine of information.

Now ask a question about your future. Receive answers from any of those inner voices that want to speak. Keep listening quietly as the members respond—to you and in dialogue with each other. Follow through on this dialogue until you're left with either a sense of resolution or a new question. The resolution doesn't need to be a neat action plan; it can be an emotional opening, an acceptance of something you've been holding at arm's length, or a new image to work with.

When you feel finished, thank each board member and dismiss them, for now. Work on this level can hold surprises of many kinds. As psychologist Molly Young Brown points out about inner dialogues in which you are reclaiming lost aspects of yourself, "A process like this can be very emotional. The combined relief and pain of reclaiming and caring for a 'lost' part of oneself is often enormous. If this is the case for you, take the time you need to allow these feelings to run their course before moving on. Practice a centering technique . . . or write about changing feelings in your journal."[12]

Your Gifts: Accomplishments,
Skills, and Resources

We have been looking in some depth at what you value and how that changes with circumstances. This has been the first priority in self-assessment because values are an underpinning. But by themselves, they do not determine the most useful or interesting path. As soon as you have some preliminary insights on values from the preceding section, enough that you feel energy and interest in moving forward, it's worthwhile to begin taking stock of the tools you have to work with in serving those values. This is the part that comes first in many conventional career planning programs. I promised we'd get to it.

There are three kinds of gifts that can be put to good use, in conjunction with your values, in choosing your work: accomplishments or the record of experience and learning that you have to go on; the skills and talents you can offer; and other resources, from musical instruments to fat Rolodexes to basement workbenches to supportive families.

We will look at each one of these, as it is now and as you would like it to be. Then we will sweep back through this section and organize the results for use as you begin describing the kinds of working conditions in which you have the best possible chance to flourish.

Exercise: Accomplishments Inventory

Review your work history using a résumé and any of the exercises in this chapter. Consider all the times you have encountered a problem, whether defined by someone else or in your own mind, and have taken action to solve that problem. Pay special attention to the result you achieved, whether it was improved procedures, customer satisfaction, a technical innovation, a less chaotic office, happier colleagues, whatever. Write down as many accomplishments as you can. Don't stop when it first gets difficult. These accomplishments can be tiny little things, and they don't have to be recognized by other people. They only have to have meaning for you. This can also be done with the help of someone who knows and loves you, who can pull more memories out of you and act as a "mirror" to help you focus.

Choose a manageable number of your accomplishments to work with in some detail. Write them up, résumé style. In this process, action words like the following are often recommended: initiated, created, developed, designed, invented, managed, led, analyzed, built, screened, hired, trained, supervised, saved.

These bottom-line-oriented verbs are useful in self-promotion (communicating to others), and in self-valuation (in your own mind). It's especially important to pay attention to them if you tend to be self-effacing. But they're not the only achievements worth noting. For example, are there times when you have quietly helped someone else to come through on a responsibility that was important to you both? That is, when you encouraged, mentored, guided, collaborated, coordinated, facilitated, organized, shared.

There is a third category of achievements that deserve your very serious consideration, even though they may have gotten you the least recognition in conventional terms. These are the ones that have involved going against the grain, whether a little or a lot, to be true to values or information you held in high regard. Depending upon the kind of career path you're planning, you may or may not choose to elaborate on these on your actual résumé. But it's very important to notice and celebrate these personal achievements as seriously as any others, and to learn from them about the kinds of situations where you're likely to run into conflict. What accomplishments can you document in which you challenged, resisted, refused, redefined, proposed an alternative, exposed an abuse or other wrongdoing?

Finally, what other accomplishments have brought you satisfaction, whether or not they fit into any of the categories I've used?

Please note that a lot of people in career transition these days are struggling hard with self-image and self-esteem. If this applies to you, this exercise may be difficult, and may even make you furious. It may be that your biggest accomplishments during some critical period were to put your socks and shoes on every day, to keep your kids fed, or to function in an impossible situation without bursting into tears. Hear me: This is heroism. If you're having trouble accepting that, talk it through with a counselor or friend.

Before going further, give yourself some time to write in your journal, meditate, talk with a friend, do visual art, or just ponder any of the above experiences that remain emotionally charged for you. Then consider the following questions:

- Which accomplishments do you value most highly? Which accomplishments are most highly valued in work situations? How have you handled any tension between those two value systems in the past? Are there other possible strategies?
- Are there any ways you could expand your options by consciously orchestrating specific accomplishments, either in a job you currently hold or in other contexts?

- How does examining these parts of your history affect your ideas about your future work?

Celebrating Your Skills

For each of the accomplishments you've named above, you've used a certain set of skills: manual, intellectual, creative, interactive, organizational, or self-reflective. Survey your accomplishments, giving priority to those that seem most noteworthy and/or most relevant to the path you want to be on. List the skills you used. Now underline those you see as your particular strengths. Also underline those you particularly enjoy using.

You might have listed some skills for which you've gotten specific training, skills that are woven into the description of jobs you've held, such as operating a switchboard or a lathe, making pastries, or drafting legislation. But you probably also noticed skills you simply have, as part of living. These can be hardest to recognize and evaluate. But you've probably used them all the time in your work, and you can draw on them in significant ways in the work you'll do next.

Consider these skills, for instance:[13]

adapting to change

aesthetic sensitivity

analyzing problems

assessing resources

coaching

communication (written, verbal)

computer literacy

concentration/focus

coordinating projects/tasks

counseling

critiquing

detail orientation

developing prototypes

disciplining fairly

drawing ethical lines

entertaining people

establishing procedures/ rules

expressing feelings appropriately

facilitating

imagination

infectious enthusiasm

inspiring

interpreting data

learning new skills

listening

maintaining systems

making decisions

managing crises

meeting deadlines	research
meeting people easily	resolving conflicts
mentoring	seeing possibilities
negotiating	selling
observing accurately	strategizing
organizing/planning	supervising
persisting	synthesizing information
persuading	teaching
physical stamina/	understanding complicated ideas
diligence	working on a team
precision	working with numbers and formulas
public speaking	

other skills not on the above list:

After identifying the skills you possess, the next step is making sense of them. One way is to sort them by categories—for example, working with things, working with people, working with ideas.

- Do your skills fall predominantly in one of these areas?
- If so, are there any other areas you're curious about and would like to explore?
- Have you ever been told you couldn't or shouldn't work in any of these areas? Have you been told that you absolutely must work in any of them? How have those messages affected your choices?

It's also useful to rank your skills in terms of strength. For example, you could use a scale of one to three, where 3's are activities at which you excel, 2 means you're average, 1 means you can do it in a pinch. In looking at the 1's and 2's, you might make a further division. On one hand, there are areas of skill where you really think you've peaked out; you're as good as you're going to get, or the effort required to strengthen the skill is more than you're ready to bargain for. For example, I have a decent singing voice for use when friends are playing their guitars late at night. But I'm completely at peace with the fact that I'll never sing at the Met. On the other hand, there are skills we each have that we're continually trying to improve. Where those are concerned, you don't want to miss opportunities to keep developing, and you can benefit from being as explicit as possible about the improvements you seek. For me, those are writing, public speaking, and advocacy. For you, they might be the core skills you use, or skills you expect to use in the next phase of your work. Some will probably leap out of the list above. Others may occur to you as you continue with the remaining steps in this book.

- What are your core skills with which you're comfortable just as they are?
- What are the skills you could benefit from developing some more? How much more? Realistically, how might you do this in the next year or two?

If you're feeling unsure after this exercise, you might benefit from some formal aptitude testing.[14] Consult the resource list for sources. Aptitudes are the innate strengths that give rise to skills and achievements.

Surveying Your Resources

This is one of the most open-ended parts of the self-assessment process. The question here is, "What other resources in myself or my community can I use?" This can include any that can play a role in launching you in the work that reflects your highest values. For instance, a basement that can serve as office space, or could host meetings for community groups whose members you'd like to get to know better; a flair for thrift-shop bargains that can outfit you for a new role; a small chunk of savings that can keep peanut butter on the shelf while you develop new products or services; a network of people with whom you barter skills. There's no right way to do this. Anything you consider to be a resource belongs on this list.

Two Out-of-the-Ordinary Questions

Now we are entering unorthodox territory, even more than we have been. The two lines of questioning that follow have something to do with values, with skills, and with the conditions under which you accomplish most easily. But they don't fit handily into any conventional career development category because, conventionally, they are considered nonissues. Yet they both have enormous significance if we are talking about making a living, making a difference, and making a life that is coherent and rewarding.

I. How do you understand your sense of place and geographic needs?

These days, it is often assumed that we are infinitely adaptable in choosing where we will live and how. Migrant workers, venture capitalists, and others have become what a friend calls "global nomads." Certainly willingness to relocate is a key in many a career development scheme and has a positive side: flexibility, cross-cultural awareness, the possibility of friends in exotic places. But the costs of this flexibility are also becoming apparent, and they can be high: disruption of the rhythms and relationships of life, lack of cultural and ecological grounding, and networks of people we care about that are too dispersed to keep the friendships healthy.

During the years when there was an implied mutual commitment between working people and corporate employers, geographic mobility was an accepted part of growing with an organization. A few years of living out of a suitcase was a kind of rite of passage. We could laughingly admit that IBM stood for "I've Been Moved" because it also stood for "I've Been Making Out Okay." Now that the implied contract between employer and employee is a relic for many of us, we have an opportunity to reassert our own values and standards regarding the degree of mobility that makes sense in our lives. In other words, if you're going to take all this responsibility for your career, you might as well do it in a place where you feel at home.

There are still reasons to accept a mobile lifestyle. But there are also compelling arguments for staying put and sinking roots in a community. This is another side to the potential of telecommuting at its best. Roots benefit and hone the individual, in poet Wendell Berry's words, by allowing us to grow "whole in the world, at peace and in place."[15] If a more rooted way of life were adopted by significant numbers of people, it might even benefit the planet—for example, by minimizing fuel use and road building, and by making it harder for any of us to keep one step ahead of our own bad decisions.

Consider these questions:

> In what ways has geographic mobility enhanced the quality of your work life?
>
> In what ways has it detracted?
>
> What parts of the world do you feel particular affinity for?
>
> Have you been able to live and work in those places as much as you would like?
>
> What experiences have shaped your attitudes about geographic mobility?
>
> Have these produced any particular attractions or aversions in you?
>
> If you were fully healed from any painful aspects of those experiences, how would your attitudes about geographic mobility be different?
>
> Are there steps you could take now to increase your ability to work in a place that you love, and/or to work for the people and ecology of that place from where you are?

II. What role does technology play in your value system and in your career?

Does this question give you the creeps? Do you feel it's sacrilege to suggest that not every invention offered for our consumption is 100 percent user-friendly and well thought out? I'm not talking just about whether a given machine works well or irritates the hell out of you. I'm talking also about its impact on the way you process information, set priorities, organize your work, and make sense of your role, rights, and responsibilities in an organization.

To question something isn't necessarily to reject it. I am typing these words into a computer as my stereo soothes me with a digitally mastered tape of Gregorian chants, produced by monks living the simple life in an abbey in Spain. John Naisbitt's romantic vision of "high tech and high touch" can be true, on the good days. But I have also held my TV watching down to about ten hours per year over the last twenty years. So I speak from experience when I assert that it's possible, and sometimes a blessing, to say no to what people around you are saying yes to.

Tens of thousands among us are now living with injuries—from infertility caused by IUDs to carpal tunnel syndrome—because we did not claim the right to ask tough enough questions about technologies offered to us, often in good faith, by enthusiasts who were running out of control. I am speaking here with a skeptical voice because we all get plenty of positive messages in our daily media diet. One of the most powerful, provocative, and well-researched antidotes to easy acceptance of technology is Jerry Mander's *In the Absence of the Sacred*.[16] In it, the author of *Four Arguments for the Elimination of Television* proposes a list of "Ten Recommended Attitudes About Technology":

1. Since most of what we are told about technology comes from its proponents, be deeply skeptical of all claims.

2. Assume all technology is "guilty until proven innocent."

3. Eschew the idea that technology is neutral or "value-free." Every technology has inherent and identifiable social, political, and environmental consequences.

4. The fact that technology has a natural flash and appeal is meaningless. Negative attributes are slow to emerge.

5. Never judge a technology by the way it benefits you personally. Seek a holistic view of the impacts. The operative question is not whether it benefits you, but who benefits most? And to what end?

6. Keep in mind that an individual technology is only one piece of a larger web of technologies, "megatechnology." The operative question here is how the individual technology fits the larger one.

7. Make distinctions between technologies that primarily serve the individual or the small community (e.g., solar energy) and those that operate on a large scale outside community control (e.g., nuclear energy). The latter kind is the major problem today.

8. When it is argued that the benefits of the technological lifeway are worthwhile despite harmful outcomes, recall that Lewis Mumford referred to these alleged benefits as "bribery." Cite the figures about crime, suicide, alienation, drug abuse, as well as environmental and cultural degradation.

9. Do not accept the homily that "once the genie is out of the bottle you cannot put it back." Such attitudes induce passivity and confirm victimization.

10. In thinking about technology within the present climate of technological worship, emphasize the negative. This brings balance. Negativity is positive.

Just as there is increasing variety among work situations in terms of the geographic mobility they require, there is also a growing degree of stratification among workplaces in terms of the complexity of technologies they embrace. The job opportunities aren't all the same in this respect. An employee has some choices. These include choices about specific technologies for manufacturing and information processing, and choices among employers with differing attitudes about employee rights to question technologies on the job.
Consider these questions:

- In what ways have technologies been a help to you in creating work that reflects your highest values?
- In what ways have technologies created barriers in that effort?
- Have you ever been in a situation in which a technology "saved" you from work you were willing to do or skills you wanted to exercise?
- How did you reconcile that situation?
- Have you ever been in a situation in which you were uncomfortable using a technology, but everyone else around you seemed to accept it, so you went along? Looking back, how do you feel about that experience? Was there any other approach you could have taken?

Your Evolving Self

So far, we've been looking at you as you are. The next exercise is to get a handle on the ways you're changing, and particularly the changes you want to encourage. This can be done with a lot of thought, or quite informally as a way of seeing what ideas are "on top" in your thinking about your path. This is a very open-ended exercise. There is no one right way to approach it. That's the point. You get to consider all the different ways you've been thinking about the patterns in your past and the direction in which you're moving.

On the four timelines below, note major phases and changes in your values, your skills and strengths, your accomplishments, and the characteristics of a favorable work environment. Each line starts at the beginning of your career and goes just a little beyond the present time. Along each axis, note major themes and milestones. In that inviting blank space after "today," note ways in which you think you're growing and changing, especially those you'd like to encourage.

when you   *today*
started

values

skills and strengths

accomplishments

characteristics of a favorable work environment

In each of the four areas, how would you describe your growing edge (how you're developing and the areas in which you could benefit from more conscious effort)?

Beyond the Basics I:
Healing and Growing

These questions lead us from your present situation to one of the most challenging questions: "So what?" Putting the pieces together requires a good working understanding of your own development, in the terms that matter to you.

Systems for classifying personality traits, motivation, and the patterns and stages of development are widespread. Many are useful, as long as their simplifying assumptions are recognized. You are obviously more than any set of personality factors, and more than your conscious mind. But any classification scheme that piques your curiosity is probably a good starting point in self-assessment.

Psychologist David McClelland created a clear and useful system when he sorted people's motivations on the job into three categories: power, achievement, and affiliation.[17] But that test, a product of an earlier generation, does not discriminate in some ways that are becoming more obvious today. Are we talking about power through domination or power through relationship? Achievement as defined by a social group or in our own independent view? Affiliation as merging, or as relationship from a base of secure self-respect?

Another classification system covering work motivation comes from Michael Maccoby's study, *Why Work?* He identified five common types, based on work motives and hoped-for rewards: the innovator, the expert, the helper, the defender, and the self-developer.[18]

For those who find personality typing useful, Robert Frager's anthology, *Who Am I?* contains twenty-one systems to explore.[19] They range from the popular Myers-Briggs Type Indicator to the chakra system of eastern religion and medicine. There's the mystical foursome of earth, air, fire, and water, whose symbolic value should not be overlooked, as well as a variety of interesting "business and leadership typologies."

These images provide a bridge from conscious self-image to the unconscious or mythic level. Tools for further exploration at this level include the Enneagram[20] and various archetypal systems, such as the "heroes at work" model developed by psychologists Carol Pearson and Sharon Seivert.[21] Heroes are bigger than ordinary life, but spring from it. As Pearson writes,

The hero's task has always been to bring new life to a dying culture. . . . Heroism for this age requires us to take our journeys, to
find the treasure of our true selves, and to share that treasure with the
community as a whole—through doing and being fully who we are.
To the degree that we do so, our kingdoms are transformed.

Pearson and Seivert's heroes have characteristic personalities and characteristic battles they need to fight in order to complete old business in
life and move on to future stages. You might see your path as the
Warrior's, calling forth courage, discipline, and assertion. Or as that of
the Caregiver, characterized by surrender and sacrifice. You might be an
Orphan, educated by loss or tragedy to be compassionate. Perhaps
you're the Ruler, grounded in responsibility. Or the Magician, creator of
new realities, the archetype that represents interdependence. Each
archetype also has a set of negative qualities which can reign if effort is
not made to integrate the shadow or unconscious side: the Warrior can
be self-serving and aggressive, the Orphan a whiny victim, the Magician
manipulative, the Ruler autocratic.

All these schemes provide structure and can help bring patterns into
awareness. But they can also give rise to a misleading sense of certainty
and can minimize your consideration of any qualities and impulses that
don't fit the general patterns. Often it's those faint signs rather than the
more visible patterns that point the way to openings for change.

Studies of the life cycle are an additional source of perspective on
the motifs and metaphors of your history. There are many schools of
thought about how adults evolve (after we're supposedly done growing).
But the majority of them include a trio of common elements: getting
established (commonly seen as the task of the twenties); achieving and
stretching (thirties); and contributing and nurturing future generations
(forties and beyond). Businessman Alan F. Kay refers to these stages as
"on, honor, honest." Career counselor Deborah Knox adds, "When I
work with people in their twenties, they tend naturally to focus on
identifying and demonstrating their skills. With people in their thirties,
it's about achieving, building their careers and lives. But by the time they
hit forty, if they have any life in them, they're focusing on values and
purpose."

As the stories in these pages indicate, though, the hunger to contribute and the will to take responsibility for life around us are not put on
hold until midlife. Psychologist Benina Berger-Gould suggests that the

quality of generativity: interest in service, caregiving, and passing on values to future generations—identified in Erik Erikson's classic developmental scheme as characteristic of the later years—is now being demanded of many of us at earlier and earlier points in the life cycle.

As we reclaim abandoned memories—including painful ones and others that are merely unexpected, confusing, funny, or outrageous—we can understand more fully how our development has been held back. This supports building an accurate self-image that includes our potential to contribute. It allows us to bring more conscious direction into finding or creating a work situation that will bring this potential to life.

This principle is illustrated by a client of mine, a talented teacher and curriculum developer who was weighing two possible jobs. One job, in a multicultural community, attracted her much more than the other. But she felt it was out of reach. "My big reservation is that I just know I can't learn Spanish," she said. "I'm slow with language. I don't retain it. I tried and tried in a class a few years ago."

I pressed her: "Was there anything about that class that stood out in your memory?"

"Oh, it was just a terrible experience. There was a lot of pressure, and the teacher made me feel really stupid and slow when I didn't get it."

"Do you think you would have more potential to learn Spanish if you were taught with more respect?" I asked.

"Hmm. Never thought of it. Maybe," she said, leaving with a commitment to think about the possibility. Two weeks later, she had made another call to her potential employer to discuss her reservations about Spanish and ways to handle them and had landed the job.

For the most part, the process of reconciling personal history and opening new options is no more and no less than paying attention, and using psychological and spiritual resources to remove the barriers to that attentiveness. The exercises that follow may help you—first, in homing in on episodes when you were emotionally hurt in a work situation and/or had to hide a significant portion of yourself; and second, in imagining a more powerful and healing conclusion to that story.

Exercise: The Résumé Vérité

Here's an exercise created by Richard Saul Wurman to help you get in touch with aspects of your work history that remain unresolved in your psyche.[22] If the résumé is the sanitized, upbeat version of your working-life story, the résumé vérité is the underside. It's a look at your working life that's mercilessly honest, irreverent, ironic if you like, and as funny as possible. This exercise helps you expand your awareness of the vulnerabilities you have dealt with in your career. It provides a handle on the reasons you bluffed your way into that supervisory position and then pulled all-nighters to get up to speed before you were caught; and why you impulsively took the job with the catering company and then got so depressed after two weeks that you stopped showing up. When I tried this, my first entry was:

1974   Howard Johnson's Restaurant
Fired as hostess for attempting to do labor organizing while still on probation.

A friend came up with:

1980   Wine steward in elegant restaurant. Managed to ricochet a champagne cork off angular ceiling and into distinguished patron's soup.

The résumé vérité is not only about remembering traumatic or embarrassing work experiences. It can also put the fun back into memories you've artificially rendered harmless, like the energy consulting job I described in Step 3:

1980   Worked for tiny business trying to save world through energy conservation. Climbed on roofs of skyscrapers on the pretext of measuring insulation depth. Held all meetings in the park, with ice cream.

Get it? Play with it. Think of the way you tell those disaster stories in the café or the pub, and take it from there.

Exercise: Rewriting the Script

Now go through the entries in your résumé vérité and the results of any other relevant exercises you have done so far. Notice the areas that trigger strong feeling, or that present new knowledge. *Let a fragment of your life-work story find you.* Reread it, out loud or even to a friend if you like. Take your time with this, and notice your physical and emotional state.

Now let that fragment become the basis of a new story. You can play any role, not just yourself. You can speak or imagine action. *Rewrite the script to come up with an ending that feels more fair, more empowering, more creative.* You might do that sitting quietly or walking along a route where you feel at peace, or at a typewriter, or talking into a tape recorder. This can be a powerful experience, so don't worry if you feel a little discombobulated. Give the feelings time to ripen.

Summary:

1. If I wanted to shape my work to make the most of my personality strength and the ways I hope to develop, I would:

2. If I want to overcome past experiences where I haven't been able to be myself in my career, here are some kinds of action that would help:

3. The bravest, most liberating things I've done on the job are:

4. If I wanted to take a more empowered stance on the job from this moment onward, some useful approaches might be:

Characteristics of a Favorable Work Environment

Each of the factors we've been examining has some implications for the kind of workplace in which you will find satisfaction and contribute. When you have digested the fruits of the exercises above, you'll be better able to organize some key points in a way that lets you step back and look for useful patterns. The table below is a tool for doing this. It is organized around two ways of considering the working conditions you want: those that feel safe ("your comfort zone"); those that might stretch you in ways you want to be challenged ("your stretch zone"); and those that represent an unacceptable stretch ("no way!"). This table can be filled out in two ways. You can assume that your gut response is the truest, and write what first comes to mind. You can sift through the results of the preceding exercises and see what they may suggest. Or you can do a little of each.

Characteristics of workplace with regard to:	Your comfort zone	Your stretch zone	No way!
size			
structure			
culture			
tools and technologies			
compensation (material, nonmaterial)			
travel and overtime			
location			
flexibility			
ways of enforcing policies and performance			
physical appearance, layout, aesthetics			
mix of people in workforce			
possible career paths			
other considerations			

Beyond the Basics II:
Contributing

Even the most hardened individualist hungers for connection and context, for grounding in community and the ability to pass on ideas to a new generation. Human development has a lot to do with community building, with alignment of the individual and the group by mutual honing and adaptation.

These interwoven webs of relationship, from the intimate to the global, are far too complex to figure out and at the same time too important to ignore. Our awareness of them can force us into a new state of receptivity to unexpected ideas. A couple of the exercises earlier in this section were focused on applying your values in these various relationships. Let's wrap up by looking more closely at your connections to others—people, organizations, cultural groups, nations, species—as a source of focus and vitality in choosing the work ahead.

From your sense of place in the world comes a strengthened sense of purpose and possibility, because you're in closer touch with the work to be done and the resources available for doing it. You come to see yourself as naturally including your connections and your caring about the world and, in the words of Joanna Macy, this expanded self-image "brings into play wider resources—courage, endurance, ingenuity— like a nerve cell in a neural net opening to the charge of other neurons."

Suppose you're not used to considering your working life in such a broad context. Either you've naturally considered them to be separate realms, or the circumstances of your life have forced a degree of separation. How does one develop, or renew, authentic commitments and priorities with respect to the greater good? Here are some exercises to start that process. To carry it forward, commit yourself to taking some action, however modest, on the insights you get through these exercises.[23]

Exercise: Lifeline[24]

Draw a line to represent your life (from birth to death, if you can handle it, or from birth to the present time). Now mark the major events that stand out in your memory for any reason. Indicate, also, periods or phases that are well defined in your history, however you think about them ("the security-guarding job from hell," "postgraduation euphoria," or "going-out-with-Kevin madness," for example).

Now draw another line, parallel to your lifeline with the same beginning and end. This represents events in the world that stand out in your memory, for whatever reason. They could be local or international, political or ecological—the idea here is to look at the context in which your life has unfolded. Don't forget to pay attention to events in the nonhuman, natural world.

Finally, examine the connections between those two progressions: your life's unfolding and the historical backdrop.

Did any of these events shape your expectations about your life? Your sense of possibility or limits? Your moods? Your belief system? Do any of the events you see in recent history suggest new options for your life and work? How have the fields of work that interest you changed to adapt to growing ecological concerns? How else might they need to be adapted? How could you contribute to that process?

Exercise: Mindfulness and the Daily News

One approach is to start by noticing the way these broader concerns intersect with your daily life, choosing to pay some extra attention to the connections and the feelings they trigger in you. You might set aside a week to do this, and remind yourself in every way possible to keep the practice going. Watch the news or read the paper with concentration; if you find meditation helpful, you might do it for a few minutes before or after. If you get your news from print sources, visualize the stories as you read them. Notice the feelings, from compassion to outrage to humor to inspiration, that each story awakens in you. Write down as much as possible. Note especially the way these stories suggest paths for action ("Why doesn't somebody do something?").

Your first responses might be quite immediate and close to home, but these may not be the most compelling ones in the long run. So stick with the exercise beyond the point when you've gathered what feels like "enough" information.

Exercise: Stepping Out

Step out into the world, equipped with a set of special lenses. Before this or any other exercise suggested in this book, it may be helpful to meditate for a while. Pick a part of town (or country) where you don't routinely go. Take a walk there, with plenty of time to linger in spots that attract your attention. You can do this alone, or with a friend who's a good listener. Pay attention to what's new; what's beautiful, inspiring, hopeful. Pay attention, also, to what's falling apart, what's struggling to survive, what's dangerous. Whenever something moves you for any of these reasons, stop. Really stop. You could be gazing at a playground, a dilapidated house, a lush garden, a wall filled with graffiti, an eroded stream bed. First, just look closely, from as many angles as you can. Then write and/or talk into a tape recorder:

What do you see?

What's important to you about it?

Who else does it matter to (note all possible answers)?

How is this image a reflection of work done or not done? If it's a sign of hope, whose work created it? If it's a danger sign, what kind of work could help to eliminate it? What kinds of organizations do this work? What kinds of people?

Don't prejudge the options you're generating. They're just that: options for consideration and further research. When you feel "done" with these questions at any one place, keep on strolling until something else catches your eye. When you get home, review the insights of the day before they get stale. Write down, or tell somebody, the next steps they suggest to you.

Exercise: If . . .

If you were infinitely fearless and powerful, and could set up your life's work any way you wanted to in order to address the concerns that you've been noticing, what would your career look like? How would it unfold? What would you be doing to lay the foundation? What would you hope to accomplish, concretely? Daydream and/or record your thoughts in a journal. Now, what gets in the way of making some of those daydreams come true? How do you feel about those barriers, and about those opportunities? What are you going to do about it?

Summary Worksheet 1

1. The primary values I want to commit myself to in my work are:

2. How will I recognize the possibility of serving those values in a work situation?

3. Other characteristics of a workplace I'd like and can grow with:

4. Specific categories of workplace suggested by 1-3 above:

5. Skills, strengths, and resources I can use in my work right now:

6. Skills, strengths, and resources I'd like to cultivate:

7. How I want to develop as a human being through my work:

8. How I want my work to affect the world I live in:

9. Specific kinds of work suggested by the questions above that use my present skills, strengths, and resources:

10. Specific kinds of work suggested by the questions above that use skills, strengths, and resources I'd like to cultivate:

When you've completed this worksheet as best you can, review it and ask, "Does this really tell my story?" If not, keep asking yourself what the missing elements are and modifying the summary sheet until you are satisfied that it's the truest picture of yourself that you can paint at this time.

Step 6:

Identify the

Essence of Your

Work in the World

Blessed are they who have found their work. May they seek no other blessedness.
Thomas Carlyle

The first three steps in this program were devoted to preparation. The next two covered assessment of the work that's out there to be done and of your own direction. In this step, you will begin to integrate what you've discovered. You will try out new language to describe yourself, your aims, and what the elements of meaningful work are for you.

Mission Without Obsession

The most commonly used language for these essential principles is the personal mission statement. This is a concept with strong plusses and minuses. To work with a sense of mission can be nourishing, even transformative. It can provide a valuable anchor. But, if romanticized or taken up uncritically, a sense of mission can also provide an escape hatch from the mundane but necessary day-to-day questions about how to live. It can lead to exhausting fanaticism, inflexibility, and setups for failure. Whatever focuses you so much that it leads you to brave obstacles and change your ways of living can also fixate you and blind you to life-saving feedback along your path. As "anti-career" counselor Rick Jarow observes, "Many people who are *absolutely* sure what they want to do with their lives are clinically crazy." [1]

The concept of mission has a place in many spiritual traditions. It's called vocation by Christians, dharma by Buddhists. It is based on the assumption that each human being has a set of unique qualities which unfold over the course of a healthy life cycle. From this it follows that uncovering these qualities, and choosing actions that test and strengthen them, is the path of maximum satisfaction and growth as well as contribution.

The famous "pink pages" in Richard Bolles's *What Color Is Your Parachute?* are an eloquent meditation on Christian vocation in three parts. [2] The first is simply living in the conscious presence of the holy spirit. The second is doing whatever is possible in a given situation to help and heal. The third is identifying a specific line of work that uses the skills and gifts that are uniquely yours. The spirit of *Parachute* is a spirit of humility and common sense. The idea of personal mission is tempered by the belief that everyone's mission is assigned and brought to life by the involvement of a higher power.

But other commentators have expressed serious, valid concern that organizing a career around a statement of mission, especially in a Western culture, can be a source of dehumanizing pressure rather than liberation. As Jarow puts it, "It's too intimately tied to Calvinist doctrine, the idea of original sin and the view of work as a path to salvation. That leads to a valuation of the performance over the person. It can end up preventing people's development rather than fostering it."

An authentic mission unfolds out of deeper and deeper self-knowledge and self-testing. It's revealed, not adopted. If your workplace burned to the ground and you had to rebuild from scratch, with the freedom to start over any way you wanted, your sense of mission is the raw material you would build with. In Jarow's words, "If you really have a mission, you can't not do it. Your whole being wants to do it, and the only question is becoming more open to it."

Of course, paid labor is only one aspect of this path. Joe Dominguez and Vicki Robin, the inspired financial consulting duo, sound a cautionary note against automatically equating life's mission with the work we do for income.[3] That can lead to undervaluing unpaid work, from caring for loved ones to taking care of our health.

At its best, though, a mission—freely and enthusiastically chosen—can provide coherence, guide choices, and present challenges we can rise to. Some of the most effective people and organizations around are mission-driven. For example, the Greyston Bakery in Yonkers, founded by Zen priest and former aerospace engineer Bernard Glassman, provides gourmet baked goods for hotels, restaurants, and retail sale.[4] The bakers are recruited from the ranks of Westchester County's homeless; with training, they are employed and housed at the nearby Greyston Family Inn. The Greyston umbrella also covers a construction company which has rehabilitated nearby buildings to provide low-income housing.

In other words, Greyston's *products* are baked goods and housing units. Greyston's *programs* also include drug rehabilitation and counseling services. These are means to an end. Greyston's *mission,* around which the business is organized, is nothing short of ending homelessness in Westchester County by the year 2000. That is what animates the daily work of everyone in the project.

Identifying the Essence

Lots of people think there is an automatic "fit" between qualities they see in themselves and kinds of work they could do. They think that self-assessment and investigation of the options, by themselves, will force a choice to pop out. But choosing work is not a logical activity. It's an informed gamble as to which of the available possibilities will really draw the most from you. This chapter offers suggestions for narrowing down that infinite range of possibilities, a little at a time. It begins with an open-ended exploration of all the available options, even those that seem unlikely. If you know you're facing a career change, this is a necessary strategy. But the same objectivity can be useful in making a more subtle shift, or even in renewing your commitment to work you're involved in already.

Summary Worksheet 1 gave you an opportunity to identify many ingredients of your optimal work situation. Reflecting on these will equip you to answer one more question. Which of the characteristics you've written down are nonnegotiable? (That is, if they weren't present in your working life, you would have very little desire to look at yourself in the mirror in the morning.) Which are attractive but not essential? This is not a choice you make once, but over and over again as you learn more about the realities of your field of work and the benefits and costs of your chosen path. But it's still a choice that's best made explicitly. Even if your nonnegotiable principles aren't totally clear, it can be helpful to hear yourself saying out loud what you hope to stand for and how you see yourself. There are many ways to organize this information.

For example, Steve Kropper, the small business owner we met in Step 3, created a matrix for evaluating job opportunities when he was working for other people; it can also guide him in business opportunities today. It has two dimensions: a company's growth and its impact.

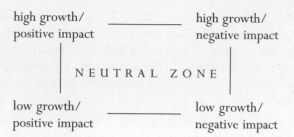

high growth/
positive impact   high growth/
                                               negative impact

NEUTRAL ZONE

low growth/
positive impact   low growth/
                                               negative impact

He explains: "I figure that a growing enterprise will be best able to afford to be generous, both with opportunities for me and in letting me use my position to do good for other people. So I look for businesses that are growing, or at least stable. They also have to be at least neutral and preferably positive in their impact, as I see it. I won't work in a company I think is doing harm, no matter how much it's growing. I'll work in a place where the impact is lukewarm, if the business is expanding and the culture allows me, personally, to have a positive effect through my work. That formula is simple enough that I can put it into practice and still find work. And it generally keeps me out of big trouble."

Consciously stating the minimal conditions you will accept in a work situation can be an act of psychic self-preservation, especially in those times when a sense of positive purpose eludes you. But continuing to pay attention to what you have to offer, and to the relationship between your own development and the needs you see around you, makes it most likely that a more focused sense of purpose will crystallize sooner or later. You always have a choice about whether to embrace it; but if you aren't looking for the possibilities, then you lose the option of saying yes.

Many of the people who seem most effective in doing work that matters to them, and in charting a coherent course in spite of chaos or obstacles, have a simple way of putting into words the essence of their work. This can come up in a thousand kinds of language. What have been the underlying characteristics or themes of your working life regardless of the jobs you were doing? What have been the primary roles you have always played, and loved most? What have you found a way to do in almost any situation?

Here's an example. One friend of mine started her adult life as a music major and choir director. Then she married and spent some years as a mother and homemaker. As her kids grew, she became more and more active in the community, hosting a TV talk show and getting involved in the civil rights movement. Moving back into paid employment, she joined the field staff for a national nonprofit organization concerned with peacemaking. Then she became a fund-raiser for another grassroots organization. Through all these shifts, people who have known her for years say she has always done essentially the same work: gathering people together for sociability and celebration, for learning about each other and working together to solve common problems. In every job, she has used superb social skills and a sensitivity to group dynamics. In every job, she has learned a new set of technical skills to do her work in a new way. She could describe herself as an entertainer and be telling a multifaceted truth.

I've been listening lately to people's simple statements about their work, and hearing powerful messages about who they think they are and can be. Craftsperson, communicator, organizer, healer, advocate, technical innovator, marketer, and builder are one-word descriptions that speak volumes, not only about the specific job but about the values and priorities that animate it. Many career counselors advise a slightly more detailed, but still simple, descriptive statement, not only for self-definition but for self-promotion as well:

"I'm a teacher who loves working in multicultural settings."

"I'm an engineer with ten years' experience in transportation systems, and I like to see projects through from start to finish."

"I'm a building contractor with an interest in sustainable architecture."

"I'm a nurse with a fierce commitment to patient care."

My favorite sound bite, though, is from the manager of the computer department for a small nonprofit organization who introduced himself to me with the statement, "I'm the guy who does everything around here that doesn't require social skills."

Some fortunate (and committed) people are able to work their way into clarity about their life's vocation by saying yes, intuitively, to opportunities that attract or creatively challenge them—and then learning about themselves by reviewing the patterns behind these acts of faith. Opportunities seem to choose them, and to pull them forward, in ways they could not reject without rejecting something fundamental about their own identity. In figuring out how to say yes to these opportunities realistically, they may need to test the waters a great deal.

They may thrash about for a time. But ultimately they accept the work and accept a self-definition as "one who does this work." Their commitment may be to a particular population in need, to a form of service or activism or innovation; or to using a particular talent for purposes which are continually refined based on the needs which present themselves. They speak of this commitment in many kinds of language, but what's constant is an understanding of "the work to be done," which takes on a life of its own.

Ken Geiser, an environmental scientist who directs the Toxics Use Reduction Institute at the University of Massachusetts at Lowell, illustrates this kind of path. He has this to say about the way his work came up and grabbed him:

> I didn't intend to do this work. I was trained as an architect. As a young man, I was involved with Frank Lloyd Wright and went off to Berkeley to become an architect. However, I've always had a huge commitment to social justice and community rights. As I became more involved in civil rights and antiwar work in the 1960s, my commitment to architecture became very complicated, and I left it after two years.
>
> I went to M.I.T. to study urban planning, and did a lot of grassroots organizing there. I helped stop a highway. I helped set up a home-based school. I had a growing interest in the environment and working-class life. That drew me into working with trade unions, and into a kind of working-class environmentalism—a notion which, in those days, made no sense at all.
>
> By my early thirties, I had begun, seriously, to find out what my work was. I realized that jobs and projects were ancillary to the work. They were a means of getting the work done. For me, "the work" meant saving us from annihilating ourselves, whether that meant focusing on urban rats or on racial injustices in exposure to environmental hazards—whatever the specifics. Toxic chemicals became my primary vehicle, because that was the most ripe area for organizing.

Geiser spent years integrating an awareness of the condition of human society into his life and identifying different approaches for doing something useful. He had a strong, but general, commitment to the greater good, but was able to entertain many different ideas about how to serve that good. Over the years, through action on his commitment and a whole lot of paying attention, he fine-tuned his views about how to do the work.

Organizing the Options

Once you have made the clearest and most honest possible statement about what's essential to your work in the world, this will provide focus as you translate that into practical possibilities. I am not suggesting that you can order up a workplace that matches your criteria down to the finest detail. However, knowing your ideal as a vibrantly living thing helps you to choose among real-life situations with sophistication and subtlety, and to recognize opportunities for moving closer to your ideal when they appear.

The self-assessment activities of the previous step provide a gestalt, a set of elements which form some kind of pattern. But there is no single right way to identify that pattern. There's just you and the pattern, and your intuitions about what it means. The elements you choose and the relationships you see among them are equally important. What kind of work can be done by a person with this set of values, skills, history, and resources? What kind of workplaces will be compatible with this person's highest values and provide fertile ground for this person to make a strong contribution?

One powerful way of getting input on these questions, or reality checking your own ideas, is to show some of your self-assessment efforts, such as Summary Worksheet 1, to a friend who knows you well and has some familiarity with the kinds of work you're considering. Invite that friend to think out loud on the questions, "What kind of work could be done by the person described on this sheet, and in what kinds of settings would that person be best off?" This series of questions will give you multiple answers, probably some that fit with your history and assumptions about yourself and others that come as a surprise. For example, suppose these are some elements you listed:

Values: honesty, environmental sustainability, productivity

Skills I have now: fast typing, Spanish, switchboard, computer graphics

Skills I'd like to cultivate: conflict resolution

Other characteristics of a favorable workplace: humor, flexibility

Ways I'd like my work to have an impact: show that "support" functions have dignity and importance in a business; find and share new ideas for managing an office in an environmentally sustainable way

These elements can be combined to yield quite a few different images. For example, you could be a secretary or administrator for a cutting-edge business or nonprofit. Or a translator for an environmental export business or grassroots group. Or an advocate for office workers committed to environmental sustainability, maybe even a transnational group. Or a self-employed desktop publisher of materials in environmental education and conflict resolution. These fields vary, of course, as to the availability and quality of jobs. That is all the more reason to identify a wide range of possibilities and investigate them with some care, in order of your priority. You don't need a lot of jobs; you need one. But it has to be one for which you're uniquely qualified, and it has to be one that will lead you on a path with long-term possibilities.

The question is not only "What are the possibilities?" but "Which ones will stretch me in the most interesting ways and allow me to make the greatest contribution?" Answering this question requires a healthy blend of imagination and research, but it's often less complex than it might appear. In many cases, the options that call forth the most growth and risk-taking in you are also the ones that allow you to contribute the most. And you can recognize those on any list of possibilities by the way they make you feel.

Constellations of Roles

Here's another way to think about the images of possibility which you're generating: in terms of roles you can play, or have tended to play, regardless of the specific job description you've held. Even if you're just starting out or if you've held one position for a long time, chances are you've played a number of roles. The following worksheet is a place to give names to these and explore further options for work which they indicate. It's also a place to explore the areas of overlap among roles and options, and the synergies which might be created out of them.

Write down all the roles you play, or "hats you wear," that apply talents which could be useful in your future work. There are no fixed ways to describe these—any language that has meaning for you is fine. You can have several roles in a single job, and even more when you consider your unpaid activities as well. The roles may be more mythic than literal; they may be related less to the formal requirements of the job than to its meaning in your life. For example, when I try this, I get these categories:

1. Storyteller. I gather, edit, and retell stories in a way that builds community and helps people celebrate what they're doing. Sometimes I do this in articles and books; other times I do it in front of audiences.

2. Shop foreman. I make "do lists" at meetings and push people to take responsibility. I do this as a volunteer in community projects, and when I'm consulting.

3. Advance person. I call up strangers and offer them proposals for lectures, panels, and workshops. I do this for my own work, for colleagues in groups I belong to, and for people I meet whose work I think is wonderful.

4. Information broker. People call me for the contents of my address book and files—everything from model book proposals to names of mediators to articles about socially responsible investing to addresses of mathematicians in Nicaragua.

5. Counselor. I serve as a sounding board to people who are deciding about their professional futures or working through blocks in writing. Sometimes I work solo, and other times I pull together personal focus groups to concentrate more creative attention on the problem and produce a breakthrough.

Now, take those categories and spread them around on a piece of paper, in any order except a straight line. Leave some space around each word for what comes next.

storyteller

advance
person

shop foreman

information
broker

counselor

Now, under each term, list other kinds of work situations besides your present (or last) one, and other job descriptions which could use a similar skill set. Augment your own imagination by asking friends to brainstorm and/or by consulting occupational directories. For example, I can imagine turning my skills and typical roles into the following kinds of work:

storyteller

- performing artist
- speechwriter
- reader of books for the blind
- trainer for business or nonprofit

advance person

- PR professional
- salesperson
- canvasser
- fund-raiser
- community organizer
- entrepreneur: 1-person business

shop foreman
- political campaign manager
- business manager
- personal coach/administrative assistant

information broker

- newsletter publisher
- consultant
- database or network administrator

counselor

- career adviser: private practice
- outplacement specialist
- university career center staff

These are not all things I'd want to do, and they're certainly not all things I would be good at. But they're paths I could explore. In some cases, they would require me to develop additional skills or get certifications I've managed to live without. So the next step in this exercise is to sort your possible roles into two categories: those you could assume without too much retraining (although you might need an internship or volunteer stint as part of your marketing strategy) and other roles that would require more long-term investment to develop additional skills and qualifications.

How might you develop those additional skills and qualifications in the course of doing some of the work you've identified as possible right now?

There's one more way to identify new possibilities with this exercise. That is to explore the synergy between these roles in which you see yourself, the ways to add power by combining elements. The combination of "storyteller," "counselor," and "information broker" gives me the role I'm playing as I write this book.

These images of possibility are valuable, and can only be assessed by doing real-world research. But all the ready-made categories are necessarily imperfect. What you want to do has never been done before—not the way you're going to do it, maybe not even close. Use job descriptions you find through research as starting points. Use role models the same way—and pop-culture icons, mythic images, anything that has life in your mind. But use all that as a starting point. Many of the juiciest ideas people have about their work don't fit into established categories because they bridge, transcend, or redefine categories of work. In many cases, that's what's important about the idea. And an essential part of bringing the idea to life has been naming it and describing its power in language that explains the limits of the old definitions and categories.

Beyond Square One

 Identifying your work is not just a matter of choosing a content area and a set of skills to use. It also means determining the levels of expertise, seniority, earning power, and influence at which you will operate. In fact, one of the criteria for choosing a field of work may well be the extent to which you can grow in responsibility and influence within it. Whether you choose to emphasize that a little or a lot, taking responsibility for your effectiveness and influence is a real part of doing your work.

Questions about status, power, and influence are fraught with significance. They touch the essence of your self-esteem and personal power, not to mention your ability to make ends meet. They are also connected to the meaning of your life and work to the world you live in. Your relationship to worldly power is determined in part by forces outside your control. But is it also a matter of choice and strategy.

Once upon a time, there were formal career paths in most fields which at least provided benchmarks for planning. Not that everyone followed them, or that the top was accessible to everyone who tried to get there. Given the pyramidal shape of most organizations, defining the path to success as a vertical climb assured that significant numbers of people would fall off as they progressed. In that sense, at least, the contemporary reality may be more humane. Lateral moves and discontinuous leaps are not only possible—they're the essence of realistic career strategy. As such, they require continuous preparation and attention.

Even though linear evolution is not the only game in town, it is a reasonable starting point in considering the levels you might hope to attain. There are certainly many organizational settings, large and small, in which it is possible to identify a series of more and more influential positions, and to have a shot at moving from one to the next. There are fewer guarantees than ever, but the possibilities have not necessarily diminished. A helpful tool in charting a path is a four-stage model, developed by University of Utah professors Gene Dalton and Paul Thompson and presented in their book, *Novations.*[5] Because this model does not assume that organizations will be organized in any particular way or that people will navigate through them in any particular sequence, it is ideal for these times of uncertainty and reinvention. The four stages are:

1. *Apprenticeship:* primarily learning to make an individual contribution under the direction of a mentor or supervisor;

2. *Individual contribution:* accepting direction and meeting goals (deadlines, budget, and performance criteria) but able to function autonomously;

3. *Reciprocity or the "mentor stage":* expansion of your role beyond individual contribution to include project responsibility; motivating and communicating with others; training and development; selling programs; and interfacing with others outside your immediate working group.

4. *Director:* setting the overall direction for an organization, division, etc. Selecting key people for development; setting priorities; representing the organization externally; exercising power and providing the vision for leadership.

Before focusing on where you are in this sequence, and where you might want to move, take a moment simply to imagine yourself in each role, in any field of work you're considering. Which ones seem most natural? Which ones have you tended to gravitate to in the past? Are there levels that seem "off limits" to you, perhaps because they're too high or too low? If you perceive barriers about the levels of influence that are possible for you, are these accurate reflections of current reality, or old tapes you haven't yet been able to turnoff?

Conventional career planning has been ruled by the belief that moving forward through these four stages in sequence is the most desirable, coherent form of evolution. This is no longer obvious. In reflecting on the path that is open to you if you choose a particular field of work, then, here are some guiding questions:

1. In terms of the four-stage model, what is your current level, or the level at which you would enter the field if you're not yet part of it?

2. How does this level compare to your expectations and hopes about where you would be at this stage of your life? How does it compare to the expectations of your friends and loved ones, and to their status on the job? What are some ways to increase the peace between your current reality and these "shoulds"?

3. Maybe your current level of responsibility is a place where you could remain throughout your time in this field. If so, is that

possible, or is there an expectation that you will move "up or out" (for example, in academia and in some corporate roles)? If a "steady-state strategy" is possible, is it desirable?

4. Maybe you want to develop greater influence and/or earning power. If so, can you visualize some paths forward using the four-stage model? Can you then reality check those images by reading up on the field and doing informational interviews? At each stage, what would be your likely levels of influence and ways of exerting that influence? What would be your likely levels of compensation (monetary and non-)?

5. As you consider moving into increasing levels of responsibility, what are some alternative directions that you could take at each stage in case your ideal path is restricted by unforeseen circumstances? How will you build some of this contingency planning into your career development?

6. How might you develop your career meaningfully without moving in a straight line through the four stages?

7. As you consider any of these career paths, in what ways can they serve your personal development in a creative and spiritual sense?

8. As you consider the career paths that are open to you, which ones would probably allow you to maximize your positive contribution in the world, and to do so in the way you find most exciting? Which ones would allow you to minimize harm? (The vexing part of many choices is that situations with high positive impact may also have high levels of undesirable side effects.)

None of these questions can be answered with precision. This is true because the options will be evolving continuously, and because you will be changed by the process of pursuing them. The greatest success, though, seems to come to people who do not fixate on the details of a given opportunity, but who keep their eyes on the prize of their basic definition of their work and its coherent evolution.

Finally, one of the most powerful ways to pull yourself forward into a new vision is to see how it fits with the world you'd like to live in. The following exercise invites you to do that.

Exercise: Your Role
in a Positive Future[6]

Relax with a few deep breaths, and get ready to visualize an unknown time. Imagine the world of the future—far enough ahead that big changes have had time to take place, but soon enough that you can still expect to be in the picture.

Lots of scenarios are possible for this world. You may well see suffering, deprivation, injustice, and darkness. But there may also be light in this future world, and that's the thing to focus on right now.

Where have things gotten better? Where is there compassion? Where are new models of living and working taking hold? Where is the environment restored? Let yourself fantasize these developments for a while without judgment. What kinds of dwellings, communities, schools, foods, ceremonies, and festivals are there? How do people travel, communicate, govern themselves? Focus in on positive things that are taking place in this world of the future, and begin to ask the question, "Where do I fit in this picture?" Don't force yourself into any niche, but keep looking for a place that welcomes you. Even a place that awakens your curiosity will do. It could be a community, a physical location, or a particular work setting. Now imagine yourself there, and let a story arise in your imagination about the work you're doing in that community. How does this work express your values, talents, and personality as they are now? How have you changed to find your place in this future world?

Whatever is clear—the whole picture, or a fragment—let it be known. Tell yourself, and then your friends, whatever you know about the essence of the work you choose to do from now on. Then keep building on that core definition. And keep paying attention to the ways you can organize your life around work that is animated by that vision.

Step 7:
Commit Yourself
to Doing Your
Work in
Some Form

Sentiment without action is the ruin of the soul.
Edward Abbey

One of my lifelong heroes is the character played by Dustin Hoffman in the 1984 film *Tootsie*. He's a struggling actor so committed to his craft that he takes on a female identity and auditions for a soap opera role. He is chosen, and becomes dangerously successful. In a mythic sense, he illustrates the need to suspend even your most cherished assumptions about who you are and how you can live, in order to create something that expresses your deepest core. This story is also a reminder that one of the most frightening aspects of commitment is the specter of success. But my attraction to the movie is actually more mundane. It has to do with one critical scene, just before the famous gender switch. Hoffman is teaching an actors' workshop in New York. He's skinny and intense. Stalking the room, he says to a mesmerized group, "Look. You're in the most competitive industry in the world. You're in the toughest city for that industry. We have ninety-five percent unemployment. But none of that matters. Find a way to work."

Find a way to work. That is what we're all up against: a situation that doesn't let us get away with being our ordinary selves, but calls forth the extraordinary resources we all suspect we have down deep but haven't quite found a way to tap.

Find a way to do your work, however you understand it at any given time, whether or not anybody else in the world is willing to pay for it or even understands it. This may seem like the ultimate unfair proposition. You can't just go out and work without a structure, a title, financial resources, accountability, and the sense that you're part of a system that will make use of the fruits of your labor . . . can you? Admittedly, you can't do it all by yourself. You can't build an aircraft carrier in your basement. You can't play the oboe part of a symphony alone onstage. You can't be a literacy teacher if there's nobody there to learn from you.

But you can make proposals, attract collaborators, demonstrate ideas, and create structures for moving ahead in many kinds of work while you're waiting for a more formal opportunity. What's more, doing so will help you attract that opportunity.

It's too easy to forget all that you *can* do, without waiting for permission. Because unconditional commitment to one's work is powerful, it is also terrifying—so terrifying that many of us screen it out of our awareness at all costs. If necessary, we do this by sneering at the very idea, or by clinging to anger at the all-too-real injustices that have held us back until now.

This philosophy isn't only recommended on tactical grounds, but because it calls forth so much from you and pays back so much as well. Writer Natalie Goldberg's words about the development of her craft really apply to any line of work that is done with soul and commitment:

> I told my writing students that practice is something done under all circumstances, whether you're happy or sad. You don't become tossed away by a high weekend or a blue Monday. It is something close to you, not dependent on high-tech gyrations or smooth workshop-leader talk. Writing is something you do quietly, regularly, and in doing it, you face your life; everything comes up to fight, resist, deny, cajole you. Practice is old-fashioned, not hip or glamorous, but it gets you through Monday, and it lets you see the ungroundedness of hyped-up New Age workshops or quick ways to write a best-selling novel that you end up never writing.[1]

We have all had painful experiences of having to commit our time and attention to activities that did not sustain us or seem worthy of the investment. The toxic side of the work ethic in so many cultures, Eastern and Western alike, makes it very important to distinguish between duty and commitment. And a disciplined commitment to build something new can be much, much harder than criticizing the existing situation. In this respect, we are all grappling with the East European lesson described by Ivan Havel, brother of the Czech president, speaking of the Czech and Slovak people: "Before the revolution, I never realized how much more difficult it is to create than to destroy. Our task as dissidents was to question authority, to disturb the peace, to attack the basis of totality's existing structures. Now that they're gone, though, it's suddenly on our shoulders to create something workable in their place."[2]

Many effective people who find ways to integrate personal and planetary concerns in their work show a distinctive kind of purposefulness that is not driven or forced. Its essence is not deprivation. It is a strength of will that comes from self-knowledge and a delight in developing and expressing oneself. This strength makes it possible, through constant experimentation, to uncover a personal vision and gently but steadily direct inner and outer resources toward bringing that vision alive.

Healthy commitment has several important characteristics.

First, it comes from within. It is articulated as part of your process of determining what's important in your life; it isn't primarily dictated by the culture or an employer or even a loved one.

Second, keeping such a commitment offers a path for self-expression and actualization. It may require deferring gratification in significant ways, but it doesn't require "stuffing down" your essential self.

Third, the kind of commitment that animates you in a sustained and sustainable fashion is quite often grounded in something larger than private satisfaction. It has a purpose: building something of value or leaving a legacy that will touch other lives.

Attentiveness to this purpose can often shift the balance of our lives to make an otherwise difficult commitment possible and even nourishing. Laura Sewall, a psychologist working to develop new tools for environmental education in an experimental college with limited resources and massive hopes, reflects:

> When I get hung up in making a commitment, it's always the same old thing that gets in the way: ego. Wanting to wait and see. Wanting to keep those options open. It's such an old, stale game. And the only thing that gets me out of it is remembering that I'm not doing this just for me, for my tenure or my reviews or even just my students. I'm doing it for the Earth. When I get a grip on that fact, my ego is able to rest and the commitment flows.

In this way, commitment helps you concentrate and focus your personal power. That is Marsha Sinetar's point in *Do What You Love, The Money Will Follow:*

> When we are pursuing our Right Livelihood, even the most difficult and demanding aspects of our work will not sway us from our course. When others say, "Don't work so hard" or "Don't you ever take a break?" we will respond in bewilderment. What others may see as duty, pressure, or tedium we perceive as a kind of pleasure. Commitment is easy when our work is Right Livelihood.[3]

Unconditional commitment is not the same as addictive attachment. Quite the opposite. Commitment to doing your work, whether or not you're being paid, does not mean giving up on making a living at your chosen work eventually. This is an especially important point for people who have traditionally been underpaid or have volunteered their efforts without setting boundaries.

You can be totally committed to your work while continuing to exercise critical judgment about acceptable means for doing it. No matter how much you want to gain experience in corporate communications, for instance, you may decide against volunteering your labor for a profitable company that has just laid off several hundred of your neighbors. But you might design an internship with them, and seek out a scholarship fund that would pay you a stipend. On the other hand, you might prefer to learn the same skills by proposing an internship with the outplacement firm that's helping those laid-off workers find other jobs, or with an agency concerned with economic development, or with a community group fighting to save jobs. In most situations, there are multiple paths to the same goal.

Commitment is not just a state of mind; it's a pattern of behavior. It requires not only caring and will but a set of survival skills that are becoming increasingly apparent. These include communication, consensus building, project management, marketing, fund-raising, and organizational self-defense.

Commitment means opening up to possibility and removing barriers. It is also a matter of intent, which focuses and disciplines our actions, whether we are capable of a lot or just a little at any given time. Finally, that spirit of commitment means discovering the kinds of actions that let you move toward a goal with as much satisfaction and even joy as possible.

Creating an Incubator

If you understand personal power as primarily competitive or hierarchical, then it's natural to think of commitment in terms of overcoming obstacles, pushing through barriers, toughing out the opposition. That's part of the picture. But when you gain a different understanding of your power to make a difference—one that's grounded in inner wisdom and cocreative relationships as well as sheer force of will—the meaning of commitment also changes. It doesn't mean going it alone, but aligning yourself with the people you want to serve and others who can help you achieve your goals.

Commitment and support go hand in hand. Commitment in isolation may be unthinkable; commitment in community doesn't guarantee success, but allows an idea to bear whatever fruits it contains, and allows the idea holder to move through the development process with some grace.

William Drayton, whose public service "incubator" program, Ashoka, was described in Step 3, points to three stages in the development of successful projects and the people who run them:

- apprenticeship, a time of "learning how your field and the world work, in a nitty-gritty way"
- launching, the time of start-up, testing, and fine-tuning
- maturation, the phase in which a model can be replicated and the original seed funding can ultimately be replaced with other sources of support

These principles apply whether you're volunteering in a shelter for the homeless and looking for a job as a policy advocate, or developing a piece of software on weekends for eventual marketing. Incubation and start-up of projects are not vague concepts; they're not a euphemism for procrastination. They involve a range of learning activities that are highly individual and are directed toward articulating a goal. It's important to give them time and attention, and to notice the subtle changes your activity is producing.

Ashoka and other incubator models are ways of formalizing these activities. David Griswold, a former staff member at Ashoka, learned the power of that approach when he left his Washington-based office job to accompany Ashoka Fellow Arturo Garcia for a year of work in Mexico's coffee country. "I went down with my wife, who had a year's job working for a nonprofit. I thought I might pick coffee or something. But soon the coffee farmers—who were organized into small cooperatives—started opening up to us and saying, 'What we really need is some help in marketing our crops in the U.S.' " Griswold and Garcia toured the U.S., visiting dozens of coffee wholesalers and being rejected by them all.

Amid the rejections, though, were seeds of future projects. A visit to Ben & Jerry's led eventually to a coffee ice cream partnership. The pair's first success, however, came when they knocked on the door of Paul Katzeff's northern California business, Thanksgiving Coffees. "Not just a cup, but a just cup," is the slogan of Katzeff's mail order business, inspired by the former social worker and job trainer's visits to Nicaragua in the mid-1980s. Thanksgiving is committed to buying from farming cooperatives, and to supporting organic farming methods, in the interest of safety for both consumers and workers.

Griswold, Garcia and the Mexican Co-ops formed Aztec Harvests Coffees, a coffee brokerage in the U.S. that buys the top-of-the-line beans from nine Mexican cooperatives, supporting some fifteen thousand farmers. These are sold to Ben & Jerry's for a new flavor, Aztec Harvests Coffee; and to Thanksgiving and 35 other roasters as the Aztec Harvests blend. So serious were they about empowering the coffee growers that they incorporated on behalf of the cooperative owners and made themselves salaried employees. At times in the first few years, even this salary was deferred.

For Griswold, the gamble was manageable because his family— with Peace Corps and Presbyterian missionary ties—backed him from the start. But he has been drawn into a much deeper commitment than he ever expected. He reflects, "I thought I would set up this little business and then move on, maybe go to law school or business school. But in the process, I developed a relationship with a lot of people in Mexico who had stuck their necks out to work with us. One collaborator in Oaxaca, Francisco Zavaleta, drew me aside once during a very difficult period. He said, 'Down here, in the rainy season, when the rivers swell, the campesinos know that you can't turn back if the water is too rough. You have to keep going and get across.' He drove home the point that there were a lot of people down there counting on me. Every time I would feel ready to bag it and go to business school, they would take me by the lapels and say, 'Hold on, gringo.' "

Griswold's commitment, in turn, has made him able to attract other high-powered resources at very little cost. "I have friends who are consultants, lawyers, graphic designers, and so on who have a great interest in what I'm doing. And they're always willing to pitch in, whether it's to design a logo or stay up late to ponder business problems."

Two Models

 The approaches to the challenge of coherent, life-sustaining commitment are infinite. But they all build on two "archetypes": the volunteer and the entrepreneur.

A volunteer works without pay—but not necessarily without a role, respect, and other forms of compensation. Volunteers are not all envelope stuffers. Some serve on boards of directors. Others are strategic advisers, speechwriters, computer helpers, project managers, and more.

Entrepreneurs, like volunteers, are stuck with many stereotypes, and may defy them all. "Entrepreneurship is the answer," said a Taiwanese businessman who had been listening to a lot of Westerners. "The problem is, we don't know yet what the question is, and we spout on about entrepreneurship whenever we don't know any other answer." An entrepreneur is simply a person who works without a boss—or, more accurately, becomes her or his own boss. Entrepreneurs are not all lean and hungry marketeers. They may be piano teachers or Amway salespeople or acupuncturists. Some build up their practices through word of mouth in a single community, while others work by mail order or computer network on a national or even international scale. Increasingly, there is an entrepreneurial element in the nonprofit sector: individuals and small groups who raise funding to pay themselves subsistence income for service projects. The stories of two figures in my current pantheon of inspiring entrepreneurs will indicate the range of this activity taking place.

"If We Can Make It Here . . ."

George Bliss, a carpenter, began thinking seriously about the ecology of his own lifestyle in New York City. He made a commitment to live with absolutely minimal waste. That got him interested in ways that scrap materials could be reclaimed and reused. He began restoring bicycles and tricycles out of "appreciation for all the labor that went into things, labor that should not be discarded so casually." Soon he had a business going, gathering discarded hardware of all kinds in a van for repair and resale.

In New York, however, the van was the weakest element in the system. The day it was towed in the middle of a run, Bliss became a fanatical advocate of human-powered transportation. He now presides over a workshop where specially designed delivery bicycles are built. That workshop has become a business incubator for Pedal Express, a delivery service employing four or five part-timers, and Pony Pedicabs of New York, a ten-person for-profit cooperative that hopes to bring a modern variation of the rickshaw straight into the financial district. Similar businesses already thrive in Denver, Toronto, and other medium-size cities.

"This project can employ people with very little training, and can pay fifteen to twenty dollars per hour for work they can feel good about," says Bliss, who at this writing was working to raise the $2,000 per vehicle needed for construction, storage, and insurance. He has devoted years to experimenting with designs, finding work space, creating a business structure, and seeking funding. "New York is the hardest place in the world for getting this idea to work," he admits. "New Yorkers are very prone to lawsuits, very jumpy about insurance issues. Storage space is at a premium. And there are no institutions that have a stake in seeing locally produced alternatives vehicles. So I figure that if I can get it to work here, it can work anywhere."

Beyond Traditional Security

Paula Gutlove is director of the Balkans Peace Project, a project that sends conflict resolution specialists to areas outside the war zones of the former Yugoslavia to train community leaders. They hope to help keep the conflict from spreading and to share tools for building a stronger civil society.

Gutlove is the project's only paid staff member, working out of a home office and funded on a project-by-project basis by grants she writes herself.

"Conflict management as a profession is really taking off," she says. "But it sure isn't because it's easy to make a secure living in it. People are attracted to the opportunities for service."

Gutlove graduated from dental school, trained as an oral surgeon, and joined a practice part-time. But the widespread concern about international security in the early 1980s captured her interest in a way that dentistry never did, and she became executive director of the Boston chapter of Physicians for Social Responsibility (PSR). There she began a characteristic way of working, "identifying a felt need and coming up with a good idea on what to do about it."

Gutlove and colleagues designed a speaker's training for PSR chapter members, which became a prototype for other citizen groups. She moved on to direct another nonprofit concerned with researching the social side of the arms race, and became interested in a project called Promoting Effective Dialogue. She and two colleagues offered dialogue workshops in Russia, Hiroshima, and other areas of historic conflict.

As time passed, her colleagues shifted their focus to domestic issues, but Gutlove remained concerned about the international situation. When the war in the Balkans started, she made a low-budget trip to the region on behalf of three colleagues. On her return, she set out to fund a series of programs that she and her collaborators called the Balkans Peace Project. At first, even the most tenacious search for financing led nowhere: "In 1991, foundations just weren't funding work in the former Yugoslavia. It wasn't on their charts." But she began telling funders, "I am going to do this work somehow, whether or not you support me." That commitment finally won out.

"How do you think about success?" I asked her.

"Differently every hour," she replied. "It's a real struggle, especially the insecurity. Why a person who has the kind of security issues that I do has chosen such an insecure path—I don't know. But maybe this is my way of thumbing my nose at traditional security, which isn't all it's cut out to be."

As the mother of two young daughters, Gutlove struggles with more than financial insecurity. She faces a work-family struggle of spectacular proportions.

> I'll get into the taxi to go to the airport for these mammoth journeys, with one of my kids clinging to each leg saying "Don't leave." I'll get into the taxi asking "Why am I doing this? This is insane. I don't want to go." I meet up with my colleagues, who are saying the same things. Then, after the workshop, we know why we're doing it. Seeing the people there and participating in the process—it feels like what we're doing could make some change. Bringing together a group of people from Serbia and Croatia, and having them hear each other—that's success for me.

Finally, Gutlove has begun to see some more conventional signs of success. She was awarded a prestigious Bunting Fellowship on the basis of her work. She has even represented the U.S. State Department in two international conferences, discussing the role of the "N.G.O. entrepreneur" in peacemaking.

Bliss and Gutlove both illustrate a spirit of total responsibility for defining, promoting, monitoring, and adapting their work to the needs they see in the world. They are especially hopeful images because they have sunk roots in fields that are not quite commercial, and have helped define those fields in a way that could very well create many more jobs in the long run. Conflict resolution and human-powered transportation are fields with potential to promote social change and employ people in every community.

People who become truly caught up in a cause often work as a volunteer and an entrepreneur at the same time. They do whatever is needed to keep the work going. In more everyday situations, you have the luxury of thinking ahead about which image, the volunteer or the entrepreneur, will be your best organizing principle. Both orientations require high levels of initiative and commitment. But both can feed your spirit richly, calling forth strengths and resources you never dreamed you could tap.

Each of these paths has strong advantages and disadvantages. Volunteer situations often provide considerable freedom to experiment. Because it lacks the perceived high stakes of a paid position, volunteer status allows you some room to try on new personalities and styles, and to test out new skills in a safe environment. Because you can walk away from a volunteer position with fewer repercussions than from a paying job, volunteer opportunities are settings where you get to learn a great deal about how to motivate yourself when there's not a whip cracking.

Volunteering and the Path of Service

There can be rich harmonies between volunteering and career development. Sally Crocker, a Rhode Island career counselor who volunteers with a Samaritans suicide-prevention group in her community, catalogs the experience she has gained: "As a volunteer leader, I serve as backup for the people who staff the hot lines, helping them make decisions in crisis situations. I get to wear a beeper, which is kind of a kick. And I respond to emergencies, which is a privilege and a constant source of learning. I have gained experience in training, served on strategic planning and search committees, and learned a lot about community outreach and fund-raising."

Sometimes, she adds, the benefits are even more direct. Most members of the agency's small staff started out as volunteers, a path that is "typical of human service agencies which run with a small number of paid staff and a lot of volunteers." In those situations, volunteers and staff develop close, cooperative working relationships. Volunteers are among the first people to be considered when job openings arise, particularly since many positions in service organizations are never advertised. They are filled by volunteers who have shown leadership and love of the organization. Says Crocker, "This is one of the clearest examples of the hidden job market."

Volunteer activity can be an entry point into diverse populations and cultures, helping you build networks that can differ significantly in age, race, gender, capacities, and worldview from the crowds you've been hanging around with at work. In almost any volunteer group you get involved in—whether it's the League of Women Voters, the Coors Literacy Challenge, or the National Toxics Campaign—you'll meet people who make their living in unexpected ways, and they can become part of your future job-finding or job-creating network.

In fact, there are fields in which it is almost impossible to be hired without significant volunteer experience. Fair or not, there are reasons why this is true.

- In the arts, you simply have to cultivate and free up your talent before you're employable.
- In many service fields, such as human rights and crisis counseling, there is no shortcut for the experience necessary to tap into the inner resources that make you effective. This path lets candidates show potential employers (and themselves) that they can not only perform but cope.
- In many start-ups, whether of businesses or nonprofit organizations, months if not years of time can be invested in defining, testing, and articulating a concept in a way that will attract financial backing.
- Similarly, researchers often invest unpaid time in developing proposals for funding. And even the most experienced journalists spend some time putting together article proposals on speculation.

Be warned: in some of these situations, the fields are structured in ways that quite unfairly demand freebies from the budding professional. Still, the challenge remains—without feeding these trends and without letting oneself be exploited—to find a way to work.

By accepting full responsibility for launching your work in this spirit, you are reclaiming the initiative, powerfully. You're shifting the focus away from the apparent barriers onto the emerging possibilities, cultivating will and focus. You are also presenting yourself to the world as a doer, not a wannabe, and this shift can be mirrored in your self-image. This is a guaranteed way to stand out, to learn fast, and to attract all kinds of support that can help move you toward your goal. There is no better way to get to know leaders, innovators, and other allies in the field, increasing your access to information about ways to do your work for pay.

Volunteering helps you develop your knowledge and skills for doing a job and for job hunting. It strengthens your commitment in the same way that exercise strengthens your muscles. It identifies you publicly as an initiative taker. Finally, especially in the case of major innovations and the fragile new organizations that often come into being to support them, your volunteer efforts may help to bring a movement or a profession into being. That effort, in turn, may radically alter the job picture five or ten years from now.

In fact, at the risk of sounding crass, I know of no better network for cultivating job and project opportunities than a movement for social change. Movements unite people of different ages and backgrounds, different professions and trades. This means they're great places to find people who work in fields far different from yours, but who share your values and may well want to support you by sharing resources and contacts. Veteran activists often relate to each other with high levels of trust, a common ethical culture, and a history of cooperating in the name of a larger goal. That tribal spirit spills over in the sharing of guest rooms, information about upcoming events, introductions, and more. The guest rooms and address files of the peace, environmental, and women's movements have been the greatest nonmonetary resource in my professional life, and my office is equipped with a futon so that I can give back in kind.

Of course, this works only if you are authentically involved in a movement and have shown commitment in tangible ways, not if you are cruising it for contacts. That strategy will fool nobody.

Still, there are some cautionary notes about the volunteer path.

Volunteers are used in many settings to handle work that requires little training, and that can be put down and picked up as needed. Nonprofit organizations and businesses are becoming open to proposals from people wanting to apply their skills in a new setting by creating higher-level volunteer projects that benefit both the individual and the organization: research, communication, and demonstration projects all fall into this category. These may last a few weeks or a year.

Depending on the organization, you may or may not receive quality supervision and leadership. You may or may not be regarded as an equal member of the team. In many organizations, it is up to the volunteer to define the relationship, or at least to set limits on it. Finally, it is always important to examine the consequences of volunteering in an organization where one wants to work for income in the future. Depending on the circumstances, the volunteer experience could be seen as a strong plus, or it could lead you to be identified as "different" from the paid staff.

It's worth putting some thought into the possible role confusion between the "you" that volunteers and the "you" that wants to be paid for your labor. These days, the use of volunteer opportunities to build up career contacts is so widespread that some community groups have begun to suffer from the load of unrestrained individual agendas. When a friend of mine was between jobs and wanted to move into the environmental field, she sensibly got involved in a community group devoted to the issue. After a few meetings, though, she noticed a strange atmosphere. People in the group seemed to be devoting an inordinate amount of time to speaking about their personal interests and expertise, and trying to build consensus for group projects in their pet areas. They were also handing out an awful lot of business cards. Finally she realized what was going on: "All but one or two people in the room were out of work, and they were all there to network—or, worse, to try to create jobs for themselves out of group projects."

The Entrepreneurial Path

 Entrepreneurship, and especially small and home-based business, can properly be talked about as a social movement these days. While plenty of people choose this path for strictly economic reasons, plenty of others find it the only acceptable alternative to giving up their decision-making power to others. There is a humane and experimental spirit among many self-employed professionals and small-business people which has nothing to do with whether they're in a start-up phase or have been at it for twenty years. Barbara Winter, a self-employment expert and author of *Making a Living Without a Job,*[4] sees this trend as stemming from the reassertion of personal values. She reflects:

> People are becoming self-employed because their self-esteem is in good order and they want to learn more about what they can be as human beings. For a lot of them, that's connected to a vision of a different kind of world they'd like to build. I see this as the most powerful force in entrepreneurship and a tremendous source of commitment. It makes things like driving an eight-year-old car or working on weekends seem real unimportant.

Launching yourself as an entrepreneur has some predictable benefits and costs. In many business settings, the entrepreneurial approach gives you higher status and credibility than volunteering. In many nonprofit settings, the reverse is true. But increasingly, each of these sectors is opening its eyes to the benefits outside its own subcultures. Businesses are realizing the feats accomplished by low-resourced, high-stakes nonprofit work. Nonprofits are noticing the degree of cooperation and creativity it takes to do well in business.

You can learn a lot, and fast, by dealing with the practical questions an entrepreneur must face: how to price a service or product, and how to market it in a systematic fashion. This, however, also suggests a downside to the entrepreneurial path; you may have to pay excessive dues in terms of learning new skills like bookkeeping, advertising, marketing, and so on, that are not directly relevant to your primary goals. However, knowing these skills may open up new possibilities for doing the work in the future.

The skills you can develop as a volunteer or an entrepreneur include desktop publishing, direct mail, database management and other computer applications; filmmaking, video and still photography; public speaking; writing and editing; research; interviewing; advertising and marketing; event and program planning; proposal development; recruitment; supervision; fund-raising; lobbying; technical expertise on virtually any issue; leadership and strategy, to say nothing of time and stress management, and self-reliance in the extreme. Whatever field you may be moving into, these are powerful skills to bring with you.

Your choice of one of these paths, or a balance between them, may depend on such factors as

- the areas where you're trying to cultivate access
- your financial needs, and the range of alternative ways to meet them
- your comfort zones in terms of work culture and style
- the time frame involved, and the relative commitments required (you can arrange a two-month volunteer stint much easier than you can start a business in two months)
- your analysis of the ultimate market for your work

There are also many ways to integrate these paths. Stipended volunteer positions, paying living expenses or offering room and board, can be found through nonprofits, universities, and religious groups, as well as through organizations that promote internships and experiential education in specific fields. Some of these select candidates based on qualifications or background, others based on need, and still others based on personality match between the volunteer and the work to be done. Consult the resource list at the end of this book for helpful organizations.

However you see your first steps and their direction, some principles will be useful in blending vision with practicality.

1. Make a finite, sustainable start. As Barbara Winter counsels, "build small fires and tend them carefully."

2. Choose a product or service that can be applied in many settings so you're not dependent on too specialized a market.

3. Give your idea a name people remember. Fund-raising expert Laurie Blum draws attention to her books and consulting services with the title "Free Money." Winter supports self-employed people she calls the "joyfully jobless." A tailoring service near my house caught my eye with the name "Clothes Clinic."

4. Let lots of people know what you're up to. Educate them about its significance. And tell them how they can help.

5. Build your operation sustainably in both environmental and managerial terms. Pay attention to the pace you can maintain and to healthy working relationships. Walk the talk.

6. Apply a consistent standard of professionalism in all your activities, whether or not they're generating income.

One of the simplest, most effective ways to raise the voltage of a commitment is to state it out loud. This is the principle behind "graduation pledge" ceremonies, affirming ethics in job decisions. These have arisen in colleges and universities from Humboldt State to Harvard Medical School, and are easy to orchestrate in many settings.

Concerning commitment, there is only one guarantee: without it, not much happens. On countless bulletin boards, refrigerators, and office doors, a quote from Goethe has been popping up:

Concerning all acts of initiative [and creation] there is one elementary truth, the ignorance of which kills countless ideas and splendid plans: that the moment one definitely commits oneself, then Providence moves too. All sorts of things occur to help one that would never otherwise have occurred. A whole stream of events issues from the decision, raising in one's favor all manner of unforeseen incidents and meetings and material assistance, which no one could have dreamed would have come along.

It isn't necessary to be a mystic to believe this. It is only necessary to notice that making choices changes the self-image of the person who chooses, and increases the mind's attentiveness to the factors that bring the commitment to fruition. Commitment may help you notice the kindred spirits and resources that have been around you all along. All that's left is the decision to walk that path.

Most commitments that withstand time are not made suddenly or with bravado; they're quiet responses to an inner creative force, to the imperative of an idea or an image. The bravest aspect of a commitment is often the initial decision to let it into your life. After you say yes, opportunities for action have a way of presenting themselves. Rob Yeager, a record producer who spent twenty years too busy with other people's music to write his own, felt a stronger and stronger desire to express more of himself through music. But his responsibilities to his job and three children did not vanish. For months, Rob felt drawn to songwriting, but was too overwhelmed to take any action—except, in a moment of inspiration, to move his three guitars out of storage and arrange them in his office. Committing himself only to face them every day, he soon responded to their silent presence. Rob began to write songs.

Exercises: Barriers to Commitment

What positive memories do you associate with commitment and self-discipline? What negative memories? You might do some journal writing on each set of memories.

What commitments, related to your working life directly or to your personal development, have you had trouble with? How would your life change if you were able to keep any one of these commitments? Is there anything scary about moving into that new life?

What barriers to these commitments could you set about dismantling? What kinds of help would you need to do that?

Exercises: Strategies for Commitment

Make a list of all the activities that could be part of doing your work without pay. Include ideas that are big and small, wild and cautious. Identify the ones that are possible in light of your current situation. Now, among those possible actions, identify the ones that seem to have the most potential for moving you along in a sustainable fashion. Do any of these seem exciting?

Choose items from this short list—possible actions that have greatest potential for moving you along your path. One at a time, consider what might happen if you took this action. You might write a little story about what you did and what resulted. Which of these scenarios provide a basis for realistic action? What steps could you take to expand the options for realistic commitment?

What steps could you take as a volunteer? Where could you find out more about those possibilities? How would you support yourself financially if you followed this path?

What steps could you take as an entrepreneur? Where could you find out more about those possibilities? How would you price your services if you followed this path?

Step 8:
Let Go
of Assumptions
About Doing
Your Work

There are at least two kinds of games. One could be called finite, the
other infinite. A finite game is played for the purpose of winning, an
infinite game for the purpose of continuing the play. . . .

Finite players play within boundaries; infinite players
play with boundaries.

Finite players are serious; infinite games are playful.

A finite player plays to be powerful; an infinite player
plays with strength.

A finite player consumes time; an infinite player generates time.

The finite player aims for eternal life; the infinite player
aims for eternal birth.

James Carse,
Finite and Infinite Games

The anarchy of these times has at least one positive consequence. New ideas are being adopted, and new rules written, by thousands of people without conventional status or successful track records. Originality has never been more of an advantage. Shift your line of sight even one degree away from the obvious, and you will almost certainly notice unexpected possibilities for new careers, clientele, styles of working, and ways to contribute.

Denise Caywood, a newly certified massage therapist, was running dry in her job hunt until she had a dream about trucks and set up a muscular therapy practice in the Triple T Truck Stop outside Tucson.

Jim Malloy, a business professor, taught a successful course on entrepreneurship to members of the Boston Bruins hockey team who were preparing to retire.

David Whyte makes his living teaching poetry in major corporations.

Scott Weikart and David Offen are computer programmers who wanted to give something back to the community without saying goodbye to their profession. They started Community Data Processing in Oakland, California to help social-change groups increase their impact by using computers.

These stories show the power of approaching your work as an infinite game. No finite attitude, no matter how generous or how right it may be in some circumstances, is adequate to deal with the degree of flux and complexity out there. What's more, no finite attitude can match the complexity in you, and open you up to the inner resources you need in order to respond to the shifting context.

In the last two chapters, we have been exploring two sources of focus and direction. The first is to identify, as simply as possible, the essence of the work that matters to you. The second is to commit yourself to doing that work, in some form, regardless of the circumstances. But most of us have some experience with the pain and wasted effort that can result from inflexible commitment. That's why it's time to talk about flexibility.

This chapter will start with a brief reminder of the practical reasons for letting go of assumptions. First among these is the uncertainty that is intrinsic to career planning today. But even before these chaotic times, there were some people who tended to color within the lines and others who opened themselves up to the unusual. It can be argued that the accelerated and exaggerated qualities of today's uncertainties are only pushing us into a state of openness that has always been desirable for its own sake. We will talk, then, about functioning in an assumptionless but very attentive state, awake to unexpected sources of insight and opportunity as we continuously craft our working lives out of the materials that are available around us.

The Need for Assumption Busting

The career paths and strategies that used to go unquestioned are not just questionable today; in many cases they're discredited. Try to play the competitive corporate game that was taken for granted not too long ago, and you can end up offending co-workers and even bosses who have become converts to teamwork. Tell a job interviewer that you want to stay with a company for twenty years and rise to the level of vice-president, and you're likely to see a furrowed brow. The survival value of finite games is being more widely questioned than ever, and the survival value of the infinite game is growing more apparent. Many people know this in general, but nobody is exempt from the need to keep examining the specific implications of specific changes in each specific situation.

There was a time when we at least had convenient stereotypes to cling to, whether or not they were accurate: work in a big company or for the government if you want stability; work in a nonprofit or small business, or try self-employment, if you really want to be true to yourself.

No more. Security is no longer to be assumed in large organizations. However, creativity is not necessarily stifled in them either. Corporations come centralized and decentralized, with sharp or flat pyramids, virtual and modular and flexible, with anonymous absentee investors or employee owners or anything in between. Working people face a menu of full-time and part-time options, as employees or contractors, with workers empowered by unions and/or self-managed work teams, sometimes garnished with telecommuting and job sharing and flextime and career mosaics as well. All these flexible approaches are highly experimental, and the results of today's experiments will determine the nature and desirability of tomorrow's jobs and business opportunities in every sector.

In spite of this range and flux, I have sat in circles of people who never questioned the assumption that they belong in a business and only a business. Or a nonprofit. Or government. All these views are severely limiting. And this set of three categories ignores a fourth approach, which just happens to be as full of promise as any, that of starting your own organization, whether it's a one-person operation or something larger.

Corporate life, nonprofits, government and public service, small business and self-employment—you may find that each of these options fits you in one of the several careers you can expect to have. What allows you to move among these worlds coherently is the basic definition of your "work in the world," discussed in Step 6, and the commitment you were invited to make in Step 7.

In terms of career planning, then, these times call for four particular kinds of assumption busting:

1. Don't assume that the organizations, sectors, and job fields that have been your home in the past will continue to be hospitable.

2. Don't assume that the organizations, sectors, and fields you have ruled out in the past will continue to be off-limits.

3. Don't assume that the outward manifestations of a job—the forms and formalities—are a major indicator of security or satisfaction. There is much more going on, and some of it is positive.

4. Don't assume that there's a single right next step or even a single right path for you. You get to choose.

Assumption busting helps us to be attentive to the opportunities that are right here, right now. This vision can make all the difference in determining whether you have many options, or none. Jan, a social worker, realized this a few months after she was laid off by a service agency that had employed her for many years. She spent part of every week playing the role of an unemployed person: collecting her check, answering job ads, having weighty conversations about the future. Another part of her life was devoted to activities she loved: a small private practice and a satisfying volunteer role in her community, producing cultural activities such as cabarets and storytelling festivals. But the enjoyment didn't feel right. "I have to stop all these free-floating projects and figure out my career!" a voice in her mind kept screaming. Then, in a workshop, she had an opportunity to list her strengths and skills and examine the possibilities they presented. Scanning them, she realized: "These projects aren't a distraction from my work. They *are* my work! I can make a living by marketing these ideas."

Assumption busting helps you notice what you have in hand; it also helps you reach out and grab the opportunities, when necessary, and tap your powers of self-preservation to the utmost in times of change. Fenna Hanes, an educational consultant, illustrates the power of what I call "committed flexibility" in this way. A few years ago, Hanes was an employee at a Massachusetts agency called the Bay State Skills Corporation. Her role was bringing together educators, employers, and people in need of job training, in order to design programs that would be responsive to all their needs.

When funding dried up for her salary, Hanes was "driven by necessity" to identify another way to keep working. Knowing that the organization had money in other accounts to hire contractors even when it could not afford employees, she developed a proposal redefining herself as a consultant and showing how she could continue to handle projects the agency needed on that basis.

That idea kept her working, but the arrangement was short-term by its nature. So Hanes used the time to develop another marketable proposal. She decided to create an information resource that would be of use to the clients she had been working with, and to her overall educational mission. Focusing on the biotechnology industry, one she knew well, she proposed a statewide directory of biotechnology firms, educational resources, and career information to support the industry. She gained support from an industry association, the Massachusetts Biotechnology Council, and persuaded the Bay State Skills Corporation to fund and publish it. There was clear benefit for each party, and for Hanes, who was able to strengthen her overview of this emerging field. It's worth noting that desktop publishing has made it possible for her and many other knowledge workers to produce and market information products without lining up a commercial publisher. The partnership worked. The book was well received, and so was its sequel, a directory of Massachusetts environmental firms.

The books, in turn, gave Hanes the professional definition and the network she needed to step into a more solid combination of opportunities—all as an independent consultant, but with ongoing relationships as stable as many other people's jobs. She works three days a week at the New England Board of Higher Education, another non-profit agency involved in education and curriculum development. She also consults to community colleges and public agencies, does independent projects supported by grants, and teaches community college courses. Like many other consultants and employees, Hanes knows her situation will change with time; but she is also confident in her ability to move through transitions and create each next opportunity.

Coping with Chaos
(But Not Necessarily Thriving)

To be anchored in a community of shared values and a sense of personal purpose is a necessary replacement for other kinds of anchors that are no longer reliable; such as structured career paths, generous organizations, and assumptions about where security lies. Yet because most of us are redefining and renegotiating the conditions of our work, most of the time, we are dealing with a constant stream of new working relationships that we need to assess judiciously. This has radical implications for our ability to figure out whom to trust, and what the nature of our working relationships will be. We are all, continuously, "checking each other out." Even people we've counted on in the past can be transformed by circumstances—for the better, sometimes, and other times for the worse. In *Leadership Is an Art,* furniture executive Max DePree reflects on a conversation with a well-to-do executive who deeply regretted the frequency of mergers, acquisitions, breakups, and other turbulence going on around him. "All this uncertainty means I can no longer feel comfortable giving my word," he explained. "Without being able to do that, I don't know who I am anymore."[1]

In many cases, these changing circumstances are outpacing people's ability to adjust to loss and to their images of themselves in the world, and their ability to interpret events constructively and coherently. Nobody really knows the effect of this kind of continuing radical uncertainty on human development—on our institutions, ethics, community relationships, perceptions, and cultures.

Although I have been recommending letting go of assumptions because so many of them become obsolete so fast, there is a corollary: an open, assumptionless attitude is key to seeing the essence of a situation and doing what's needed with grace. This is nothing new, but its survival value grows in turbulent times.

On one level, the decision making that shapes a life's work can be reduced to a series of resolutions to dilemmas: Shall I work as an employee or entrepreneur right now? Shall I take this weekend workshop or go to the mountains? Shall I gamble on my future in this organization by committing to another extra project, or update my résumé and spend my free time networking? Shall I stick my neck out on these administrative battles now, or save my energy for the environmental initiative we're planning next month?

Behind every either-or decision, though, is a series of more fundamental questions about values, needs, priorities, and strategies. While rising to the daily decisions, we are challenged to go deeper, in order to become increasingly clear on our core values and increasingly true to them. This is another way of describing the shift from a fragmented to a holistic view, of taking seriously the idea that everything is interconnected, and paying attention without judgment to the integrated web of ever-present opportunities and constraints. Only with this recognition do we have a prayer of assimilating change and getting to the roots of conflicts, moving through changes, and embracing opportunities on their own terms.

All this requires a flexibility of response and a deeper flexibility of mind, anchored by a set of core values and loyalties that are continuously clarified. You can't fathom the resources that will come into your life. You can't predict the time frame for change. You can't guess the kindred spirits you'll meet, or the complementary organizations and projects you'll discover at conferences or even in the course of doing your work. You can only keep on carrying the ball, using your best skills, and pay attention to changes around you—including those that result from your actions. But doing "only" this can have a near-miraculous impact on learning and creativity. Here's Natalie Goldberg again, discussing the way discipline and openness intersect in meditation, or any other practice (such as the practice of clarifying one's work):

I've watched meditation students come and go. They use anything as an excuse—"My knee hurt," "The teacher said 'he' instead of 'she,'" "The schedule just wasn't good for me." There is no excuse: If you want it, go for it. Don't let anything toss you away. The other extreme is to accept blindly everything a teacher does: He's sleeping indiscriminately with the women in the community and you think, "Well, it's part of the teachings." It is best to stay alive, alert, trust yourself, but not give up, no matter what the situation. Get in there, stay in there, figure it out. If we want the teachings, we have to let ourselves be hungry. If a green pepper is offered, eat it. If it's a steak, devour it. If it's something indigestible—a turd, a cement block, a shoe—figure out what to do with it, but don't back away.[2]

Obviously, then, this kind of flexibility is not a passive or indecisive stance. It's about showing up and "waiting for instructions" in a very alert, disciplined, responsive, and playful spirit—paying attention to the subtleties of every decision, doing your best to be well prepared to respond to the right opportunities and even taking initiative to test out the wrong ones. It means treating each situation as unique, and making the fullest possible use of all the faculties you have developed in response to it.

Fewer Assumptions,
More Decisions

That is, use all you have, and give all you can, without depleting yourself in a way that makes it impossible to bounce back. The ideas in this step will serve you best if you have taken seriously the recommendations in Step 2 for stabilizing your life. When you have fewer assumptions to fall back on as a source of structure, the arts of limit setting and dynamic decision making become much more crucial to living through times of uncertainty. Saying yes and no appropriately are both acts of self-affirmation. Hyperadventurousness—trying new things in a way that's out of proportion with your ability to assimilate them—is just as damaging as hyperprotectiveness. To get a fix on whether I'm being open to a given opportunity in a spirit of relaxed faith or of compulsiveness, I rely on a handful of questions:

Am I looking at my options from the standpoint of what's needed right now to meet my goals or to address a specific problem, or am I driven by old business such as proving something to someone?

If I don't do this, will it be picked up by somebody else who is in a better position to accomplish it in a sustainable and healthy way? If nobody takes the action or initiative in question, will harm result?

Is there a simpler, less risky or labor-intensive, means to the same end?

Part of healthy limit setting is realizing that all you have to give will not be enough to bring to life the great visions you're capable of seeing. Not enough by itself, that is. But tiny, isolated acts of unpredictable significance can often be a key element in helping major changes to take place. In Gandhi's words, "What you can do may be too small to matter, but it is very important that you do it."

In any decision you're facing, consider what you really know. Then consider all you don't know—both the dangers and the factors that could work powerfully in your favor. In a system with so many dimensions and so many unknowns, tiny, marginal changes anywhere can have enormous ramifications. Just think of the number of elections that are won or lost by a few dozen votes; the number of businesses that have stayed open or folded based on decisions of a few customers or one critical investor; the number of decision makers, in government and industry, who spend their lives on the fence, listening for the messages from citizens and workers that will shape their policies. That's one reason why it is so often necessary to act without having a clue of the potential of success, and to give "minor" actions the same weight as "major" ones in your value system. Grasping the importance of actions taken in this spirit means knowing that you are not acting in isolation, that you can be contributing a tiny but critical piece of a very big puzzle.

Many spiritual traditions—Christian, Buddhist, and Native American, for example—recognize the notion of letting oneself be "acted through," serving as a conduit for developments more significant than you could be expected to know. This may or may not be the case at any given time; that is another reason for being open to it all the time. And it's certainly a more gracious way to understand commitment than an attitude of all-or-nothing drivenness. Thomas Merton said it this way, in 1966, in a letter to peace activist Jim Forrest:

> Do not depend on the hope of results. When you are doing the sort of work you have taken on, essentially an apostolic work, you may have to face the fact that your work will be apparently worthless and even achieve no result at all, if not perhaps results opposite to what you expect. As you get used to this idea, you start more and more to concentrate not on the results but on the value, the rightness, the truth of the work itself. And there too a great deal has to be gone through, as gradually you struggle less and less for an idea and more and more for specific people. The range tends to narrow down, but it gets much more real. In the end it is the reality of personal relationships that saves everything. . . .[3]

Life and Work
Beyond the Rule Book

Whenever you meet people who seem to understand this process, ply them with pastries and get them to talk about their lives. It is these stories, rich and unpredictable, that provide the best antidote to that arid, fearful quality that invades too many career discussions. Be warned: this life can seem (and be!) very scary. That is because it involves letting yourself feel more of your responses to the choices and limits in your life, and using those feelings as a homing device, whereas a more structured and less individualized approach makes it more possible to stuff down those feelings. Be warned, also: one of the scariest feelings known to humanity is fear of success. Letting go of assumptions includes letting go of self-imposed limits.

My first memorable exposure to the art of assumptionless evolution was a meeting in Managua, Nicaragua, with a Seattle woman on her way to Alaska indirectly. I am going to tell you this story in some detail, because it runs counter to every form of "rational" career planning and yet has a logic that I believe is characteristic of a growing number of people's paths today.

In Central America for a conference, I happened to be sitting on the front porch of a small guesthouse when someone I'd interviewed years before pulled up to the curb. Not knowing I was in town, she was looking for a fellow guest I hadn't met yet. That is the co-incidence that introduced me to Janet Levin, a teacher and writer with a "useless degree" in educational psychology. In the days that followed, she told me about "her work" as she had come to under-stand it.

In the final years of the Contra war, Levin was a shoestring traveler working with children, parents, and teachers in communities touched by the war. Her project was simple but psychologically sophisticated: getting kids to draw pictures about their lives, and talking with parents and teachers about the meaning of those drawings for the children's development. That set her apart from a majority of her fellow North Americans, who registered discomfort with the U.S. military interven-tion but would not have put their belongings in storage, as she had, and transplanted themselves to the region in order to become agents of healing. It also set her apart from a majority of international aid workers, who concentrated on more tangible offerings such as shipping medicine or rebuilding schools. She was in the incubation phase of a new life as a traveling teacher and healer.

Levin knew that when people experience trauma, their ability to heal and reclaim their lives is increased a great deal if they are able to give some voice to their emotions soon after the fact. Given an undi-rected invitation to draw, Nicaraguan children portrayed gunfire, houses burning, people running and screaming. So did children in Guatemala, where she had already spent time. By helping adults to recognize and support the children's need for catharsis, she was also creating a struc-ture for communities to find their voices.

Levin's leap of faith—or, as she called it, "the kid pictures project"—resulted in a book called *Guatemalan Guernica,* a traveling exhibition, media appearances, and expressions of gratitude wherever she went. It led her on to demonstrate the same idea in a Russian village of resettled refugees from Chernobyl, and in an Alaskan fishing village with high levels of domestic violence. Finally, the classic social entrepre-neur, Levin found her way into a tailor-made job in Alaska, directing a citywide counseling program to combat community violence. But the job was a by-product of saying yes to an open-ended quest. Here is how she tells the story:

My work and life have been a spiral. Now that I'm forty-five, I can see from this vantage point how I've chosen each step. Each successive five-year period beginning with twenty, I was involved with work and place I didn't know existed five years earlier. A five-year plan? I don't think so.

It's taken years of groping in the darkness to realize that I actually had a system, even when I thought I was just groping. I don't recommend my process to everyone. It's hard. It's utterly organic, so sometimes it stinks, and sometimes it has the perfume of roses.

She started out with a life as conventional as it gets:

The blueprint I got from Mom and Dad in Philadelphia was "Teach. Marry. Have kids. Teach." I started out teaching kindergarten in the inner city. I was good enough to be a demonstration teacher, to be videotaped on clumsy equipment long before that was common. They called it an effective and innovative open classroom model, and I developed it in a pretty traditional setting.

That classroom contained the major elements that Levin would carry with her in the years to come: "comfort and curiosity in a culture not my own, children, families, community, poverty, innovation." And the tendency to take very thorough "breaks" from work every five years or so. Levin's first break was a trip southward, with Mexico as the carefully planned destination and Guatemala as the real end point.

Traveling taught me to follow my feet. Yes, have a good map. Be knowledgeable about the surroundings, ask about safe places and restaurants. Talk to the locals, and to the travelers. And then be still. Feel where you're drawn, and move in that direction. When the street curves or dead-ends, look around; pay attention; go toward your curiosity. Consistently a place or person of interest is there.

My experience in Guatemala affected my senses, but my mind didn't understand. That taught me the power of my own sensate experience. I didn't have to understand. My attention was firmly grabbed. I felt at home. At first, I thought it had to do with the geography and the Mayan culture. Now I'd say it's a state of being I learned there.

On her return, Levin had the predictable second phase of awakening that awaits most international travelers: reverse culture shock. One of the gifts of cross-cultural experience, in fact, is the insight it provides about where you feel at home and where you don't. Levin settled in the Pacific Northwest and held a series of jobs in early childhood education, learning for herself what worked and what didn't.

> I mourned having to conform to a nonorganic life. I couldn't follow my senses. I had to show up. But I didn't have to work full-time, so half my awake time was passed strengthening "traveler's senses."
>
> I didn't really know what to do in this new situation, so the traveler in me went with the organic approach and the evaluations were much like those in Philadelphia. I seemed to have followed my feet long before I'd articulated the concept.
>
> The ending of a grant coincided with a birthday visit to eastern Oregon, an introduction at a party, and by the end of the weekend, a job. A temporary one for five months which would leave me eligible to collect unemployment and my thoughts. I wanted out of the classroom. I wanted to work with terminally ill children. But it didn't happen on my timeline.
>
> I spent five years as director of a university day-care co-op in Seattle, loving the people but not the work, all the while learning budget management and staff supervision. On my own time, I volunteered with the hospice, drawing with the kids and talking about their feelings. What was desire for change at thirty was a fever pitch by thirty-five.

Note that all the "organic" approach in the world did not get Levin off the hook for learning budget management and staff supervision, and being fully present to the left-brained aspects of her job. Nor does it take the place of planning and active prospecting for opportunities when it's time for a change. This is a principle that can't be overemphasized. Most of us favor either the intuitive/receptive aspects of life or the analytic/ active aspects, and see these two sides as competitive rather than complementary. But opening up and taking action are both important parts of taking complete responsibility for the unfolding of our work, as Levin testifies.

> I have a drawing on my wall. It's a straight line, with a spiral, like DNA, going around it. The straight line stands for the planned actions I took to hunt for a job. I read the paper every day. I wrote letters, wonderful fictions, for jobs I didn't really want. I went to the

employment service. I networked. As I was doing all these things I had the distinct feeling that they were baby steps, but very necessary.

Then there was another, simultaneous, process: the spiral. It accounts for what I would call the outside influences, what's bigger than my ego or my perception. All the surprises. They're part of me, too, but they're bigger than my conscious mind could handle.

These two processes converged to lead Levin to Central America, and on the saga set in motion by the drawings. As her fever grew to leave Seattle and day care, she knew only a few things about the future. She wanted something really new. She knew it would be a good idea to be in an unfamiliar place, "in order to pull the newness out of me." She imagined returning to Mexico to write, and began networking to learn more about the region. She saw a slide show about Guatemalan refugees in Mexico, containing children's drawings that moved her.

I thought, "Somebody should do a book of kid drawings in Central America, and let the kids speak for what's happening down there." Then I met somebody who knew somebody who knew the bishop in southern Mexico, who was visiting in the U.S. I was introduced, and the bishop invited me to come with him and meet people who could get me into the refugee camps. All this I did. I ended up with three hundred drawings and a changed life.

You, too, have the elements of self-expression that are powerful inside you, whether it leads you to work in the humanitarian or scientific or artistic or advocacy or business realms. It's in the impulses and attractions that make no sense but are hard to shake, and that stay with you in spite of the most careful plans.

Several aspects of Levin's lifestyle have made it much easier for her to follow her feet. She lives a life of material simplicity. When she is employed, she saves money fiercely. She barters and thrift-shops. And she has built a large network over the years that provides her with vigorous support for new adventures. These are things that can expand anyone's flexibility; you only have to do them.

Try this exercise. Go around and ask people you respect, whose work you find fascinating, how they ended up in their present jobs. You will find stories nothing like the careful, planned campaigns that most of the how-to books advise. You will find people who try to be organized, and try at the same time to be authentic, and slouch into all sorts of unexpected opportunities as a result of those combined efforts. You may even notice people straining to put their experiences into logical sequences, when the real plotline was anything but straight. For that matter, how have *you* found jobs? What has been the mix of rational planning and unexpected magic?

Real career development is about getting out of our own way, acknowledging and accepting opportunities rather than hiding from them. It's a process of constant horse trading and gambling, with reassessment from each new point along the path. Every plan, no matter how carefully made, is laced with coincidences bordering on the miraculous. The people who use this knowledge well are the ones who stay open.

One of the biggest assumptions in need of busting is the idea that we don't matter. At the root of so many battles people face in taking charge of their work is the struggle to value themselves, their intuitions, their sensibilities, and their desires to be useful, in the face of a barrage of "be-realistic messages." It's common to assume that if what we're doing isn't working, the proper response is to think smaller.

At times it seems to me that the industrialized economy contains millions of exquisite human beings, scrambling to hide their beauty and potential in order to fit into jobs which all, on the surface, seem so finite. It's worth remembering that increased self-esteem is a root of both creativity and responsibility. Only when we learn to hold on to the awareness of our own value, when we can be guided from within by the quiet but growing voice of our vocation as we understand it, can we free ourselves from the devaluing messages of the workplaces where we have been considered expendable. Only with that freedom can we set about finding or creating more worthy alternatives. When a "finite" door closes in your life, then, pay attention. There may be an "infinite" one waiting to open.

❧

Can you think of any aspects of your career that have "always been this way" and seem unchangeable?
How about industries, professions, trades, or parts of the world you've always been in? Roles you've always played?
Definitions of success that have always attracted you?

Where and how did you decide that these were necessary?

Is there anyone you're trying to please, or rebel against, by hanging on to these assumptions?

When you have been in the most open, assumptionless, states in your life, what conditions have helped you function that way?

What has it been like to work, and make choices about work, in that state?

❧

Step 9: Mine Your Experience for Gems

*O*ften *I am asked, who taught me how to write? Everything, I want
to say. Everything taught me, everything became my teacher, though
at the time I was not aware of all the tender shoots that helped me
along, that came up in Mr. Clemente's class, in Mr. Cates's, with all
the teachers I can't remember anymore, with all the blank times, the
daydreaming, the boredom, the American legacy of loneliness and
alienation, my Jewish background, the sky, the desk, a pen, the
pavement, small towns I've driven through. The list could go on and
on until I named every moment I was alive.... And we can't avoid an
inch of our own experience; if we do it causes a blur, a bleep, a puffy
unreality. Our job is to wake up to everything, because if we slow
down enough, we see we are everything.*[1]

Natalie Goldberg,
Long Quiet Highway

A Moral Center

Margaret Burnham, a cofounder of the first African-American women's law firm in Boston, has no problem recalling the moment when her life first turned toward the law.[2] "I was a teenager in Mississippi in 1964, passing out leaflets in Jackson. A police officer took a leaflet and rounded me up as an illegal demonstrator. I was sitting in jail, contemplating my existence, when a woman showed up. She was my lawyer. I had never seen a lawyer, much less a black woman lawyer. I said to myself, 'This has got to be magic.' "

Since then, Burnham has been an attorney, a judge, a teacher, a mother, and a community activist. Through it all she has "tried to live as part of the freedom movement," remaining true to those early moments and to the life that has unfolded as a result.

Certain experiences become guiding metaphors for our lives and work. They connect us to our inner power and integrity because of their symbolic role in making sense of our lives. They provide a steady context in times of flux. Not all those transformative experiences have the drama of days spent in jail for exercising citizenship. There are quieter kinds of drama that resonate just as richly. We all have these defining moments. As sources of direction, they are far superior to any aptitude test. As Burnham puts it, "That time set up the canvas on which I've painted my life. The moral center of that experience recurs in everything I do."

The theme of this chapter is the necessity of continuous learning, about work options and about oneself. This means weaving together a richer and more accurate sense of where you have been, and cultivating the skill of seeing, without judgment, where that past could take you. Continuous learning also means addressing a dimension of your history that is sometimes ignored: your role as a social being whose background in a particular generation and cultural group and region and family that has shaped the meanings you derive from your work. Finally, continuous learning means reinterpreting our personal and professional lives in light of changing conditions in economy, society, and ecology.

Most discussions about using ongoing experience for shaping future work center on fields that are commonly considered creative: writing, performing, composing, speaking, inventing, discovering. But creativity is wherever creative people are: in cooking, community organizing, counseling, auto repair, interior decoration, landscaping, administration, law. Not every personal breakthrough is material for a career reassessment, and it's not necessary to have made complete peace with your history before moving on the work front. In fact, the opposite can be true; moving forward with career choices, especially challenging ones, can be a source of rich revelation about who you are and what you need.

Crystallizing Moments

For many people, a handful of crystallizing experiences provides enough material for a life's worth of career development. When you're paying attention to where you've been and to your intuitions about the future, the puzzle pieces have a way of fitting together, often with a spark. Consultant Judy Otto describes a slow evolution of her professional focus, from industry to health care, during a period when friends of hers were facing life-threatening illnesses and the health care crisis was becoming national news. Those events brought numerous possibilities into her mind, but at first they did not easily translate into a course of action. She was able to give the options time to unfold, since her working life was proceeding comfortably enough. One day, though, she was struck by a line by the poet Antonio Machado: "What have you done with the garden entrusted to you?" She knew it was time to take action on some of the opportunities that were presenting themselves, and let experience lead her from there.

Some of the meanings she drew from her situation were highly personal; others were connected to the broader crisis, in health care, that she saw around her. For Otto, as for many people, working in health care was compelling because it made sense in terms of her personal history and in terms of the social context.

Many of the moments that help crystallize career directions have to do with our own healing and development. People or experiences that throw us a lifeline have a special way of capturing our attention with a sense of new possibility. Will Fudeman, a social worker and musician, recalls what happened when all the more or less reasonable parts of his life did not add up to a satisfying whole:

> I had three great jobs. I was a therapist part-time. I worked in an educational nonprofit part-time. I was a Sunday school program director. On top of that, I played in a klezmer band. And I was saying to myself, "What do I want to be when I grow up?"
>
> In fact, I said this to myself at great length at two in the morning, when I should have been sleeping. Now, you can give me the obvious response, that I was doing too much and my body was out of balance. But I've been overcommitted before, and this restlessness was new.
>
> I've studied a lot about the immune system and the energies of the body. So I took myself to my acupuncturist, who told me I've got a yin deficiency—too much fire in the head. Whatever else that may mean, it meant I got to lie there with needles in me for half an hour, which made me feel a lot more grounded. The worries of my life didn't go away, but I'm better able to deal with them.
>
> So I want to work with people in more tangible, physical ways. I don't plan to give up being a counselor. But I'm now studying acupuncture and herbal medicine so that, when the need arises, I can offer people something more tangible to go with the counseling.

Some crystallizing moments, like these, are the sources of satisfaction and healing so memorable that you want others to know them firsthand. Others come out of the ambiguous moments and dark times whose memories can put up barriers to forward movement until they are faced. There are sometimes obvious connections between insults and struggles in the past, and perceived limitations in the present. At times, dipping into those painful memories can even bring unexpected reassurance. Experiences that seemed like pure failure can take on a very different meaning in time.

For example, in the early '80s, Rose Diamond was a secretary, mother of three, and part-time college student in North Carolina. She could not have predicted the sequence of events that would lead her, by the middle of the 1990s, to be training as an art educator in Boston. Diamond had only a faint sense of what was ahead—a fascination with the arts, a drive for more education, and an exploring nature. Her memory of that era illustrates the way many of us really move our lives forward—by leaping into opportunities that are somehow compelling, even if we are not always being able to make full use of them right away:

> I had always wanted to work in radio, and they were just starting up a National Public Radio station in Charlotte. I went in and volunteered. I had an idea for a huge project: a storytelling show for children. Storytelling was just starting to come back into the culture, and there were wonderful mountain stories. My son's friend's father was a great storyteller. I got the go-ahead to get a pilot show together and apply for funding from IBM.
>
> I had never done anything like this before. I was scared to death. But I went ahead. I developed the proposal. I got the story recorded. And then I went to do an interview with a local literature professor whose backing we needed. I took my tape recorder but pushed the wrong buttons. We did an hour-long interview. But when I went to play it back, there was nothing there.
>
> I got so scared. I thought, "There's no way I'm going to make this happen." I backed out, and I was so embarrassed that I didn't follow through for years.

During those years, Diamond put one foot in front of the other to keep her children fed and uncover more of her skills and strengths. She finished college with a major in art history and museum studies. Her marriage ended. She worked for a time in a museum. Then, temporarily disabled by a car accident, she was forced into an entirely different rhythm of living for many months: resting, physical therapy, and days that were wide open for writing or drawing or working with clay. During her convalescence, she was showered with attention by co-workers in a way that profoundly increased her own self-esteem. Eventually she was able to say, "I guess I'm an artist," and some time later, "I suppose I could be a good teacher." No single event led to either of those acknowledgments; they grew organically out of the life she was leading and her openness to new images of herself.

Curiosity drew her to a more urban setting. Moving to Boston, she discovered a small graduate school whose programs integrate the arts and education. Everything that excited her seemed to be there, and her application was soon accepted. By coincidence, the college was home to a national center for oral history and storytelling, bringing her around full circle to that earlier interest. Viewing the potential and unknowns at the beginning of the program, she was able to say,

> I'm finally going to find out where Rose's creativity is. For the first time in my life I'm able to take the risk and not worry, just take one hurdle at a time. Since I've stopped to pay attention to my inner life, I don't have the need to be an overachiever anymore, so I'm much more free to act. I know now that I wasn't ready, back in 1980, to do that public radio show. My self-esteem wasn't high enough. That's why I quit.

Only by making peace with that earlier "defeat" could she see herself rising to the present challenge. This cyclic quality is quite common in the process of self-discovery and self-deployment (that is, "putting yourself out there"). This applies equally to career identification and career development. There are active times and reflective times, phases when the work to be done is formulating questions and other times for more actively testing out answers. In discussions of creativity, the term "incubation" often arises to describe those times of waiting and watching, figuring out what to observe, and learning the language of the questions that matter now, which may not be the language that has worked in the past.

You might work for a while in a particular area, gathering observations and insights about what fits and what's not quite right; this might be followed by a time of mounting energy and escalating tension between you and your surroundings (including the ultimate escalation, when you move on or are ejected); next might come a time to mourn the loss and identify the resources you have to work with now. Only then is it possible to apply those new understandings effectively to a new phase of work.

❧

When, in your life, have you experienced generosity or unexpected possibilities?

If you brought the spirit of those moments into your working life, how would it affect your choices of jobs and the ways you do your job?

> *When, in your life, have you experienced defeat or failure?*
> *How has that experience helped to establish the direction of your*
> *work? In what ways have you outgrown the limiting*
> *influence of earlier defeats?*

For some people, those clarifying moments are defined by strictly personal concerns. However, particularly potent insights can come when we see our lives in the broader context of our life cycle or the position of our generation in history. This was the case for Heather McLeod, Chloe Breyer, and Leslie Crutchfield when the three Harvard graduates started *Who Cares?*, a magazine about service and social change for twentysomethings. This down-to-earth publication, by and for "slackers," covers practical ways to make a difference, from national service to activist photography to political organizing.

A similar principle applied at a different life stage for Bob Graham, an agribusiness executive who decided in midlife to go "fifty-fifty at fifty." Graham began to divide his time between business and public service projects such as the Katalysis Foundation, which provides village microloans in several developing countries. As a successful businessman concerned about setting his children up with solid values about money, Graham used philanthropic projects as a way to work with them on those issues. More personally, though, social commitment was a natural expression of his deepening spirituality.

Integrity as a Creative Force

One of the powerful driving forces in adult development, including career development, is the quest for internal consistency, or at least coherence, between what we profess to believe and what we live. Granted, we differ vastly in the degree of consistency that's required for comfort. We differ, too, in the degree to which the circumstances of our lives have placed limits on what seems to be possible. Sometimes, the realities of a job seem to require us to be a different person, in significant respects, from the person we are outside the office. But leaps forward tend to take place when we can ask challenging questions about the reasons we assume those contradictions are necessary, and the resources we have to work with in transcending them.

Until 1990, Abhay Bhushan was living two lives that were morally and logically consistent, but quite different. For his livelihood, he was a successful strategic planner and system architect for Xerox Corporation in Palo Alto. In his leisure time, he pursued an interest in sustainable development in his native India, raising money and doing educational work in support of village economic projects. That commitment had been steady ever since 1978, when Bhushan took a paid social service leave from the company and went with his family to visit the area in northern India where his grandfather, a public defender, had founded the Institute for Engineering and Rural Technology to promote sustainable development. But somehow it had never occurred to him that his two lives could, or should, have much to do with each other.

The line between them began to blur around the time of Earth Day in 1990, a celebration that attracted sponsorship and public statements from many major corporations. Preparation was also in high gear for the 1992 U.N. Earth Summit. "Corporate environmentalism" seemed less like an oxymoron and more like a necessary idea.

That entire season could be described as one big crystallizing moment for Bhushan as his two worlds began to blend. Bhushan knew people at Xerox who biked to work and pushed for recycling and other initiatives. But there were no companywide initiatives to deal with the paper, chemicals, and packaging that were at the heart of the company's business. The idea just hadn't come to life yet.

Bhushan decided it was time for someone to remedy that situation. He developed a proposal to devote a part of his time to launching a coordinated company-wide initiative. He got enthusiastic approval from top management, and in a few months was asked to take the responsibility full-time. Bhushan remembers the incredulous responses of colleagues who saw the job as a professional backwater. In fact, it has been just the opposite. What's more, his twenty years of extracurricular interest and commitment made him the ideal person for a job whose creation, sooner or later, was inevitable.

He could see this because he did what corporate strategists are supposed to do (and what individual job holders, whatever their level, also benefit from doing). He looked at the possibilities in a dynamic way, as part of a flow of history. He looked at the changes under way, in markets and regulations and product possibilities and public sentiments, as they affected both the company's potential and his own. And he thought through the alternatives until he came up with an intelligent synthesis that would let him meet a recognized company need while bringing more of his values and interests into his work.

~

Are you leading multiple lives?

If so, what are the benefits and costs of this approach?

What areas of overlap do you see between your career and other "lives" you lead?

What do these suggest about ways to cultivate greater integrity and impact?

~

An Evolutionary View

I've been indulging in some storytelling to illustrate ways in which the whole of your life, your personal history, and the larger context can provide extremely important information about who you are and the conditions you need to be at your best in your work. In finding the gems in your experience that will help you to value your work fully and accurately, one of the most important processes is learning to see yourself in an evolutionary sense, dynamically rather than statically. This is part of learning to learn. If you find it easy, consider yourself lucky. If there are aspects of your self-image that seem frozen in place, you're not alone. Without continuous reassessment, new experiences don't become part of your evolving self-image; you may test and prove yourself endlessly because you've never paused to notice real accomplishments; you may find yourself stuck, at midlife, in the self-image of a beginner.

Adapting your self-image as you change involves comparing the present with the past; it also involves some perspective on the future. For example, whether a particular change constitutes progress or not depends on where you want to be and how you expect to get there. One of the most useful life-planning skills, and one of the most difficult to cultivate, is the ability to maintain a lively awareness of both past and future, and a sense of continuity between them.

Keeping a journal is a powerful method for developing this awareness. Boston writer and career counselor Kendall Dudley of Lifeworks, who has spent over fifteen years using autobiographical writing to help people uncover new life directions, points out the value of this tool for seeing the subtle aspects of changes as they occur. For example, he notes,

> It's very useful to ask, "Who am I becoming? How am I different now than I was ten years ago?" You can follow that up by going back to times of major change and asking, "Who was I then? At seventeen? At twenty-four? What did I want?" Writing from the point of view of the person you were at each stage can be very valuable.
>
> That same opening question—"Who am I becoming?"—can also be carried forward by searching for new images of yourself as they are emerging. One way to get through your barriers, and get your unconscious mind involved, is to write (or draw) a self-portrait a year, or two, or longer in the future. Often the language people come up with to describe themselves is rich with implications about where they're going and what they need.

The further in the future you can imagine and focus your intention, the more power you will have to make really significant changes in your situation. This point was brought home to me by my friend Bill Page, who was director of corporate planning for Polaroid under the leadership of Edwin Land. "I'm really getting organized," I once bragged to Bill. "I just made a detailed three-year plan for my life and work."

"No good," he responded. "You have to carry it out at least five years before you get into anything interesting." And, of course, you have to keep reassessing and reintegrating as you move through those years.

Seeing the future and making peace with the past are highly complementary processes. Discoveries on either front will help bring the other into focus. That means it's neither advisable nor possible to work out everything in the past before moving forward, as the self-improvement junkies among us try to do. Often, in fact, facing the future actively, and finding sources of authentic enthusiasm in it, can provide the needed energy for sorting out the past.

Of course, all this consideration of time takes time. If you don't find yourself making that time spontaneously, it might be worthwhile to do it in a more structured way. Some people go so far as to reserve time for reflection about their evolution, on a regular basis or as the cycles of their lives dictate. Especially if you are involved in a major passage, it is important to take stock of the ways you have changed during this phase of your life, and to make the best statement you can about where you see yourself going. For example, here are some questions for taking stock in a time of career transition.

1. How have you grown in your present or last work experience?

2. What did you set out to accomplish, personally and professionally, in this situation?

3. In what ways did you accomplish these things?

4. What were you most appreciated for on the job, and by whom?

5. What strengths of yours were not given the acknowledgment they deserved, and how has that fact shaped your ability to move into the next phase with confidence?

6. What were your characteristic struggles on the job?

7. In what ways were these a reflection of the work environment, and in what ways were they a reflection of your style and psychological needs in the situation?

8. What did you learn from those struggles that could help you to achieve the same goals with less suffering?

9. What accomplishments in this job are you most proud of?

10. How do these suggest new areas of responsibility, and new sources of marketability, for you in the future?

A Time to Let Go?

Now it is time to talk about the situation facing a special working population: those who have cast their lot with organizations, or with entire industries or professions, that are now, for various reasons, not the sources of opportunity they once were. You may be recovering from a layoff or anticipating one. Either way, you are entitled to feelings of vulnerability, confusion, grief, and rage. The reasons may be primarily economic, such as a downturn that shows no signs of reversing itself. They may also have to do with changing views among consumers, regulators, or investors about the value of a product or service. To use an obvious example, there are a host of reasons why tobacco marketing is no longer an uncomplicated career choice, even for people who are ethically comfortable with it. It is neither a secure profession nor a popular one. Its future depends mightily on public opinion and public policy. As one salesman for a large cigarette company said after being laid off and finding a new job in a different industry, "I wasn't really motivated to make a move on my own. But it does feel better to be out of there. I was getting tired of being kicked by little old ladies in the supermarket."

Suppose you find yourself in a field whose outlook has changed dramatically, in terms of financial success or public popularity or ecological sustainability or all of the above. Suppose you went into this field with solid reasons for believing you would make a positive contribution. Suppose further that, over the years, you sensibly enough paid primary attention to doing your job, not to the broader trends. But now you may be feeling less certain that the strategic minds at the head of the industry have a full grip on the situation. It may be time to assess whether you're still meeting the needs that drew you into this work, and are still being true to the values that matter to you.

All the questions above apply to this process. So do a couple of others.

What do you wish you had been told, or had asked, about the industry before you joined it?

How will you use this awareness to ask more useful questions from now on?

Suppose you stay in your present position or make a conservative move elsewhere in the industry. What will your working life be like in five years?

Suppose you take a leap into a new field. What kinds of work might let you serve the values that matter to you now?

What would it take for you to feel comfortably "finished" with this phase of your life?

Summing Up: Four Principles

Decisions about vocation make use of much more information than we can conceivably deal with using logic alone, but not more than we can hold in our awareness using imagery and intuition. By seeing wholes instead of parts and seeing each decision in the context of individual and community life, we can find our way into a much broader world than the one defined by the obvious alternatives around us. This is a world in which values, accomplishments, skills, strengths, resources, and most important, a sense of purpose are all naturally integrated. You can't put it all on your résumé, but you really are everything. And when your working life is on track, you feel best able to make use of all that you are.

In the last four steps, we have been exploring four principles that help to guide the process of moving your life's work forward, beginning with a definition of the essence of your work that is as clear as possible, making a commitment to taking whatever action is possible along that path, letting go of assumptions about the best ways to do the work, and a serious respect for life's experiences as sources of unfolding direction.

Ken Geiser, the environmental scientist who spoke about the identification of his work in Step 6, illustrates the way these four principles fit together. Geiser defines himself as an environmentalist, a simple but powerful statement about the principles that organize his work in the world. He commits himself to concrete action in an unorthodox but powerful fashion. The idea came to him after a few years in the fray.

I realized that I needed to code this thing in a new way, so to speak. Jokingly at first, and then more seriously, I said I needed a metric for measuring what I was achieving, so that I would be able to take stock at the end of my life.

I chose one that seemed rather silly, but that I've actually taken to heart. I've developed a list of toxic chemicals that are generally agreed to be environmental health hazards of a very significant magnitude. I've decided that the world isn't big enough for them and me. So they have to go. I have dedicated myself to the removal of this group of chemicals from commerce. That way, I can mark my success not only in terms of this passion, but also in very clear behavioral terms.

While pushing ahead fiercely to accomplish goals as he understands them at a given time, Geiser has learned to avoid making assumptions about the ways his life and work will unfold. He has arrived at this point through experiences that could not conceivably have been planned for, including the end of a marriage and the hard choice to leave an earlier career in architecture.

The losses that I've suffered have tended to be some of the best material I've gotten to work with. It took me a long time to realize that the things I was losing were really kicking me along in a way that was very, very powerful.

It's all in the perception you have of yourself, and your ability to hold some things steady even as others change. If you start thinking there's a grand plan—and then you discover that architecture is not going to satisfy you, and the wife that you have is going to leave you, and suddenly you have this collapsed image of yourself—you have to say, "I guess I was wrong. I'm going to have to start over."

If it weren't for those external pushes, it might have been much harder for Geiser to let go of aspects of his life that were making him comfortable but not challenging him at the highest level. Like many people who feel they have found their life's work, Geiser is continually coming to terms with its high demands. "I never intended to have this kind of life," he admits. "For years, I constantly looked for it to flatten out and become normalized." That hasn't happened. But if the work demands a lot from him, it gives back much more.

Full Circle

What's more, this commitment has brought Geiser around, full circle, to new possibilities in using the design training he thought he had abandoned when he left architecture. Now he is applying the same skills and knowledge toward finding new, nontoxic materials for building and industry. He sees this as "a design task, and it's one that can tap the most creative forces in the society for building a much better house for the future," metaphorically and literally.

This illustrates a common experience among people who allow themselves to be led by an unfolding sense of purpose, and who, within the limits of real-world alternatives at any given time, do their best to choose jobs that help them do "their work." New ideas and images come, and are integrated sooner or later. Obsolete understandings are shed. It is not a process any of us can control. We can only pay attention and use what we know about ourselves to shape our strategies, holding on to as many elements as we can and letting go when we have to. Somehow, doing that can lead us back to new ways to make use of the experiences and commitments with which we started out.

Unless he is forced to do so, Geiser does not abandon one set of self-images or goals when others come into focus. He thinks the way a designer does in his work to promote the use of less toxic materials. In addition, he is spearheading a major program to get Massachusetts moving in materials recycling. In that project, he sees himself in another role he developed back in college, that of a community organizer. He explains,

> I've always brought themes forward from each era in my life. I think that's really critical. We're like books, and the first chapter shouldn't be forgotten. There are metaphors and reasons that come from those early experiences that help make sense of what comes later.
>
> One of my models early on was Nat Owings, founder of one of the biggest architectural firms in the country. In his late forties, he and four other guys walked away from an office in Chicago that they were in trouble over. They all uprooted themselves and went to San Francisco to start over. I always thought, "Well, that's very romantic—but foolish." In my mind, you don't throw out what

you've learned. You are one person. You might as well bring the lessons forward. Actually, it has a lot to do with one's respect for oneself, belief in oneself, and, quite frankly, love for oneself.

From Self-Knowledge to Strategy

Love, of self and of the world, is the essential power source for the self-discovery, initiative, and adaptation necessary to craft a career with purpose and impact. The self-knowledge recommended in this chapter goes beyond simple work history and future plans. It's about purpose and principles, strengths and vulnerabilities. It's about drawing on the totality of your history to find a way to tell the most interesting possible story about who you are and what you're really working for. The benefits of this degree of self-knowledge are immeasurable, but they are also quite tangible. You gain in the very qualities that help you most in finding and doing your work: clarity, articulateness, self-confidence, and the ability to stand out with a positive presence.

As you decide on a path and a strategy, deeper self-knowledge helps you make use of everything in your background, including the gems of experience that put the rest into clearer context. Some of these gems are hard-won accomplishments. Others come directly from darker times when you were forced to face yourself and take stock of your values.

Times of difficulty on the job are often times of major learning about the conditions we need in order to work sanely and productively, and about the ways we fail ourselves by accepting unacceptable conditions. By recalling those experiences with a nonjudgmental attitude, doing the best we can to respect our own limitations and those of others in the situation, we can ask very useful questions about the negotiating positions we would benefit from taking with respect to future work. For example, these include questions about trade-offs between money and quality of work life, security and fascination, power and risk, the ease of finding jobs and their safety.

These elements are not all within the control of every working person in every situation. But it is always possible to ask, before saying yes to a new work situation, "What is my full range of alternatives here?" These alternatives may include relocating, self-teaching a new skill, choosing a period of self-employment, or investigating opportunities in a completely different field before saying yes to a job you suspect will make you miserable. They may include taking an undesirable job for a specific period of time, while promising yourself that you will find a way out of it.

On the other hand, if you say yes, you have some voice in exactly what you're saying yes to. More than pay and standard benefits can be negotiated in many situations: schedule and nature of performance reviews, bonuses, tuition assistance, flexibility of scheduling and other aspects of control over the way you do your job. Often minor changes in an overall employment package—for example, freedom to telecommute one day a week, or to work four long days instead of five average ones—can make major differences in terms of child-care costs, life balance, ability to pursue education, and time for self-renewal. Only by knowing yourself very well can you know the subtle negotiating points that will make a difference.

Likewise, self-knowledge is an underappreciated asset in marketing. Mining your history for gems, including the unpolished ones of failure and struggle, is a powerful antidote to the feelings of vulnerability that stick to many job changers. The knockout questions that blow your confidence in an interview often have such deadly impact because they direct attention toward your real vulnerabilities. Every step you take to make peace with those nagging memories and reclaim self-esteem will make a difference in your ability to respond to hard questions with candid, mature, specific, relaxed answers that set you apart. Standard job interview guides advise you to respond to questions about your vulnerabilities in some standard ways: by describing weaknesses that will be perceived as strengths, or by deflecting the questions entirely. These are sometimes necessary strategies to fall back on. However, answers to tough questions that show courage, creativity, individuality, or growth will be appreciated by some employers—including, perhaps, those you most want to work for. Especially in the entrepreneurial world, there are many hiring managers smart enough to value an applicant who has learned and grown through failures much more than one who minimizes their importance by acting impervious.

Exercise

Think of a rocky time in your work history. Write the story out, or tell it to a friend or a tape recorder. You can do this any way that seems authentic, with one rule. You have to talk about yourself in an active voice. That is, do not focus on what happened to you or why you were so powerless, but on the choices you made, the actions you took and the perfectly legitimate reasons you had for responding as you did.

Once you've made some peace with the difficult times in your history, you will probably have much more access to pleasant memories as well. The strongest reason for making peace with your history is that doing so is a foundation for fully valuing yourself and your experience. Challenges you've faced, turning points you've passed through, previous careers that have built up your experience and networks—these are the factors that make you unique, and uniquely qualified for a work experience that you target with these elements in mind.

You have just put into words some of the most important hopes and wishes and plans of your life. You have identified what you think you really work for, and how you expect to build on that work through the next phase of your life. From here on, you're in charge of the experiment.

Summary Worksheet 2

This worksheet sums up Steps 6 through 9. You might want to review the work you have done in earlier chapters, and fill in any gaps on questions you've been pondering, before moving into this series of summary exercise.

1. How do you describe the essence of your "work in the world" right now?

2. What kinds of jobs or business ventures would allow you to do some of that work in a satisfying way in the near future? (If you're not sure about that, refer to Step 4 and Step 6 for ideas about relating your personal qualities and history to specific kinds of work.)

3. What kinds of workplaces would be the best fit for you, based on all you know now about yourself?

4. What are some steps you could take now to act on the ideas, above, that you're clear on? Consider what you could do as a volunteer, as an entrepreneur, or in a particular kind of job (including your present one if you're employed).

5. What are some steps you could take now to test out any of the ideas above that you're not so clear on?

6. What commitments will you make to move your work forward?
   a. Volunteer activities:

b. Entrepreneurial activities:

c. Learning more about options:

d. Skill development:

e. Removing barriers:

7. What are some other open questions in your mind about the ways you would like to do your work? For example:
   a. Questions about scheduling and organization of work: (e.g., "Would I do well in a telecommuting situation, or do I need closer supervision and support?")

   b. Questions about the sector(s) you can most effectively work in (business, government, nonprofits, or a mix): (e.g., "I want to work internationally and have a fair amount of responsibility. Would a business, a government agency, or a nonprofit be more likely to offer that opportunity given my background?")

   c. Questions about the level of seniority and responsibility that's appropriate for you: (e.g., "I've never been called a manager, but I was a shop steward in an earlier job and I've coordinated some complex projects. How does this translate into managerial experience?")

   d. Other questions:

8. How will you go about answering the questions you just identified?

9. What major elements of your history do you especially want to carry forward in your work? Consider commitments, kinds of contribution and accomplishment, relationships, ways of defining yourself, strengths.

10. What major elements of your history are you ready to let go of in your future work?

11. What past experiences and interests could provide further focusing, contacts, and selling points in taking the actions to which you have committed?

Step 10:

Be a Co–creator

of the Workplace

You Want to See

It is natural for any system, whether it be human or chemical, to attempt to quell a disturbance when it first appears. But if the disturbance survives those first attempts at suppression and remains lodged within the system, an iterative process begins. The disturbance increases as different parts of the system get hold of it. Finally, it becomes so amplified that it cannot be ignored. This dynamic supports some current ideas that organizational change, even in large systems, can be created by a small group of committed individuals or champions.

Margaret Wheatley
Leadership and the New Science

Be ye therefore wise as serpents, and harmless as doves.
Matthew 10:16

So far, our focus has been on choosing a situation in which you can make a living and a contribution. We have looked at some approaches to preparation, research, and self-assessment. We have discussed charting a course with a realistic balance of purpose and openness. We've looked at a variety of examples of an expanded work ethic in operation.

At this point, you may be feeling a mix of enthusiasm and resistance. Even if you like the basic principles and are excited by the possibilities in fact, especially if you're excited—you might be cutting to the chase by asking, "How do I make all this work for me?" You may be comparing the picture painted in these pages with the one you see around you and feeling a bit skeptical.

So let's be honest about one thing. Most of the available alternatives out there are highly imperfect. There are more jobs from hell than there are dream jobs. The same is true for business ventures and self-employment opportunities.

Nobody says we have to take creative initiatives against these odds. And nobody can rise to every challenge. But the options will only get better when many of us accept an active role in improving them. Since you're still reading, I am going to assume that you're a spunky sort. This chapter is about promoting healthy change, moment by moment, in the course of doing any job. I apply the term "cocreation" to this kind of activity to indicate that whatever you do is an experiment and a collaboration with others.[1] The process of making significant changes at work almost never follows a formula, and it is almost never a solo act.

For people who are used to having "objective" job descriptions and measures of performance—standard fare in many workplaces—cocreation is a new way of thinking about responsibility. Clearly defined roles are great for supervision, performance evaluation, and determination of pay scales. But they're lousy for promoting initiative and collaboration. Most of us redefine and renegotiate our jobs all the time, and we can expect to do so even more in the future. You might as well do it with your eyes open.

Adding Value, Wherever You Are

There are many ways to add value in your workplace. Let's start with a sampling. Depending on your situation and your personality, you might:

Promote workplace flexibility. Whether you're an employee, a small business owner, a professional, or a corporate manager, you can free up people, including yourself, to keep a more flexible schedule. This may take the form of worker self-management, which naturally gives rise to flexible scheduling, compressed workweeks, telecommuting, and job sharing. Some of the largest organizations—AT&T, Bank of America, Xerox, and the U.S. government—have gotten out front by at least experimenting with flexibility. Research by the consulting firm Work/Family Directions indicates that while many employers have these options written into their personnel manuals, far fewer take full advantage of them. But those that do report significant savings in productivity, employee retention, and loyalty.[2]

Engage in high-impact hiring. If you are in a position to hire employees, even a few, you have an opportunity to make a strong statement about the values of your organization. Do you look to hire ordinary people, or extraordinary ones? People who have followed a straight path, or those who have gone their own way? People who look like those you already employ, or a wide enough range of cultures and perspectives that you might just be challenged now and then? Over the long haul, these seemingly routine decisions are among the most crucial you can make.

Los Angeles building contractor Baxter Sinclair is a wizard of high-impact hiring. Sinclair uses informal referrals from the court system to hire ex-convicts who want to change, and offers them a climate of hard work and support. It's a tough path, and he warns others, "If you try it, don't think everybody will love you."

For Sinclair, as a black business owner, it's part of restoring community pride by countering stereotypes and ingrained powerlessness. In the aftermath of the L.A. riots, Sinclair's company came into the affected neighborhoods and laid 10,000 feet of pipe, using a crew composed equally of black, white, and Hispanic faces. "To make this work, you have to be in partnership with the correctional system, and unions, and the community," he adds. Since 1979, he has employed some 300 people with criminal records; today, he can vouch for 120 of them as productive, tax-paying, and clean—better statistics than any prison system.[3]

Price and market your services in a way that reflects your values. What is the implied contract you make with the people you choose to serve? And how do you select that population anyway? How do you combine economic analysis and social vision, short-term thinking and long-range view?

Suppose you work in a bank. Are loans made equitably to wealthy and poor neighborhoods?

Suppose you work for a drug company or, for that matter, a corner pharmacy. Are the medicines affordable? Are products developed based on need as well as profitability?

Suppose you have historically undervalued your labor. What can you do to take a fully developed sense of self-worth with you into every salary negotiation?

Suppose you're in a line of work that pays well. Do you price your services based only on your own lifestyle goals? Or do you stretch to find ways to meet the public's needs?

The Guild of (Financially) Accessible Practitioners (G.A.P.) is a network of healing professionals in New England—acupuncturists, massage therapists, counselors, and others—who are committed to making their services affordable. They offer sliding scales and even free treatment to clients who cannot pay full fee. But rather than setting up formal structures that are easily abused, the group works to involve clients in taking responsibility for their part of the transaction. According to Dan Menkin, a founder, "The approach works in surprising ways. When we ask clients to get involved in thinking about the value of the treatments to them and their ability to pay, they tend to act responsibly. While some really can't pay, others find ways. It balances out."

See the public as a partner, not as the enemy. Social responsibility isn't a matter of checking the right box on a multiple choice quiz, but of continuously negotiating in order to respect the rights of many publics at the same time. One powerful tool for achieving this is the CERES Principles, developed by the Coalition for Environmentally Responsible

Economies. By 1994, some eighty companies had signed, including large corporations such as the Sun Company and General Motors, who pledged to:

1. Minimize the release of pollutants.

2. Conserve nonrenewable natural resources through efficient use and careful planning.

3. Minimize the creation of waste, especially hazardous waste.

4. Use energy wisely.

5. Diminish environmental, health, and safety risks to employees and communities.

6. Sell environmentally safe products.

7. Accept responsibility for environmental harm and make compensation.

8. Disclose potential environmental hazards.

9. Appoint one board member for environmental interests.

10. Produce and publicize a self-evaluation each year.

A second approach to community environmental responsibility relies less on standard principles and more on the specifics of a situation. Good Neighbor Agreements are contracts negotiated between industries and coalitions of neighbors to solve pollution problems and ensure community safety. Martin Saepoff, president of the glass company Dynasil, ignored lawyers' advice by signing a Good Neighbor Agreement with a Philadelphia coalition and hasn't been sorry. He says, "First of all, if you have something to hide, don't let anybody see it. If there is nothing to hide, these are citizens with a right to know."[4]

Consider the full implications of your job description. In many professions, there's an awakening to the fact that prevention is cheaper and more humane than treatment. For example:

• In Framingham, Massachusetts, the police run violence prevention programs in local high schools.

- Syracuse businessman Marty Yenowen uses his ambulance company, Eastern Paramedics, as a springboard for community activism against drunken driving.
- For Joseph DiFranza, a family doctor in the central Massachusetts mill town of Fitchburg, practicing medicine means standing fast against influences that erode health, including the largest preventable cause of death in the Western world: tobacco. As a member of D.O.C. (Doctors Ought to Care), DiFranza fights tobacco advertising as a logical outgrowth of his commitment to community health. As DiFranza puts it, "A lot of physicians limit their vision and just take care of people one at a time. But if you get a big enough idea, you can save a million lives."

Set limits on how and where you will work. Saying yes to working from a base of values means saying at least the occasional, well-thought-out no. This obviously requires skill, care, dignity, and an ability to choose your battles. Fugazi, a nationally touring rock band, refuses to play in clubs that charge more than $5.00 admission, or to sell tapes in shops that charge more than $8.00. The band also refuses to let its performances or recordings be advertised in magazines that advertise cigarettes. Not a path to riches for guys who hadn't quit their day jobs when they set that policy. But it's a reminder—from Generation X—that you don't have to be insatiable to be successful.

When you work for other people, it's harder to maintain this autonomy—but surprising things are possible. Continental Airlines baggage counter employee Theresa Fischette, who said no to a new company "spruce-up" campaign requiring that women wear makeup, illustrates the kind of surprise victories that sometimes take place. Initially, she was fired for her stand. But nationwide protest and a high-profile lawsuit got the company to reinstate her, with a public apology, within a week.

Principled refusal takes many forms. Working parents are saying no to career tracks that require weekends at the office. Medical and veterinary students are saying no to using healthy animals for surgery practice, leading some prestigious schools to develop alternative curricula for them. In the process, they are saying yes to the idea that steering a principled course can be perfectly practical.

Come out of the closet at work, whatever you may be hiding in there. Workplaces are notorious for stamping out "otherness." Therefore, the commitment to bring your whole self to work is a potent decision for many reasons. First, it's harder for a company to disregard the sensibilities of any social group if there's One of Them present at the board meeting, and harder still if there are two. Second, coming out breaks the ice for others. Third, coming out acts as a very powerful catalyst for an organization to look at the taboos it has held in place. Fourth, coming out is essential in expanding the legal protection available to any at-risk group. The progress that has been made in providing equal insurance coverage and other benefits to same-sex spouses has required a lot of lesbian and gay employees to identify themselves and claim their due.

One of the bravest minority groups in the workplace consists of people who have suffered from emotional or psychological troubles such as depression, manic-depression, schizophrenia, addiction. Newscaster Mike Wallace and Presidential Assistant Robert Boorstin are two prominent manic-depressives who have made their illnesses public and have become powerful advocates for workplace policies that promote recovery. When *Harvard Business Review* covered the topic in 1994, the magazine received strong positive feedback from people who echoed Boorstin's hope that "the 90's could be for manic depression what the 80's were for alcoholism. [If] people are open about their illness and able to function well in their jobs . . . people will finally see that mental illness should not be a hindrance to a successful career."[5]

Be someone's mentor. One of the most direct ways to make a difference in one person's life is to serve as a mentor for a talented young person, especially one who shows an extra measure of curiosity or social concern that seems worthy of cultivation. "Mentoring is best understood as a form of a love relationship," says psychologist Daniel Levinson in *The Seasons of a Man's Life.* A mentor helps a less experienced person through a transition by means of emotional support, strategic advice, reality checking, introductions, and information, by acting as a moral guide and model. According to Levinson, this is "developmentally the most important" function:

> to support and facilitate the realization of the Dream. The true mentor . . . fosters the young adult's development by believing in him, sharing the youthful Dream and giving it his blessing, helping to define the newly emerging self in its newly discovered world, and

creating a space in which the young person can work out a reasonably satisfactory life structure that contains the Dream.[6]

Green your workplace. It's a little more complicated than spring cleaning. But the process of moving your surroundings toward sustainability resembles a more conventional cleanup in one way: it's fairly intimidating before you start, but eventually it draws you in. Paybacks may range from direct savings to streamlined procedures to valuable professional experience to positive recognition of your leadership.

It's becoming easier to get your hands on information written from the viewpoint of managers rather than outside advocates. For example, Tedd Saunders, whose family owns the prestigious Park Plaza Hotel in Boston, illustrates this with his 1992 book, *The Bottom Line of Green Is Black*.[7] In it, he tells the story of his initiatives to make the Park Plaza a model by getting rid of disposable service items, maximizing energy efficiency, renovating bathrooms for water conservation, switching to nontoxic cleaning products, and even training night security staff to do ongoing energy audits as they make their rounds. Documentation of dollar savings attached to each change, and profiles of model companies, make this a must read for the skeptical boss as well as a valuable resource for job seekers.

Make a commitment to diversity. The creation of workplaces where everyone's gifts are welcome and everyone's perspective is honored equally—this is the hardest kind of work for social change: gritty and immediate. Hardly anybody seems to be getting it right. A 1993 study by the Nonprofit Academic Centers Council reports that nonprofit organizations—many of whom are supposed to be in the business of social change and justice seeking—are lagging behind the private sector in achieving ethnic and cultural diversity.[8] Only 17 percent of nonprofit employees are nonwhite, compared with 24.4 percent in government and 20.6 percent in the private sector. In spite of recent initiatives, more than 80 percent of the nation's biggest environmental organizations have staffs that are more than 80 percent white.

The report includes these ideas for overcoming racism (and other isms):

- Develop a concrete strategy, with commitment by senior management and measurable goals and objectives.

- Identify sources of institutional racism and work to eliminate them.
- If your employer is a nonprofit organization, you might consider building coalitions with social justice groups, which tend to have higher percentages of minority staff.
- Cast a wider net for new employees, giving yourself a kick out of habitual networks.
- If you have a grants program, require recipients of funding to show they have done their best to hire minorities. (If you're a business, you could think up similar forms of education and gentle pressure to use on your suppliers and subcontractors.)
- If you are an educational institution, concentrate on making programs accessible with flexible course schedules and with minorities in responsible positions on faculty and staff.

Of course, the issue is not only hiring qualified candidates. The issue is creating a setting where everyone can flourish, from the most entrenched to the newest on board, a workplace where difference—when it's noticed—is respected and even celebrated.

Use the purchasing power of your office to promote shared values. In the world of business relationships, the most powerful vote is with one's dollars and loyalty. Businesses and public agencies are using their purchasing power to support the cutting edge of clean and green suppliers for raw materials, office supplies, and other necessities. (Needless to say, this strategy is most credible if it is accompanied by a frugal approach to using all nonrenewable resources.) Every federal government office that purchases recycled paper and plastic goods is helping to stabilize the suppliers of these products. Every small business and local government can do the same.

Green Business Letter, an excellent resource for these strategies, reports on the successes of Compaq Computers (which issued guidelines to its suppliers for components packaged in materials made without CFCs); General Motors (which has encouraged packaging methods that fit better with recycling systems); and Intercontinental Hotels (which implemented a detailed Environmental Purchasing Code for all its hotels worldwide).[9] Editor Joel Makower notes that " 'Greening' your supply chain involves a delicate dance between buyer and seller."

Adopt win-win organizing strategies. Groundbreaking labor agreements have been signed by smart companies and unions to create more collaborative relationships without co-opting the unions' legitimate functions. For example, the Bath Iron Works, a Maine shipbuilder, has navigated through a painful strike and won over the majority of a divided labor force for a new contract. Its features include worker self-management, continuously adapting work functions within a context of job protection, and pay scales that build in financial rewards for workers who develop new skills. Labor and management at Bath overcame differences to unite around a common goal for survival—the need to diversify products, clientele, and competencies in order to wean the company away from its dominant customer, the U.S. Navy, and bring it into the peacetime economy.

Promote joy and celebration. Happiness at work may be one of the world's most radical ideas, but it is being widely rediscovered. Some of the more committed alternative businesses, such as Ben & Jerry's Homemade and *Utne Reader,* get frequent press coverage for their playful work cultures. But in most organizations there are at least a few people who create opportunities for play and renewal. They may be conspicuous—the ones organizing the volleyball games and ski trips, the ones with the Halloween masks and bubble potions in their desk drawers. Or they may work more quietly. Some determined souls have even found ways to make a living making other people happy.

Wenty Kelleher makes her living making matches. A former business systems analyst with a strong psychic bent, she calls herself a "dreammaker and matchmaker." Kelleher works to help people see their blind spots "in a loving, lighthearted way."

Jerilyn Brusseau is a Seattle restaurant owner who knows the power of a good meal to promote harmony. A founder of Peace Table, a national movement of chefs who practice "culinary diplomacy," Brusseau engineers spectacular community banquets in which people taste each other's cuisines and learn about each other's cultures.

Engage in high-impact philanthropy. It's worth remembering the most common form of contribution, one which can be handled in a number of uncommon ways. Companies are paying more attention to the values their contributions are supporting and the groups they may be inadvertently offending. For instance, the Boy Scouts of America's decision not to welcome gay members caused several large San Francisco businesses, including Levi Strauss and Wells Fargo Bank, to discontinue sizable donations.

Employees who want to see their contributions to the annual fund drive working toward fundamental social change—promoting self-reliance and social justice rather than simply helping the needy—can also take the initiative to interest their employers in funds set up for that purpose. The National Alliance for Choice in Giving, a network of 33 umbrella organizations covering over 500 funds, raised over $7 million in 1992 from campaigns in workplaces that included Lotus, Nissan, Apple, Mattel, Nike, and other major employers. Many of these alternative funds are targeted toward environmental sustainability, ending racism and poverty, challenging domestic violence, and other more ambitious goals.

A strong example of a corporate aid program that promotes community self-reliance is that of Terre, a Belgian recycling cooperative, which has applied nearly all its $10 million annual profits to financing other cooperative ventures such as a worker-owned bicycle factory in Nicaragua, an irrigation project in Peru, fishing boats in India, and a quarry in Algeria.[10]

Encourage your employer to institute a green tax. The "green tax" takes organizational giving beyond philanthropy, in the direction of equity and justice. This payment—at this point, voluntary—is made by an enterprise to offset its negative environmental impact. For example, Patagonia, a distinctive clothing company, pledges 10 percent of its gross profits to support 300 environmental groups. New Society Publishers, a worker-owned nonprofit committed to nonviolent social change, has raised $12,000 in voluntary green tax payments from customers and distributed it all to grassroots groups.[11]

Let everyday experience inspire you. Finally, the most inventive ideas are those that do not fit in established categories. They arise in the moment when people let their hearts and minds be opened. For example, too many incidents of random violence on television inspired Chuck Wall, a teacher in Bakersfield, California, to give his writing students an assignment.[12] They were to think up, and commit, one random act of kindness. Then they were to write about the experience.

One student bought thirty used blankets and handed them out to homeless people gathered under a bridge. Another gave up a parking space to somebody obviously in a hurry. These are simple things. Yet they have an unknown and unknowable ripple effect on the doers and recipients alike. And they all occurred because one teacher was doing his job with an inventive, caring attitude.

Early innovation is the hardest part of any social change. Today, people wanting to try any of these ideas have models and benchmarks for guidance and phone numbers to call for direct support. Barriers to change are often strong enough that trying one idea at a time is plenty. But this sampling of living models suggests the range of things you can do to add value in a variety of work situations.

Strategies for Changemaking

There is an intimate connection between strategies to promote change in a workplace and strategies to protect and advance your own position. Most exploration of career strategies has been based on considerations highly competitive, hierarchical, and often toxic organizations and has reflected the most naked forms of win-lose thinking. This is an accurate reflection of too many established workplaces. But it disregards the islands of win-win thinking, collaborative workstyles, and hunger for new ideas which are scattered unpredictably through organizations of all kinds. It *is* a jungle out there. But a real jungle holds thousands of peaceable creatures as well as predators. It's home to stable communities. It thrives on diversity. Its relationships are characterized by massive interdependence. Survival requires a wider set of skills than competition alone.

The first step in cocreating the workplace you want is sinking roots in a job, being known as a credible and valued team member, and learning the basics well enough that you're able to devote some attention to the bigger picture. As Lawrence Otis Graham points out in his book *The Best Companies for Minorities*, "Organizations want to be understood before they are changed. They welcome change from someone who seems like an insider more than from someone who is totally different."[13] Therefore, any efforts to spearhead change in a workplace have to be grounded in a solid understanding of the organization's mission, the agendas of those you work for, and the degree of maneuvering room that exists in your job description.

Today, more than ever, job descriptions are often exercises in fiction writing. Especially in settings where there have been reorganizations, major turf battles, and/or widespread angst, job descriptions can become battlegrounds on which hiring managers and human resource people fight for power as well as principles. The fact that a job description exists does not mean the employer has a rational basis for thinking a human being exists who can fill this job. In accepting a work opportunity it's very important to negotiate with, and educate, everyone who has a remote interest in the definition of your job. This includes communicating what you're best at, your limitations and how you're handling them, how you understand your role, what you dream of contributing, and how others can most constructively give you feedback.

Just as all politics is local, all career strategy boils down to the interpersonal. It's about how you handle each assignment, meeting, memo, task list, or chance encounter in the hallway. All the forms of self-assessment that were suggested in Step 5 as tools for choosing a work situation are no less valuable on the job, for understanding your needs and those of co-workers too.

Career self-defense and self-promotion are as necessary as ever. At the same time, they're an arena for putting forth the image of yourself for which you want to be known: your preferred balance of working solo and collaborating, cooperation and competition, directedness and acceptance, flexibility and limit setting. These are the dilemmas in which strategy and values intersect. Where do you want to go? How do you want to get there? What is your position on Gandhi's famous principle that ends and means must harmonize? What factors do you pay attention to when you're assessing the potential for change, and the blocks to it, in a situation?

Images of Change

It's possible, of course, to promote change without having a conscious idea about why you're doing what you're doing. The intuitive approach can yield amazing riches. But a guiding theory can be a source of considerable focus. As consultant Geoffrey Bellman reflects in his useful book *Getting Things Done When You Are Not in Charge,* "Our hope of influencing change is increased with our understanding of it. To the extent that we have working concepts and models of what change is about, we will be able to sort out and deal with the changes that come our way." Bellman's suggestion for mapping the dynamics of a desired change consists of four elements: what is, what you want, the players involved, and you. He explains:

> Each of the four elements exists whether we are actively talking about change or not. Floating around out there are all the things people want from their work. . . . And there are many people involved, active participants, players. Their experience, opinions, feelings, beliefs are just floating, too. You are just another one of those players unless you decide to do something about the situation. The "something" you could do is initiate and take responsibility for changing things. When YOU decide to do that, your role in relation to the other players changes in your mind and in your actions. You begin to see the opportunity present in the dynamics between the want, the "is," the players, and you. The free-floating ends, and the change dynamic begins.

Bellman's primary audience is professionals in organizations who may serve as communicators, marketeers, middle managers, accountants, lawyers, or all sorts of internal consultants and who have roles and responsibilities but little formal power. What he says to these people is true much more generally: "You don't have to be in charge all the time to take charge some of the time."[14]

If you are considering your potential as an agent of change in a situation where you have little formal power, Bellman advises starting with an "authority audit" to identify the range of your authority, how well it's working in enabling you to do your job as it's presently defined, and how it might be expanded if you can show a reason in light of the organization's mission. The same audit can also explore your informal sources of power—for example, your credibility, information you have access to, and others' perceptions of you.

What you observe in that audit may depend a lot on the lens through which you see organizational life. Management professor Gareth Morgan provides a very readable introduction to the dynamics of human systems in a book called *Images of Organization.*[15] He notes that we can think of organizations as:

- *machines,* the approach that has given rise to the bulk of traditional management theory and some of the most incorrigible bureaucracies
- *organisms* with highly individual natures, which influence and are influenced by their environments
- *brains* that process information, learn, and can, in theory, learn to learn better
- *cultures* and subcultures, shaped by the societies they grow out of but with socially constructed realities all their own
- *political systems* defined by a complex crossfire of competing interests such as battles for power, resources, and recognition
- *psychic prisons*, the actualization of Plato's cave, in which what's really going on is shaped by the unconscious lives of participants
- *flux and transformation*, with process rather than content as the focus of attention
- *instruments of domination*, in which power and resources are systematically concentrated and a powerless population is required for the ongoing functioning of the organization

Each of these perspectives is supported by some evidence and challenged by other evidence. But each one is useful, at least as a metaphor. The metaphor we apply to a particular situation may strongly influence our conclusions about whether a desired change is possible and, if so, how to accomplish it. For example, if you focus on the organization as political system, you will probably become adept at seeing under the surface and noticing people's hidden agendas. On the other hand, you may lose some of your ability to trust and to notice the times when people really want to be helpful without vested interest. If you focus on the organization as brain, you may cultivate the art of presenting strategic information to decision makers and peers. However, you may run into trouble dealing with people whose style in processing information isn't the same as yours.

Seen through any of these lenses, most organizations appear dauntingly resistant to change. Even the most powerful people, or the most beloved, have no guarantees that their agendas will succeed. Still, there are signs of receptivity interwoven with the signs of resistance everywhere. This is true throughout the economy.

From Dow Chemical to the Department of Energy, bureaucracies are being overturned by people who are tired of spending their days feeling like they're part of the problem. For all the forces holding bad situations in place, there can be equal and opposite forces for innovation. Even changes that are not enough by themselves may bring unforeseeable ripple effects. Even the most toxic, unconscious, inconsistent, driven, nasty, neurotic organizations are still made up of human beings with at least a glimmer of desire for a better way to spend their days.

There are of course multiple paths to tapping into the potential of a situation. Sometimes an informed gamble pays off. At other times, wisdom dictates a conservative strategy. According to organizational consultant Peter Block, it pays to be cautious when you're new or in an untested situation; when you or the organization are recovering from major change; when the survival of the organization (or your job) is threatened; and when you're in a zero-trust environment.[16]

Just as there are many imperfect ways of thinking about organizations, there are many imperfect frameworks for considering how to make changes within them. And they're all tempered by the observation of the military strategist Clausewitz, who noted in *On War* that "No battle plan survives contact with the enemy."

Transformative Leadership

The most obvious and romantic option is the taking over of an organization, division, department, whatever. As I've noted, even people who are nominally in charge may have trouble moving things in the direction they choose. But they certainly have wider options. And in these times of flux, top jobs can be some of the highest-turnover positions around.

In industry, government, and the nonprofit sector, the rule book of leadership is being rewritten continually. There is hunger for new wisdom, and examples of it in the field are getting easier to unearth. Notice especially those areas where there's a big need for transformation. My own short list would include the military, defense, and energy industries; health care; and international aid bureaucracies. Wherever things haven't been working, look for examples of people moving into the vacuum with a fresh approach. One of the most noteworthy examples is Hazel O'Leary, the Clinton administration's secretary of energy. O'Leary earned one senator's nomination for a "Nobel Prize for guts in government" by admitting that the military had performed radiation experiments on human subjects and endorsing the idea that the government owed victims and their families compensation. O'Leary also outlawed technospeak in the department, knocked down the bulletproof glass that surrounded her office area, replaced photos of missiles with photos of wind farms and solar panels, froze contractor salaries and set standards for cost containment, started a large-scale project to declassify documents, and hired whistleblowers and grassroots critics for positions of responsibility. As journalist Francis Wilkinson observes:

> O'Leary has established trust-building as something more than a management fad or a saccharine morale booster. She has made it her department's most central and significant policy. It's the right and honorable thing to do, of course. But after so many years of secrecy and deceit, it's also probably the only route to problem solving the DOE has left.[17]

You don't have to be a cabinet officer or a corporate CEO to exercise positive leadership. Departments, divisions, committees, franchises, and work teams have their own unexpected possibilities to tap. A new kind of leader, promoting more open and effective organizations, can be found in industry, government, and nonprofits.

The world of grassroots activism is full of exemplary leaders. One of the finest is Linda Stout, executive director of the Piedmont Peace Project mentioned in Step 1. The daughter of a sharecropper in a highly segregated region of North Carolina, Stout founded the multiracial project with a vision of active reconciliation. She didn't start by talking about racial harmony. She started by forming multiracial teams and giving them hard work, such as canvassing and voter registration, with measurable goals to meet. She is a genius at linking issues and creating programs that bring people together, from a literacy project to the Piedmont Peace Project Gospel Choir.

One part shop foreman and one part choreographer, Stout and her small staff orchestrate experiences in which community members can take stock of their own needs and test out their skills in local political action. "I can go into a rural neighborhood that lacks trash pickup or water service, and I can tell exactly what's going to be involved in fighting for that service. But I keep my mouth shut and let people find their own way," she says. "There's nothing more exciting than seeing people who are discovering their own power."

In small business, too, high stakes and limited resources combine to produce leaders worth following or imitating. One of these is Bill Hanley, chief executive officer of the largest publicly held military company to convert to civilian production. Galileo Electro-Optics, a 500-person high-tech firm in Sturbridge, Massachusetts, used to make night vision systems for the military. Now the company uses variations on the same core technology to produce dozens of products: sensors on photocopy machines, medical and dental diagnostic equipment. An engineer who worked his way up through the manufacturing ranks at Corning Inc., he says, "I can tell people on the shop floor honestly that I know their jobs, because I've done just about all their jobs."

Hanley, like Stout, is demanding as well as empowering. "What I run is a benign dictatorship," he admits. "Because that's what it takes to turn an organization around." All the leaders I've highlighted here have risen in surprising settings—in the midst of highly resistant organizations or in situations with no structure at all. They have all walked in with a set of beliefs about what is possible that might have been considered naive and have proceeded, with extraordinary effort, to realize the possibility.

Bill Hanley, in particular, challenges one article of faith about the capacity of businesses to change. It is commonly believed that the CEO of a publicly held corporation is powerless to do anything but maximize short-term profits for shareholders who are clamoring for their dollars. Admittedly, this is true in some situations, especially when the investors are pension funds with inflexible investment guidelines. But in 1985, when military contracting was booming and Galileo was entirely dependent on that single customer, Hanley made a long-shot pitch to his board of directors: "This isn't going to last. Either the world is going to get more peaceful, or the world isn't going to last. We have to find other ways of earning a living here. It's going to take some adjustment in the short term, but it will put us in a much stronger position in the long term." Some board members left; others were attracted. Although the company is just now edging into profitability, it has maintained a stable population of investors who are willing to wait for the payoff, financially and otherwise.

People like this can serve as role models for those who are attracted to leadership, and potential bosses for those who aren't. You can find them by purposeful networking, following the trail of media coverage, or watching for organizations that show visible turnarounds. And some of the principles of organizational change that they illustrate can even apply, at times, when you're working to exert influence from a position other than the top.

Innovation as Strategy

If you want to innovate without being in charge of more than your own contribution, Gifford Pinchot's valuable study, *Intrapreneuring,* is filled with cases and strategies.[18] Consider, for instance, efforts by buyers at Kinko's copies to find alternative papers made from corn and hemp that would diminish pressure on forests; or McDonald's veggie burgers, first test-marketed in Europe, as a response to the ecological and nutritional downside of a meat-based diet.

As even the most bureaucratic organizations rediscover the spirit of enterprise, the title of "intrapreneur" gives a new name and dignity to a well-established phenomenon. As Pinchot points out, "Imagination or vision is perhaps the most concrete of mental tools. The better a person's imagination, the more concrete a plan he or she can produce." Intrapreneurs are idea people, but they are also action oriented and one of their most consistent traits is "the inability to accept no for an answer."

While some innovators struggle in anonymity, a fair number of others find recognition and financial rewards, especially when their ideas meet a pressing social need. One example of this is the Energy-Efficient Refrigerator Competition launched a few years ago by a consortium from government and industry. Since the humble fridge has one of the most wasteful designs ever created—a freezer on top, which constantly loses its cool to the rising warmer air below it—a painless path to massive energy saving lies in adapting this appliance. Westinghouse, the winner, was rewarded with $30 million.

Innovations are not always about making new products or offering new services. They can be about organizing work in more effective, humane ways; forging new channels of information; or finding new language that makes old problems less vexing. One of the most powerful kinds of workplace innovation is redefining the job in which you find yourself. Some people are artists at doing this informally. For example, Carol Fargnoli left a high-pressure position as an optician and followed her instincts into a position as cook in an elementary school cafeteria. Over time, her real role began to emerge: paying attention to the kids and their troubles, serving as a sounding board and an advocate. "Some of these kids are tough in a major way," she noticed. "I hope they'll still be in school when they're fourteen. In fact, I hope they'll be alive."

She has followed no plan, just watching and asking questions. She noticed that one boy, who suffered from autism, was treated roughly by a particular teacher. So she read up on autism and then spoke to the school social worker. The situation was investigated, and the teacher was finally removed. Fargnoli doesn't look for conflict; she just does her work and pays attention. "It's very simple," she says. "I'm here for the kids. They feed me tremendously. I can't get enough of them."

Now Fargnoli is getting ready to train as a teacher's aide who can be more directly involved in the work of education. She has strong endorsements from her principal and the school social worker. Some straight-line thinkers might say she has stepped backward in order to move ahead. But for her, every step has been forward.

While this informal strategy can work in some settings, other people have benefited from going through the necessary channels to formalize a whole new set of responsibilities that better serves their employer and their own career development.

Nashville judge Penny Harrington has learned how to redefine her role, piece by piece. One of Harrington's responsibilities is presiding over the nation's first countywide environmental court, a role for which she volunteered after her colleagues had gone out of their way to distance themselves from the idea. This began a pattern Harrington has repeated successfully several times since: "taking on something everyone else hated, and realizing I knew what to do to make it work."

The season Harrington ran for the bench, a community groundswell was building for a special civil court that could address the backlog of building code violations in the city and surrounding countryside. A county environmental court, modeled on a successful citywide one in Memphis, would hear cases ranging from landlord-tenant disputes to illegal disposal of motor oil to Harrington's favorite, that of a man who could not seem to keep his twenty roosters properly caged. But Harrington understands the link between local and global, as well as the need for real judicial wisdom in these cases: "When you have an elderly lady who fails to remove the trash and debris from her yard, and her yard is in the watershed of the Cumberland River, and you don't know what kinds of medical wastes could end up in that trash, it's not a simple issue."

In three years of running the court just a few days a month, Harrington has seen tangible changes. Lawyers are more willing to take on local environmental cases. Building inspectors say they get more cooperation from landlords. This feedback has encouraged her to launch a second special docket, this time on domestic violence, with similar success. Largely due to the publicity, Harrington feels, "Women are saying for the first time, 'I don't have to take this. The courts will protect me.'

"It's mostly a matter of being creative and noticing what the needs are," she advises. Of course, it doesn't hurt to be comfortable with power and self-defense. Harrington has worked extensively on political campaigns and has been a lobbyist for a statewide environmental coalition. She readily admits: "I am no political neophyte."

The potential for this kind of initiative varies from workplace to workplace. But it is not just an option for those in the inner circles. In fact, often it's the new people who have the greatest chance at redefining their jobs. This is illustrated by the story of Annette Szumaski, who joined a large Washington law firm as a paralegal. Within a year, she had her superiors' blessing to create a new position as the firm's first environmental site investigator.

Her proposal filled a troublesome gap for her employer, whose business was concentrated in environmental insurance litigation. Many of its cases involved long-standing, poorly documented claims of illegal practices, some with serious health effects. Private investigators hired from outside didn't always understand the environmental issues or the firm's needs. With a varied background that included technical writing and a period as a Pentagon analyst, Szumaski provided an intriguing combination of technical and political sensitivity.

After training as a legal assistant, Szumaski intuitively looked for "an opportunity a little out of the ordinary." She was hired into the support staff to conduct research, write reports, and travel as needed. Her workload soon grew to include research into the history of contaminated sites. On her first investigative trip, Szumaski brought back information that was critical to the successful resolution of a case. She also developed a fascination with environmental law, and a conviction that "we have to clean up these sites, and we have to get the responsible parties to pay."

With the encouragement of the partner who had hired her, Szumaski carefully drafted a proposal for a new job description. Two committees fine-tuned it. Her new role formalized some of the work she had already been doing. It also freed her up from routine paralegal responsibilities and allowed her to focus sharply on environmental issues. Besides investigating contaminated sites, she was able to carry out special research projects for the firm's 75 attorneys—such as gathering background information on the waste-hauling practices of truckers—and to organize an in-house environmental library.

Szumaski's story shows that it's possible to create fundamentally new positions, even in fields as highly structured as the law. "This process was evolutionary," she says. "I didn't try to change things overnight. It was happening, and I helped give it form." And the job, in turn, gave form to her next step, into Pace University Law School.

''Just'' Doing Your Job

In some situations, the innovation that makes all the difference is just to do one's job correctly, fairly and without corruption. In a significant minority of workplaces, this is a path of bravery. There are many workplaces where challenging abuses and reporting problems—even serious ones—is welcome. There are others where the same behavior draws swift retaliation. The inventiveness of the mischief that rewards unpopular truth-telling in the workplace is well known, and the most flamboyant stories are those of whistle-blowers. A 1987 survey by Donald Soeken, a social worker serving whistle-blowers, and his wife, Karen, a statistician, showed that 84 percent of those who worked in private industry had been fired. In government, 75 percent were demoted. Any individual who stands up to an organization on issues of credibility and ethics can expect a period of extended stress, often culminating in a career change. The average time it took for whistle-blowers in this survey to resolve their legal cases was three to five years.[19] A yearlong investigation by the *Houston Chronicle* of the nuclear industry and its whistle-blowers revealed that most of them were forced into a career change.[20]

The experience of whistle-blowing and related forms of public protest will change your life. It is almost guaranteed to change your career. However, as lawyer Billie Garde affirms, some of those changes can be liberating. Years ago, as a temporary worker in the census bureau in Muskogee, Oklahoma, Garde reported her boss for sexual harassment. He was investigated, indicted, and convicted of more serious improprieties, including conspiracy to defraud the government. The experience led Garde to go to law school, and she now specializes in the legal defense of whistle-blowers for a Houston law firm. In the short run, the episode was devastating. In the long run, however, it forced her to break through to a new level of strength. She says frankly:

> My previous life was lost. I didn't have anything to go back to. Now, working with whistleblowers who feel that their lives are falling apart, I say, "Let's review this. You lost your job. But it was in a corrupt organization that treated you like dirt. You lost your so-called friends. They ran away when your life got rough, so you didn't have much for friends anyway. What you lost was your illusions. What you do next is up to you."

If you think you see serious fraud, abuse, or illegality around you, take pains to document what you see and shore up your support system before you make a move. Consult the Government Accountability

Project's manual, *Courage Without Martyrdom: A Survival Guide for Whistleblowers,* prepared by a team of experienced lawyers and counselors.[21] Attorney Robert Backus, who works with whistle-blowers in the nuclear power industry, advises, "Keep careful records. First, they're going to say it's outside your area of concern. Then they're going to say it's not significant. You have to show why the issue is an issue." And trust your perceptions. In the words of one health care professional who was thinking of reporting possible research fraud, "I kept thinking, 'They couldn't be so transparent. They couldn't have gone so far.' The stunning part is how flagrant, how amateurish, it all seems."

In spite of resistance and harassment, 84 percent of the whistleblowers who responded to the Soeken survey said they would do the same thing again in the same circumstances. And an estimated 25 percent of whistle-blowers eventually see direct results from their action in the form of changes within the organization, and many others have a less direct impact in bringing about needed reforms. For example, in the aftermath of the *Challenger* disaster, Morton-Thiokol engineer Roger Boisjoly testified that he had reported faulty booster components to his superiors and tried to stop the takeoff. His testimony was one of the most powerful factors in reforming both the space program and federal laws to protect whistle-blowers.[22]

Many whistle-blowers experience a double whammy: resistance and sometimes harassment by the employer; and reluctance on the part of other employers to risk hiring them. But this is a taboo that can be broken, and many people reading this book can help. Anyone who has hiring power, even for a tiny department, can play a role. What is needed is the equivalent of an Underground Railroad, or Oskar Schindler's factory in the great film *Schindler's List*—a commitment on the part of courageous employers to welcome courageous employees and reach out a strong hand to assist people who have told the truth at high cost to themselves.

This leads to the subject of organizational self-defense. The legal protections and social support systems that exist today for whistleblowers have been built over decades, through tenacious and bitter battling, by whistle-blowers themselves and by activists, attorneys, legislators, and helping professionals who see these people as front-line defenders of democratic institutions. The same is true for labor and workplace law. Two valuable guidebooks for self-protection are Dan

Lacey's *Your Rights in the Workplace,* and John D. Rapoport and Brian L. Zevnik's *Employee Strikes Back!*

Court battles and appeals to regulatory agencies both tend to be nasty, brutish, and long. Their payoff can be high, morally as well as financially, but so can the investment that is required. This fact has created a groundswell of interest in a win-win approach to self-defense.

A Spirit of Healing

Fortunately, most work situations do not contain the degree of overt hostility of the ones we have been discussing. But many, if not most, suffer from some degree of paralysis brought about by conflicting agendas and personalities. As a consequence, one of the greatest ways to become an agent of change in any workplace is to become skilled at conflict resolution and to watch for opportunities to use that ability. You probably won't have to wait long. There has been an explosion in resources available for training and development of this capability, as industry and government alike begin to recognize it as less costly and cumbersome than court action.

Pete Swanson, who coordinates training in alternative dispute resolution for the Federal Mediation and Conciliation Service in Washington, notes a tremendous upsurge in interest and "an amazing diversity of people working as mediators." A graduate of George Mason University's conflict management program, Swanson developed his talents through an internship in northern India, helping exiled Tibetans study the feasibility of an institute for conflict resolution. He returned to Washington just as the government was expanding its commitment to alternative dispute resolution.

Swanson has trained and mentored staff groups in agencies such as the IRS and the Occupational Safety and Health Administration, and sees himself as part of nothing less than a "movement to incorporate and institutionalize conflict resolution in government." To the extent that government touches lives and workplaces, this skill—and the world-view it reflects—could spread quickly.

Cocreation Beyond the Workplace

There is one more major aspect of cocreation to consider. The work opportunities available to you, and the maneuvering room you have for change on the job, both depend greatly on the policy climate in which you are functioning. In the words of *Philadelphia Inquirer* reporters Donald Barlett and James Steele, authors of the exposé *America: What Went Wrong?*, the economy is shaped by a "government rule book":

> a system of rewards and penalties that influences business behavior, which in turn has a wide-ranging impact on your daily life. From the price you pay for a gallon of gasoline or a quart of milk to the closing of a manufacturing plant and the elimination of your job. From the number of peanuts in your favorite brand of peanut butter to the amount of money you will collect in unemployment benefits if you are laid off. From whether the shirt or dress you are wearing is made in Fleetwood, Pennsylvania, or Seoul, Korea, to whether the company you work for expands its production facilities in the United States, thereby creating jobs, or opens a new plant in Puerto Rico or Mexico instead.[23]

That rule book has been rewritten with a fairly crude scrawl in recent years. I believe that an acceptable range of workplaces will only be created by a two-part strategy. The first part is doing whatever is possible in each workplace to rebuild trust and true collaboration between employers and employees. The second part is redesigning the systems of worker-management relations and corporate governance so that the economy becomes an engine of social and environmental renewal rather than degradation—in Paul Hawken's words, creating a "restorative economy."[24]

In other words, if you want to expand your opportunities to perform income-producing work for human well-being and ecological health, then do all that's in your power to work for a sustainable, equitable socioeconomic order. Sustainable economic development is a powerful idea, defined by the U.N.'s World Commission on Environment and Development as progress that "meets the needs of the present without compromising the ability of future generations to meet their own needs." Sound obvious? Only if you haven't been terrified by predictions, many from industries that will be affected, that environmental protection will destroy the economy, job by job by job. A 1990 survey conducted by the *Wall Street Journal* found that one-third of workers thought it was likely or somewhat likely that their job was endangered by environmental regulations.[25] However, when economist Eban Goodstein reviewed twenty years' research on the connection between environmental protection and jobs, he found that "at the economywide level, there simply is no trade-off. . . . Moreover, actual layoffs from regulation have been startlingly small."

Goodstein also observed that environmental regulations generate jobs, especially for blue-collar workers, and that even in industries where local job-environment trade-offs are significant, such as mining and logging, a counterbalancing number of "new jobs are generated in such fields as providing substitute products for the timber or minerals preserved, in fishing and tourism, as well as in industries seeking a high quality of life for their employees."[26] Worldwatch Institute researchers add that the industries that are being most dramatically challenged by the environmental situation (such as energy, pulp and paper, steelmaking, and chemicals) are among the least labor-intensive.[27] But for working people in those industries and for regions heavily dependent on them, it is clear that the shift to a sustainable economy will require considerable retraining and well-run support systems to help workers adapt. In this respect, too, what's good for sustainability is good for economic development in general.

Besides regulations (the clumsiest approach to promoting an economic shift), a number of positive incentives have been proposed to hasten the coming of a sustainable economy. Worldwatch researchers highlight four major strategies in their study *Saving the Planet: How to Shape an Environmentally Sustainable Global Economy:*

1. More accurate indicators of human welfare than the present Gross National Product

2. Elimination of government incentives that encourage unsustainable practices, such as pesticide subsidies, and development of incentives for sustainable practices

3. Green taxes (sometimes called Value Extracted Taxes) on such practices as the burning of fossil fuels, the use of virgin

materials, the generation of toxic waste, and the overpumping of groundwater

4. Overhauling international aid programs to support sustainable development practices

This overall shift will also depend on countless smaller changes that will make workplaces more sensitive to their environments and employees, as well as more receptive to innovation. To sketch some more features of the policy climate that are ripe for renewal:

1. Labor relations and workplace laws presently protect workers from many kinds of discrimination, but not from purely arbitrary firing, and apply inconsistently at best to the growing temporary workforce.[28]

2. The North American Free Trade Agreement (NAFTA) has eroded the already tenuous rights of workers in Mexico. Several dozen firings for union organizing were reported in Mexican subsidiaries of U.S. companies in the months after the agreement took effect.[29]

3. A maze of restrictive and at times obsolete regulations limit the options of small businesses, and especially start-ups. Consider, for example, *Inc.* magazine's report of a local licensing monopoly that kept three African-American taxi drivers from starting a business to serve Denver's inner city.[30]

4. Tax laws and local business codes can wreak havoc on home-based businesses. Deva, a Maryland clothing business employing home-based craftspeople, was shut down for a time as a result of local ordinances outlawing home sewing for women's clothing, but not for men's.

5. Occupational health and safety have been seriously compromised by downsizings in many companies and inadequacies in the federal regulatory process. According to a survey of readers conducted by *Industrial Safety and Hygiene News* in 1994, 64 percent of respondents said safety was a lower priority in their plants due to economic factors; more than half said they

were performing fewer safety audits due to resource constraints.[31]

6. Finally, job migration is a continuing reality that threatens to
keep nations in conflict rather than cooperating to solve global
problems. In the U.S., protection of "our" jobs is often held
up as a singular goal, rather than as part of an integrated
strategy for global economic well-being. But as Robert Reich
and other economists have argued, it's hard if not impossible to
create a national economy that's healthy and equitable when the
global economy isn't. What's more, sustainable economic development is a planet-wide challenge in which the wealthy and
poor countries will make it together, or not at all. If we really
understand that, we will think of domestic and foreign job
creation as complementary, not competing, goals. And we will
see both these goals in the light of sustainability and social
justice.

The movement of jobs away from the developed world is more than
a matter of labor costs. Changes in U.S. tax laws have created competitive advantages for companies that move their labor-intensive operations
to low-wage zones. American companies that build plants in U.S.
possessions such as Puerto Rico can claim federal tax credits even if they
are shutting down plants elsewhere in order to do so. In addition to that,
the Internal Revenue code allows multinational corporations to shift
costs to the books of operations in high-tax countries (in order to
maximize deductions) while shifting profits to low-tax countries (to
minimize tax payments), thus making it attractive to operate a network
of plants that can each be geared up or down as desired.

Sometimes the incentives to move jobs offshore are even more
direct, and more ripe to be challenged. A few years ago, union research
uncovered the use of $100 million in taxpayers' funds—through the
Agency for International Development, the Overseas Private Investment Corporation, and other government agencies—to promote the
movement of industry out of the U.S. and into the Caribbean basin. In
1992, activists representing 21 major unions marched into Congress
with a report called "Paying to Lose Our Jobs."[32] The most flagrantly
offending funds were cut off.

These are some of the reasons why activism is not a luxury to be pursued when things are going fine at work. It's an essential element in creating a workplace where things have a chance of going fine. This means accepting that what's not working in your situation is real. It isn't going to go away by itself. We each have our own special style of denial. As Chris Carlsson, editor of the in-your-face San Francisco office workers' magazine *Processed World,* observes, "What it takes to get people to organize on their own behalf is the belief that they're stuck somewhere. The modern work force is organized now around transience and escape."

Just as there are many ways to chart a career path that makes the most of your strengths and meets your basic needs, there are many ways to take action to expand the range of possible workplaces. For instance, with negligible inconvenience, you can use your purchasing and investing decisions to support the enterprises you see as more responsible and communicate displeasure to the others. Market researcher Faith Popcorn points to "the vigilante consumer" as one of ten potent market forces that will shape business in the 1990s. And this has not always been the case. Alice Tepper Marlin, who founded the Council on Economic Priorities twenty-five years ago, remembers a kind of wistfulness in the old days when she surveyed consumers about whether or not their purchasing decisions reflected their true values. "We don't have the information to make those decisions" was the overwhelming response. "But if we had that information, we sure would use it." Since then, the council has put 900,000 copies of its pocket consumer guides, *Shopping for a Better World* and *Students Shopping for a Better World,* into the hands of people who use them to make purchasing decisions and, in some cases, to research employers.

Organized investing power, both as a market force and through direct shareholder activism, is even more significant, as the toppling of apartheid in South Africa shows. At the peak of the campaign, in the late 1980s, the value of socially screened investment funds rose to a peak of some $650 billion. Divestment alone did not topple apartheid, but South Africa's economic isolation was clearly a critical factor.

Consumer power and investor power are two ways of exercising economic clout outside the workplace. And on the job, even in an era of strained labor-management relations, the organized influence of working people is greater than their disorganized influence. If all else fails, you can get involved in electoral politics. A shortage of options is not the hard part.

However you go about choosing a focus for action, the idea is not to leap with such zeal that you put your working life on hold, but to find a balance and choose activities in such a way that a job, or job search, and extracurricular activism can complement each other. People met in one realm can be helpful in the other. Skills learned in one realm can be a major advantage in the other. What's more, the empowerment that comes from taking responsibility for the conditions surrounding your work life can make a significant difference in your self-esteem and your ideas about what's possible for you on the job.

In standing up for your rights, you can tap into a rich body of information about social movements and the ways activists within them work effectively. For example, successful activists are able to see the big picture, but also to break progress down into manageable steps. Successful activists tend to function in a supportive community. Successful activists are prepared for difficult times, but are also able to enjoy themselves along the way. Finally, successful activists learn from history, example, and personal experience. And when it comes to the movement to rewrite the rule book in the interest of job security and satisfaction, there is a strong tradition to build on.

For example, the Small Business Administration launched a bold new program to offer "microloans" for new and growing ventures in low-income communities. Unlike many federal programs, the microloan idea was articulated and marketed to a significant extent by grassroots activists.[33]

Another example: a story about citizen activism with a high-tech assist. In the fall of 1993, General Motors was identified by the Council on Economic Priorities as one of the worst environmental polluters among U.S.-based transnational corporations. The council targeted GM in its annual Campaign for Cleaner Corporations. Three thousand phone calls came into the company switchboard expressing public outrage— aided, no doubt, by the Working Assets alternative phone service, which mails monthly "action alerts" along with phone bills and which offered subscribers a free call to GM that month. In early 1994, General Motors became the second major corporation, after Sun Oil, to sign the CERES Principles of environmental accountability. Coincidence? Doubtful.

Major changes in policy, law, and enforcement are needed to create a climate in which job security and workplace rights are not an arena of constant struggle. But these big changes will be the product of thousands of smaller victories. Look around. Start with what gets in your way, and keep going from there.

An Ethic of Cocreation

All this talk about promoting change leads to a question that was posed to me a few years ago by my sister, an M.D. in an urban teaching hospital where the issues are seldom simple: "Just where do you get off thinking that you have the right to change other people?" The answer that first popped out was, "I guess I have the right to try to *influence* other people as long as I let them influence me in return."

I'm not sure that's always true, or that it's sufficient. But it does illustrate the kind of guidelines that are necessary to keep any kind of advocacy on track in an ethical sense, to reduce the likelihood that new ideas and new regimes will bring in worse abuses than those they tried to wipe out. What are some other principles that might help to guide the strategies for change laid out in this chapter? Here are a few to consider:

1. Accountability. Identify specific goals and people on whose behalf you're working, so that you get beyond ideology and have some concrete standards for evaluating your impact.

2. Disclosure. Be as open about your values and goals as you can in a situation, recognizing that there are limits to this but finding ways to build trust carefully over time and getting a grip on chronic secretiveness.

3. Responsibility. Taking risks to make change does not exempt you from the responsibilities of your day-to-day job and working relationships. If you take an extra initiative, do so with grace and acceptance of the ways it may change your life. Having an agenda in an organization means carrying an added weight and setting yourself apart. Nobody is necessarily going to respond to your

initiatives on your terms or timetable. Yours is the responsibility for meeting other people more than halfway. This in turn requires tapping your own support system off the job, for recharging and keeping perspective.

4. An inside job. If you're pushing other people to deal with their "stuff," best deal with yours. How have your opinions on the issue been formed? Who have you tried to please over the years by the positions you've taken? It's easiest to see the issue through others' eyes—which you'll be called upon to do in countless ways—if you have some appreciation of your own blinders.

5. Follow-through and ongoing relationship. In Joanna Macy's words, "You can't change what you can't touch." The best change agents root themselves deeply in the community they are trying to influence, in order to work from a base of love and shared values rather than judgment.

These principles can help to bring discipline and accountability to the process of cocreating the workplace you want. Ultimately, though, choosing an active strategy means getting comfortable with power. Principled people often have trouble with this, especially when they are used to seeing the exploitive side of power. But the power we are discussing here is very different; it's the power to work for shared values and contribute to many people's well-being, not just your own. Conscious effort to create a more humane, sustainable workplace means using power to affirm your own self-worth and that of the people you work with.

When that path gets difficult, as it will, think about Lesly Rodriguez. Like many teenagers in Honduras, Lesly quit school to work twelve-hour days in a sweater factory, earning thirty-eight cents an hour to knit sweaters sold by Liz Claiborne for ninety dollars. An Evangelical Christian, Lesly became involved in union organizing at age fourteen when she and her co-workers were required to work through the night to fill a rush order and then were paid less than had been promised. Passing notes under the work tables, she and two friends signed up ninety new union members. That effort got the attention of international labor organizers, who brought her to the U.S. in 1994 to testify about child labor in Honduras. She addressed the U.S. Congress and appeared on network news. The media campaign she took part in led the White House to reverse its policy on duty-free imports of Caribbean-made clothing and brought Liz Claiborne officials to Honduras to investigate conditions in the factories. At age fifteen, Lesly Rodriguez was ready to explore a career as a union organizer in the workplace she had already done more than her part to co-create. [34]

Part III

Afterthoughts

Afterword

Finding your work in the world is like finding your soul mate: open-ended, full of possibility, and therefore terrifying. The world is so complex and fluid that it's rarely possible to map out more than the crudest approximation of the path you need to follow. But each muddling movement along the path gives you new information about who you are, what you need, and what is required to meet those needs—if only you can keep paying attention. The ability to find wisdom in moment-to-moment reality, and to function with both adaptability and integrity, may be the ultimate career survival skill for the '90s and beyond. And, in work as in love, that constant challenge of living with ambiguity plunges some of us into a conflict between "monogamous" commitment and more pluralistic exploration of the options.

If finding your work resembles finding your soul mate, then sustaining your work, once you've found it, is something like sustaining a relationship. I say this not only because both contain struggle, compromise, and ambiguity, but because the process of sustaining commitment molds you in ways that are impossible to anticipate.

In work, as in love, you never really reach an ideal as full and pure as you can imagine. But you can keep getting closer. You can peel away layers of resistance. The peak experiences can keep getting richer. There is no limit to the strategies you can try, except the limits of your imagination.

In work, as in love, you need a proper mixture of romance and realism to get you through. Most of us err on the side of so-called realism. We keep our heads down and our options open and our résumés so very sedate. But consider the benefits of erring on the romantic side, the side that's concerned not with adapting to the old but with imagining and building the new.

These times call for what psychiatrist Robert Lifton has dubbed an "apocalyptic imagination," the ability to open up to the truth at its strangest. The steps in this book have been designed to unleash that kind of imagination, and to create a foundation solid enough to support you as you follow its guidance. The good news is that this imagination is powerful. When people do let go of expectations and focus on what they really value; when they wake up, stabilize their lives, and gather a supportive community around them; when they take a sharper-than-usual look at the subtle differences among a set of opportunities; when they face themselves—their strengths and gifts as well as their blind spots—then they tend to find ways to work, with impact and meaning, in spite of the madness around them.

The ability to make a living and a difference is not a luxury. It's the essence of a dignified life, as more and more people are figuring out. May you, too, reclaim the ordinary joy of work that makes a difference in your world.

Resources

General Job Search
and Career Development Resources

Bennett, Steven J. *Playing Hardball with Soft Skills*. New York: Bantam, 1986.

Bolles, Richard N. *What Color Is Your Parachute?* Berkeley: Ten Speed Press, 1994.

Carland, Maria Pinto, and Daniel Spatz, Jr., eds. *Careers in International Affairs* (1991). School of Foreign Service, Georgetown University, Washington, D.C. 20057.

Cowan, Jessica, ed. *Good Works: A Guide to Careers in Social Change*. New York: Barricade Books, 1991.

Kaplan, Robbie Miller. *The Whole Career Sourcebook*. New York: AMACOM, 1991.

Kleimann, Carol. *The Best Careers for the 1990's and Beyond*. Chicago: Dearborn, 1992.

Krannich, Ronald L., and Caryl R. Krannich. *Almanac of American Government Jobs and Careers*. Woodbridge, VA: Impact Publishers.

Krannich, Ronald L., and Caryl R. Krannich. *Complete Guide to International Jobs and Careers*. Manassas Park, VA: Impact Publishers, 1992.

Levinson, Jay Conrad. *555 Ways to Earn Extra Money*. New York: Henry Holt, 1992.

Lewis, Adele. *Fast Track Careers*. Glenview, IL: Scott, Foresman, 1990.

Lindquist, Carolyn Lloyd, and Diana June Miller, eds., Cornell University Career Center. *Where to Start Career Planning: Essential Resource Guide for Career Planning and Job Hunting*. 8th ed. Princeton, NJ. Comprehensive bibliography distributed by Peterson's Guides.

Mattera, Philip. *Inside U.S. Business: A Concise Encyclopedia of the Leading Industries*. NY: Irwin Professional Publishing, 1994.

New Careers Center, 1515 23rd St., Box 339-CT, Boulder, CO 80306. Mail-order catalog of hard-to-find resources with emphasis on crafting a career to reflect your values.

Petras, Kathryn, and Ross Petras. *Jobs '94*. New York: Simon & Schuster, 1994.

Sacharov, Al. *Offbeat Careers: The Directory of Unusual Work*. Berkeley: Ten Speed Press, 1988.

Sher, Barbara, with Annie Gottlieb. *Wishcraft*. New York: Ballantine, 1979.

Sinetar, Marsha. *Do What You Love, The Money Will Follow*. New York: Dell, 1987.

Smith, Carter. *America's Fastest Growing Employers*. Holbrook, MA: Bob Adams, 1994.

Smith, Devon, ed. *Great Careers: The Fourth of July Guide to Careers, Internships and Volunteer Opportunities in the Nonprofit Sector*. Garret Park, MD: Garret Park Press, 1990.

Researching Employers by Social or Environmental Criteria: Directories and Clearinghouses

The Council on Economic Priorities' pocket guidebook, *Shopping for a Better World,* rates major consumer products companies on the following criteria: Environment, Charity/Community Outreach, Equal Employment Opportunity, Family Benefits, Workplace Issues, and "Extras." 30 Irving Pl., 9th Floor, New York, NY 10003.

People for the Ethical Treatment of Animals publishes a free fact sheet on companies that do not test their products on animals, as well as a more detailed, product-by-product *Shopping Guide for the Caring Consumer* ($4.95). PETA Merchandise, P.O. Box 42400, Washington, D.C. 20015.

Nuclear Free America publishes two useful lists: the top fifty nuclear weapons contractors, and the cities, counties, and states that have passed ordinances to become nuclear-free zones. 325 E. 25th St., Baltimore, MD 21218. (301) 235-3575.

Co-Op America's *National Green Pages* lists U.S. businesses that adhere to a strict code of environmental sustainability and workplace democracy. Also: quarterly *Boycott Census* identifies offenders. 2100 M St., N.W., Suite 403, Washington, D.C. 20037. (202) 872-5307.

The National Center for Employee Ownership (2201 Broadway, Suite 807, Oakland, CA 94612) sells lists of employee-owned companies in the following categories:

- Majority Employee Ownership Companies (over 550 with at least 50 percent of stock owned by employees)
- Nonmajority Private Employee Ownership Companies (over 550)
- Public Employee Ownership Companies (over 850 public companies with over 5 percent employee ownership)

Solidarity, the United Auto Workers' newsmagazine, also publishes a column of friendly and unfriendly companies from organized labor's viewpoint. Subscriptions: 8000 E. Jefferson, Detroit, MI 48214, $5.00 a year.

The Capitol Research Center (727 15th St., N.W., Washington, D.C. 20005. (202) 737-5677.) publishes an annual volume identifying companies that it views as abandoning the free market cause in their philanthropy or other policies.

Deal, Carl. *The Greenpeace Guide to Anti-Environmental Organization* (Berkeley: Odonian Press, 1993). lists "wise use" organizations with substantial backing and funding from industry, and includes the names of sponsoring companies.

"30 Great Companies for Dads," *Child,* June/July 1992.

The Coalition for Environmentally Responsible Economies (CERES) publishes a list of organizations that have endorsed the CERES Principles of environmental accountability. In mid-1994, the list had eighty names, which included a few large corporations (the Sun Company, H. B. Fuller, General Motors), a few nonprofits, smaller companies in many fields, and one local government: Westchester County, NY. Contact: 711 Atlantic Ave., Boston, MA 02111.

The Eagle Connector, a self-described "transformational" newsletter, sells networking lists including guides to growth centers in North America and New Zealand, and an address list for 900 holistic groups worldwide. 457 Scenic Rd., Fairfax, CA 94930-1924. (415) 457-4513.

Every spring, *Inc.* magazine publishes its annual list of 100 of "The Fastest-Growing Small Public Companies."

Close, Arthur, Gregory Bologna, and Curtis McCormick, eds. *National Directory of Corporate Public Affairs*. New York: Columbia Books, Inc., 1992. Statistics and company profiles.

To identify environmentally aware local governments, ask for the membership list (over 134 cities and towns worldwide) of the International Council of Local Environmental Initiatives, City Hall East Tower, 8th Floor, Toronto, Ontario M5H 2N2, Canada (416) 392-1390.

"Ecolabels," on products that meet the environmental standards of the certifying organization Green Seal, point to companies with best practices on producing paper, plumbing and heating equipment, and a host of other consumer products. Green Seal's list of certified companies can be ordered from 1730 Rhode Island Avenue N.W., Suite 1050, Washington, D.C. 20036–3101. (202) 331-7337.

Other Directories and Guidebooks for Identifying and Researching Employers

"A Citizen's Guide on Using the Freedom of Information Act to Request Government Records" (House Report 103-104, July 1993). Order #Y1.1/8:103-104.

Council on Economic Priorities monthly Research Reports on companies and trends, and Corporate Environmental Reports on companies. 30 Irving Pl., 9th Floor, New York, NY 10003.

Daniells, Lorna M. *Business Information Source,* 3rd ed. Berkeley and Los Angeles: University of California Press, 1993.

Federal Career Directory. Superintendent of Documents, Government Printing Office, Washington, D.C. 20402-9325. Order #006-000-01339-2. U.S. Employment Service (federal), 200 Constitution Avenue, N.W., Washington, D.C. 20210. (202) 535-0157.

Franklin Research and Development Corporation's Equity Briefs ($10 each) on the social/environmental performance of 100 selected companies. Order from 711 Atlantic Ave., Boston, MA 02111. (617) 423-6655.

Graham, Lawrence Otis. *The Best Companies for Minorities.* New York: Plume, 1993.

"How Green?" Profiles of twenty-five prominent environmental groups. *Outside,* March 1994.

Human Rights Organizations and Periodicals Directory. Lists over 1,000 U.S. organizations focusing on peace and human rights, published by the Meiklejohn Civil Liberties Institute, Box 673, Berkeley, CA 94701-0673. (510) 848-0599.

Levering, Robert. *A Great Place to Work: What Makes Some Employers So Good, and Most So Bad.* New York: Random House, 1988.

Minority Organizations: A National Directory, 4th ed. (1994). Covers over 8,000 organizations. Garrett Park Press, P.O. Box 190, Garrett Park, MD 20896. (301) 946-2553.

Morgan, Hal, and Kerry Tucker. *Companies That Care: The Most Family-Friendly Companies in America.* Boston: Houghton Mifflin, 1991.

Pankau, Edmund. *Check It Out.* Chicago: Contemporary Books, 1992.

Rittner, Don. *Eco-linking: Everybody's Guide to Online Electronic Information.*

Trattner, John H. *The Prune Books* (detailed descriptions of top-level federal positions filled by presidential appointments) from the Council for Excellence in Government, 1620 L St., N.W., Suite 850, Washington, D.C. 20036. (202) 728-0418. Four volumes:

The 45 Toughest Financial Management Jobs in Washington (1993)

Fifty Jobs That Can Change America (1992)

The 60 Toughest Science and Technology Jobs in Washington (1992)

The 100 Toughest Management and Policymaking Jobs in Washington (1988)

Weinstein, Miriam. *The Making a Difference College Guide* (a directory of colleges and universities with programs supporting social change or service). San Anselmo, CA: Sage Press, 1994.

Zeitz, Baila, and Lorraine Dusky. *The Best Companies for Women.* New York: Simon & Schuster, 1988.

Job Listings

Some of these are publications devoted exclusively to job listings; others are periodicals with a significant and interesting Help Wanted section containing not-your-ordinary classifieds:

Chronicle of Higher Education. Weekly journal, with extensive ad section, on academia. 1255 23rd St., Suite 700, Washington, D.C. 20037.

Community Jobs. A monthly newspaper published by Access, 2 W. 16th St., New York, N.Y. 10011. 212-675-4416.

Current Jobs. Newsletter of organizing and social justice jobs in the southeastern U.S. and the District of Columbia, from the Southern Empowerment Project, 343 Ellis Ave., Maryville, TN 37804. (615) 984-6500.

International Employment Hotline. WorldWise Books, Box 3030, Oakton, VA 22124-9030. Monthly.

National Ad Search. Weekly "mega-classifieds" drawn from Help Wanted sections of seventy-five major newspapers, organized into more than fifty categories. Box 2083, Milwaukee, WI 53201.

National Business Employment Weekly. Dow Jones and Co., Inc. Box 300, Princeton, NJ 08540. (609) 520-4000.

"Interim Executive Jobs" (reprint, *National Business Employment Weekly,* April 16–22, 1993, address above). Contains listing of approximately 100 firms that place executive temps.

National and Federal Legal Employment Report. Federal Reports, 1010 Vermont Ave., N.W., Suite 408, Washington, D.C. 20005. (202) 393-3311.

Opportunities in Public Affairs. The Brubach Corporation, 1100 Connecticut Ave., N.W., Washington, D.C. 20036. (202) 861-0590. Biweekly.

Sound Opportunities. Public interest jobs in Washington State and Oregon. Nonprofit Community Network, 501 N. 36th St., #177, Seattle, WA 98103. (206) 441-8280.

Environmental Career Opportunities. Over 350 listings every week. (301) 986-5545.

The Job Seeker. Environmental job newsletter. Rt. 2, Box 16, Dept. CJ, Warrens, WI 54666.

GRADS. Biweekly newsletter on entry-level jobs for liberal arts graduates. Box 40550, Washington, D.C. 20016. (703) 506-4440.

Eagle Connector. "Transformational" newsletter with job listings, fundraising ideas for nonprofits, and interesting strategic pieces about social change. Address above.

JobMart. Published twenty-two times a year by the American Planning Association, 1776 Massachusetts Ave., N.W., Suite 400, Washington, D.C. 20036.

National Directory of Internships. Lists service-learning opportunities for people of all ages, indexed by location, field of interest, and responsibility. National Society for Internships and Experiential Education, 3509 Haworth Dr., Suite 207, Raleigh, NC 27609. (919) 787-3263.

Peacework. Monthly newsletter published by the American Friends Service Committee's New England Regional Office (2161 Massachusetts Ave., Cambridge, MA 02140), lists selected activist and service jobs.

Global Village News. Monthly newsletter of Businesses for Social Responsibility and the Social Venture Network, 1388 Sutter St., Suite 1010, San Francisco, CA 94109. (415) 771-4308.

Business Ethics magazine, 52 S. 10th St., #110, Minneapolis, MN 55403-2001.

Career Resource Center, Public Interest Clearinghouse, 100 McAllister St., San Francisco, CA 94102.

National Directory of Nonprofit Organizations, Taft Group, 1991. "Why Not Work for a Change?" a booklet packed with contacts on public service jobs, is published by the Advocacy Institute, 1730 Rhode Island Ave., N.W., Suite 600, Washington, D.C. 20036-3118. (202) 659-8475.

If you're interested in U.N. employment, there are four entry points:
1. Technical Assistance Recruitment and Administration Service
   Room DC1-1208
   United Nations
   New York, NY 10017
   Fax 212-963-1272
2. Professional Staffing Service (nontechnical professionals)
   Room S-2500
   United Nations
   New York, NY 10017
   Fax 212-963-3134
3. General Service Staffing Section (support and general staff)
   Room DC1-0200
   United Nations
   New York, NY 10017
   Fax 212-963-3726
4. Co-ordinator, Internship Programme (for graduate students)
   Room S-2500E
   United Nations
   New York, NY 10017
   Fax 212-963-3134

Magazines That Publish Annual or Frequent Special Issues on Careers and Salaries

Adweek

Advertising Age

Cable Television Business

Chemical and Engineering
    News

Datamation

Engineering News-Record

Federal Employees Almanac

Hotel/Motel Management

Infosystems

Lawyer's Almanac

Library Journal

Mart (retail stores)

Medical Economics

Meeting News

Money

Monthly Labor Review (U.S.
    Department of Labor)

Personnel Administrator

Practical Accountant

Public Relations Journal

Purchasing

Research and Development

The Secretary

Technical Communications

Traffic Management

Training and Development
    Journal

U.S. News and World Report

Video Manager

Working Woman

Other Major Clearinghouses for Labor Statistics Including Pay Scales

American Association of University Professors: *Annual Report on the Economic Status of the Profession*

Brooklyn Public Library, Business Library. *Business Rankings and Salaries Index,* 1st ed. Detroit: Gale Research, 1988.

European Communities Commission: *Basic Statistics of the Community*

International Labor Office: *Yearbook of Labor Statistics*

Savage, Kathleen M., and Charity Anne Dorgan, eds. *Professional Careers Sourcebook.* Detroit: Gale Research, 1990.

U.S. Bureau of Labor Statistics: *National Survey of Professional, Administrative, Technical and Clerical Pay*

Union Bank of Switzerland (global studies of wages for many trades, e.g., bus drivers, construction workers, et cetera)

Wright, John W., and Edward J. Dwyer. *American Almanac of Jobs and Salaries*. New York: Avon, 1990.

Business Start-up Resources

Blum, Laurie. *Free Money for Small Businesses and Entrepreneurs,* 3rd ed. New York: Wiley, 1992.

Cohen, Charles E. "Striking Out on Your Own," *Working Woman* (May 1994).

Entrepreneur magazine, 2392 Morse Ave., Irvine, CA 92714. (714) 755-4211. Publishes annual "Franchise 500" listing. Also annual "Small Business Development Catalogue."

Godfrey, Joline. *Our Wildest Dreams: Women Entrepreneurs Having Fun, Making Money, Doing Good*. New York: Harper Business, 1992.

GEO (Grassroots Economic Organizing) newsletter. P.O. Box 5065, New Haven, CT 06525. Phone 203-389-6194.

Holland, Phil. *How to Start a Business Without Quitting Your Job*. Berkeley: Ten Speed Press, 1992.

Huber, Janeen. "The Quiet Revolution: Homebased Businesses Command Respect," *Entrepreneur,* September 1993.

Kramer, Felix, and Maggie Lovass. *Desktop Publishing Success: How to Start and Run a Desktop Publishing Business*. Homewood, IL: Business One Irwin, 1991.

Maki, Kathleen, ed. *Small Business Sourcebook: The Entrepreneur's Resource*. Detroit, MI: Gale Research, 1994.

Murphy, Anne. "Do-It-Yourself Job Creation," *Inc.* (Jan. 1994).

Ratliff, Susan. *How to Be a Weekend Entrepreneur: Making Money at Craft Fairs, Trade Shows and Swap Meets*. Phoenix, AZ: Marketing Methods Press, 1991.

Schecter, Gail. "Environmental Business Opportunities for Low Income Neighborhoods," Amoco Fund for Neighborhood Economies/ Center for Neighborhood Technology, 2125 W. North Ave., Chicago, IL 60647. (312) 278-4800. (Feb. 1991)

Wall Street Journal Report, "Small Business: Getting Started," October 15, 1993, pp. R1–R26.

Winter, Barbara. *Making a Living Without a Job*. New York: Bantam, 1993.

Regional and International Resources

Andruss, Van, Christopher Plant, and Judith Plant, eds. *Home! A Bioregional Reader.* Philadelphia: New Society Publishers, 1990.

Bijeen (global newsclipping service/database). Postbus 750, 520, AJS-Hertogenbosch, Simon Stevinweg 17, 5223 XA-Hertogenbosch, The Netherlands. 073218970; fax 073218512.

Calvert-Henderson Quality of Life Indicators (for metropolitan areas). Available early 1995 from Calvert Social Investment Fund, 1715 18th St., N.W., Washington, D.C. 20009.

The Economist magazine publishes frequent country reports on developed and developing areas.

Germer, Jerry. *Country Careers: Successful Ways to Live and Work in the Country.* New York: Wiley, 1993.

Henricks, Mark. "Hot Spots" (twenty best small-business locations), *Entrepreneur* (October 1993).

Japanese Working for a Better World: Grassroots Voices and Access Guide to Citizens' Groups in Japan. Honnoki U.S.A., 300 Broadway, Suite 39, San Francisco, CA 94133. (415) 392-3151.

Planet Drum Foundation publishes a directory of bioregional groups throughout Turtle Island (aka North America), Box 31251, San Francisco, CA 94131. $4.00.

Sanborn, Robert. *How to Get a Job in Europe.* Chicago: Surrey Books, 1991.

"Six New Business Meccas for African-Americans," *Black Enterprise* (May 1994).

SOMO (research center on multinational corporations). Keizerstracht 132, 1015CW, Amsterdam, The Netherlands. 310206391291; fax 310206391321.

Spiers, Joseph. "Heartland Expansion Rolls On; Coastal Recessions Recede," *Fortune* (January 24, 1994).

Winsor, Anita. *The Complete Guide to Doing Business in Mexico.* New York: AMACOM, 1994.

Workplace Issues and Ethics

Blasi, Joseph, and Douglas Kruse. *The New Owners: The Mass Emergence of Employee Ownership in Public Companies and What It Means to American Business.* New York: HarperCollins, 1992.

California Commuter Transportation Service. "Telecommuting: Moving Work to the Workers." 3550 Wilshire Blvd., Suite 300, LA, CA 90010. (213) 380-7750.

Dumont, Matthew, M.D. *Treating the Poor: A Personal Sojourn Through the Rise and Fall of Community Mental Health.* Belmont, MA: Dymphna Press, 1992. (Box 44, Belmont, MA 02178)

Fox, Matthew. *The Re-Invention of Work.* San Francisco: Harper, 1994.

Harman, Willis, and John Hormann. *Creative Work: The Constructive Role of Business in a Transforming Society.* Indianapolis: Knowledge Systems, 1990.

Holland, Joe. *Creative Communion: Toward a Spirituality of Work.* New York: Paulist Press, 1989.

Jackall, Robert. *Moral Mazes: The World of Corporate Managers.* New York: Oxford University Press, 1988.

Kaye, Kenneth. *Workplace Wars and How to End Them.* New York: AMACOM, 1994.

Kaylin, Jennifer. "Downward Mobility," *Utne Reader* (July/August 1991).

Ray, Michael, and Rochelle Myers. *Creativity in Business.* New York: Doubleday, 1986.

Sinetar, Marsha. *Work as Spiritual Path* (two-tape set), Sounds True Recordings, 735 Walnut St., Boulder, CO 80302.

Stock, Gregory. *The Book of Questions on Business, Politics, and Ethics.* New York: Workman, 1991.

Weiss, Robert S. *Staying the Course: The Emotional and Social Lives of Men Who Do Well at Work.* New York: Free Press, 1990.

Workplace Rights

Kahn, Si. *How People Get Power.* Washington, D.C.: National Association of Social Workers, 1994.

Lacey, Dan. *Your Rights in the Workplace.* Berkeley, CA: Nolo Press, 1994.

Rapaport, John D., and Brian L. P. Zevnik. *The Employee Strikes Back!* New York: Macmillan, 1989.

U.S. Department of Labor, Women's Bureau, "Don't Work in the Dark: Know Your Rights." Kit covering sexual harassment, family and medical leave, and pregnancy discrimination. 1-800-827-5335.

Summary of Major Federal Workplace Laws in the U.S.

The following chart is an introduction to the federal laws that shape workplace rights, including hiring and terms of employment. Each of these contains volumes of special provisions and has generated many times more volumes of interpretation in the courts. This chart tells you where to start in figuring out whether your legal rights are being violated and assessing your chances of doing something about it.

Law	*Basic Provisions*	*Where to Learn More*
National Labor Relations Act	Protects right to organize and bargain collectively through chosen union	National Labor Relations Board
Fair Labor Standards Act	Minimum wage Overtime pay Child labor standards	Dept. of Labor
Davis-Bacon Act	Payment of prevailing local wages and benefits for laborers and mechanics employed by federal contractors and subcontractors	Dept. of Labor
Employee Retirement Income Security Act (ERISA)	Uniform standards for pension and welfare benefit plans	Dept. of Labor
COBRA	Continues health coverage for qualified "separated" workers up to 18 months	Dept. of Labor

Law	Basic Provisions	Where to Learn More
Unemployment Compensation	Authorizes funding, and guides administration, of state unemployment insurance programs	Dept. of Labor
Family Medical Leave Act	Allows 12 weeks unpaid leave for birth, adoption, illness or other emergency	Dept. of Labor
Title VII, Civil Rights Act of 1964	Prohibits discrimination by employers or unions based on race, color, religion, sex, or national origin; prohibits pregnancy-related job discrimination	Equal Employment Opportunity Com. (EEOC)
Equal Pay Act	Prohibits sex-based pay discrimination	EEOC
EO 11246	Prohibits discrimination by federal contractors and subcontractors on basis of race, color, religion, sex, or national origin, and requires them to take affirmative action to remedy imbalances	Dept. of Labor
Age Discrimination in Employment Act	Prohibits employment discrimination on the basis of age against people 40 and over	EEOC

Law	Basic Provisions	Where to Learn More
Americans with Disabilities Act	Prohibits employment discrimination against people with disabilities, and requires employers to make "reasonable accommodations" unless doing so would cause hardship	EEOC
Rehabilitation Act (Section 503)	Prohibits employment discrimination by federal contractors and subcontractors on basis of disability; requires affirmative action to employ and advance persons with disabilities	Dept. of Labor
Antiretaliatory Protections	Prevents firing for refusing specified unsafe working conditions	Dept. of Labor/ OSHA
Occupational Safety and Health Act	Work and workplace must be free of conditions that can cause death or serious injury	Occ. Safety and Health Admin. (OSHA)
Drug Free Workplace Act	Requires recipients of federal grants and contracts to take "certain steps" to maintain drug-free workplace	Office of Federal Contract Compliance Programs

Law	Basic Provisions	Where to Learn More
Polygraph Protection Act	Prohibits the use of lie detectors in hiring or employment	Dept. of Labor Wage and Hour Division
Veterans Reemployment Act	Protects right to reemployment of people coming back from active duty, reserve training, or National Guard duty	Dept. of Labor Employment and Training Administration
Immigration Reform and Control Act	Prohibits hiring of illegal aliens, and designates employers' responsibility for verifying legality; protects employment rights of legal aliens; sets conditions on seasonal farm labor	Dept. of Labor Wage and Hour Division
WARN	Requires employers to give 60-day written notice of a layoff to individual affected employees, local govt., and other parties	Dept. of Labor Wage and Hour Division

Source: U.S. Departments of Labor and Commerce: *Fact Finding Report of the Commission on the Future of Worker-Management Relations,* May 1994.

Resources for Citizen, Consumer, and Shareholder Action

Crystal, Graef. *In Search of Excess: The Overcompensation of the American Executive.* New York: Norton, 1992.

Evanson, David R., and Greg Matusky. *50 Things You Can Do to Save American Jobs.* New York: Carol Publishing Group, 1994.

Markusen, Ann, and Catherine Hill. *Converting the Cold War Economy.* Economic Policy Institute (1730 Rhode Island Ave., N.W., Suite 200, Washington, D.C. 20036), 1992.

Ward, Cynthia, Geri Langlois, Diane Feldman, and Erica Walters. *Jobs and the Economy: A Primer on Principled Economic Development for Progressive Elected Officials and Activists.* Boston: Progressive Policy Initiative, 1992.

Advocacy and Support Groups

9 to 5, National Association of Working Women, 614 Superior Ave., N.W., Cleveland, OH 44113. Job Problems Hotline, 1-800-522-0925.

Alcoholics Anonymous: If not in your phone book, call 212-870-3400.

The American Association of University Women (lobbying and citizen education on issues that affect women "knowledge workers"), 1111 16th St., N.W., Washington, D.C. 20036.

Ashoka Innovators for the Public, 1700 N. Moore St., Suite 1920, Arlington, VA 22209. (703) 527-8300.

Association for the Sexually Harassed, P.O. Box 27235, Philadelphia, PA 19118. (215) 482-3528.

American Civil Liberties Union. Briefing papers on workplace rights and model statutes, in such areas as lie detector use, drug testing, and so on.

Americans for Workplace Fairness, Suite 301, 815 16th St., N.W., Washington, D.C. 20006. (202) 842-7845. A project of the Industrial Union Department, AFL-CIO.

Business Executives for Economic Justice (organization of Catholic business executives seeking more harmony between their business lives and the church's moral teachings). A Project of the National Center for the Laity. 4848 North Clark St., Chicago, IL 60640.

Business Executives for National Security (organization focused on a well-managed defense complex and expanding the notion of security to encompass economic, social, and environmental as well as military elements), 1615 L St., N.W., Suite 330, Washington, D.C. 20036. (202) 296-2125.

Businesses for Social Responsibility, 1030 15th St., N.W., Suite 1010, Washington, D.C. 20005. (202) 842-5400.

Center for Economic Conversion, 222 View St., Mountain View, CA 94041-1344.

Coalition for Environmentally Responsible Economies (creators of the CERES Principles), 711 Atlantic Ave., Boston, MA 02111. (617) 451-3252.

Council on Economic Priorities, 30 Irving Pl., 9th floor, New York, NY 10003. (212) 420-1133.

Domestic violence hotline: 1-800-TRYNOVA, sponsored by National Organization for Victim Assistance.

Environmental Business Council, Inc. Exchange Place, 53 State St., Boston, MA 02109. (617) 367-0282.

Environmental Careers Organization (a clearinghouse and support center for internships), 286 Congress St., Boston, MA. (617) 426-4783.

Giraffe Project, 197 Second St., P.O. Box 759, Langley, Whidbey Island, WA 98260. (206) 221-7989. International society that recognizes, supports, and promotes acts of courage and service.

Global Action Plan for the Earth, 84 Yerry Hill Rd., Woodstock, NY 12498. (914) 679-4830; fax (914) 679-4834. An educational nonprofit that offers a detailed program, with training and technical assistance, for moving toward sustainable ways of living and working (helps form "Workplace Eco-Teams").

Good Neighbor Project for Sustainable Industries, P.O. Box 79225, Waverly, MA 02179. Publishes *Good Neighbor Handbook for Sustainable Industries*, a superb research guide.

Government Accountability Project, 810 1st St., N.E., Suite 630, Washington, D.C. 20002. (202) 408-0034. Provides legal, strategic, and moral support for whistle-blowers.

Graduation Pledge Alliance, c/o Student Center, Humboldt State University, Arcata, CA 95521.

Guild of (Financially) Accessible Practitioners, c/o Dan Menkin, 3 Harvard St., Arlington, MA 02174-6017. (617) 641-4469.

Narcotics Anonymous, P.O. Box 9999, Van Nuys, CA 91409. (818) 780-3951.

National Alliance for Choice in Giving (a federation of community-based alternative funds for workplace fund drives), 2001 O St., N.W., Washington, D.C. 20036. (202) 296-8470.

Public Employees for Environmental Responsibility, 840 First St., N.E., Suite 680, Washington, D.C. 20002-3633. 202-408-0041.

Rational Recovery (twelve steps without the spiritual focus), c/o American Humanist Association, 7 Harwood Ave., P.O. Box 146, Amherst, NY 14226-0146. (716) 839-5080. (Kurt Vonnegut, Honorary President.)

Samaritans Suicide Hotlines, c/o 500 Commonwealth Ave., Boston, MA 02215. (617) 247-0220.

Scientists for Global Responsibility, Unit 3, Down House, The Business Village, Broomhill Road, London, SW18 4JQ, U.K. (081) 871-5175. E-mail: sgr@gn.apc.org

Social Venture Network, 1388 Sutter St., Suite 1010, San Francisco, CA 94109. (415) 771-4308.

Southwest Organizing Project, 211 10th St., S.W., Albuquerque, NM 87102. (505) 247-8832. Publishes "Economic Self-Defense Campaign" for workers facing plant closings.

United Shareholders Association, 1667 K St., N.W., Suite 770, Washington, D.C. 20006. (202) 393-4600.

Where to Find Information on Selected "Fields of Change" (From Chapter 1)

Alternative / preventive health care
  Office of Alternative Medicine, National Institutes of Health
  Executive Plaza South, Suite 450
  6120 Executive Boulevard
  Rockville, MD 20892-9904
  (301) 402-2466

  Holistic Health Directory (published annually by *New Age Journal*)
  42 Pleasant St.
  Watertown, MA 02172

Child care
  National Association for the Education of Young Children
  1-800-424-2460

Council for Early Childhood Professional Recognition
1341 G St., N.W., Suite 400
Washington, D.C. 20005-3105
(202) 265-9090

Community organizing
Advocacy Institute
1730 Rhode Island Ave., N.W., Suite 600
Washington, D.C. 20036-3118
(202) 659-8475

Community planning
American Planning Association
1313 East 60th St.
Chicago, IL 60637
(312) 955-9100

Corporate ethics
Center for Business Ethics
Bentley College
175 Forest St.
Waltham, MA 02154
(617) 891-2501

Elder care and services
American Association of Retired People
1909 K St., N.W.
Washington, D.C. 20049
(202) 434-2277

Energy conservation / demand side management
National Association of Regulatory Utility Commissions
P.O. Box 684
Washington, D.C. 20044

Environmental education
Alliance for Environmental Education
P.O. Box 368
The Plains, VA 22171
(703) 253-5812; fax (703) 253-5811

Environmental management
Center for Environmental Management
Tufts University, Curtis Hall
474 Boston Ave.
Medford, MA 02155
(617) 627-3488

Environmental retailing and product innovation
Andrea Trank. "Global Marketplace for Green Products," *In Business*
(December 1991). The magazine also has a regular feature, "Green
Retailing."

Green Retail Association (information)
c/o Craig A. Ronai of Pranafit
(607) 277-3954
or Kevin Connelly of The Natural Connection
(802) 365-7188

National Green Pages
Co-Op America
2100 M St., N.W.
Washington, D.C. 20037
(202) 872-5307

Labor organizing
George Meany Center for Labor Studies
10000 New Hampshire Avenue
Silver Spring, MD 20903
(301) 431-6400

Land preservation
Land Trust Alliance
1319 F St., N.W., Suite 501
Washington, D.C. 20004-1106
(202) 638-4725

Language instruction
Teachers of English to Speakers of Other Languages
1600 Cameron St., Suite 300
Alexandria, VA 22314-2751
(703) 836-0774

Library careers
American Library Association, Public Information Office
50 East Huron St.
Chicago, IL 60611
(312) 944-6780

Occupational safety / health
American Industrial Hygiene Association
(703) 849-8888

Public interest law
Vermont Law School Environmental Law Center
Chelsea St.
S. Royalton, VT 05068
(802) 763-8303

American Bar Association, Public Services Division
1800 M St., N.W.
Washington, D.C. 20036
(202) 331-2276

Recycling and re-use
The Biocycle Guide to Maximum Recycling
Biocycle Magazine
419 State Ave.
Emmaus, PA 18049
(215) 967-4135

Renewable energy
Jordan Energy Institute
155 Seven Mile Rd.
Comstock Park, MI 49321
(616) 784-7595

Solar Technology Institute
P.O. Box 1115
Carbondale, CO 81623-1115
(303) 963-0715

Directory of Energy-Related Graduate Programs in U.S. Universities
The Energy Foundation
75 Federal St.
San Francisco, CA 94107
(415) 546-7400

Research on environment and sustainable development
World Resources Institute
1709 New York Avenue, N.W.
Washington, D.C. 20006
(202) 638-6300

Spiritual / transpersonal psychology
Common Boundary Education Guide
c/o *Common Boundary* magazine
4304 East-West Highway
Bethesda, MD 20814
(301) 652-9495

Sustainable agriculture
Organic Food Production Association of North America
P.O. Box 1078
Greenfield, MA 01302
(413) 774-7511; fax (413) 774-6432

Sustainable architecture
"What's Happening in Sustainable Architecture," *In Business* (July/
Aug. 1993).

American Institute of Architects, Committee on the Environment
(202) 626-7300

Personal Development and Life Management

"A listing of spiritual retreats," in *EastWest Natural Health* (September/
October 1992), p. 144. $4.00 from East/West Partners, 17 Station
Street, Box 1200, Brookline Village, MA 02146.

Amen, Daniel. *Don't Shoot Yourself in the Foot: A Program for Ending Self-Sabotaging Behavior.* New York: Warner, 1993.

Bear, John. *College Degrees by Mail.* Berkeley: Ten Speed Press, 1991.

Bridges, William. *Transitions: Making Sense of Life's Changes.* New York: Addison-Wesley, 1980.

Brown, Molly Young. *Growing Whole: Self-Realization on an Endangered Planet.* New York: HarperCollins, 1994.

Dominguez, Joe, and Vicki Robin. *Your Money or Your Life?* New York: Viking, 1993.

Gerzon, Mark. *Coming Into Our Own.* New York: Delacorte, 1992.

Green, Tova, and Peter Woodrow with Fran Peavey. *Insight and Action: How to Discover and Support a Life of Integrity and Commitment to Change.* Philadelphia: New Society Publishers, 1994.

Hanh, Thich Nhat. *The Miracle of Mindfulness: A Manual on Meditation.* Boston: Beacon Press, 1987.

Keen, Sam. *The Passionate Life.* New York: Harper & Row, 1983.

Kelly, Jack, and Marcia Kelly. *Sanctuaries* (series of books on monasteries and other spiritual retreats, organized by region). New York: Bell Tower.

Lerner, Michael. *Surplus Powerlessness.* Atlantic Highlands, NJ: Humanities Press, 1992.

Lipnack, Jessica. *The Teamnet Factor.* Essex Junction, VT: Oliver Wight, Publisher, 1993.

Mindell, Arnold, and Amy Mindell. *Riding the Horse Backwards.* New York: Penguin/Arkana, 1992.

Parry, Danaan. *Warriors of the Heart.* Cooperstown, NY: Sunstone Publications, 1989.

Pearson, Carol. *Awakening the Heroes Within.* San Francisco: Harper, 1991.

Poole, Judith. *The Little Grounding Book.* Self-published: P.O. Box 762, Watertown, MA 02172-0762.

Richards, Mary Caroline. *Centering in Pottery, Poetry, and the Person.* Middletown, CT: Wesleyan University Press, 1989.

Richardson, Douglas B. "Balance Your Life." *National Business Employment Weekly* (April 24–30, 1994).

Seligman, Martin. *Learned Optimism.* New York: Random House, 1990.

Shaffer, Carolyn R., and Kristin Anundsen. *Creating Community Anywhere: Finding Support and Connection in a Fragmented World.* Los Angeles: Tarcher/Perigee, 1993.

Sinetar, Marsha. *Developing a Twenty-first Century Mind.* New York: Villard Books, 1991.

Utne Reader (Jan./Feb. 1994). Special issue on the theme of time.

Vilas, Donna, and Sandy Vilas. *Power Networking: Fifty-Five Secrets to Success and Self-Promotion.* West Palm Beach, FL: Discovery Seminars, 1991.

Work Styles, Organizational Change, and Leadership

Barrentine, Pat, ed. *When the Canary Stops Singing: Women's Perspectives on Transforming Business.* San Francisco: Barrett-Kohler, 1993.

Bennis, Warren, and Joan Goldsmith. *Learning to Lead: A Workbook on Becoming a Leader.* New York: Addison-Wesley, 1994.

Duff, Carolyn, with Barbara Cohen. *When Women Work Together: Using Our Strengths to Overcome Our Challenges.* Berkeley: Conari Press, 1993.

Morgan, Gareth. *Images of Organization.* Newbury Park, CA: Sage Publications, 1986.

Pearson, Carol. *Magic at Work.* New York: Doubleday, 1995.

Senge, Peter. *The Fifth Discipline: The Art and Practice of the Learning Organization.* New York: Doubleday, 1990.

Wheatley, Margaret. *Leadership and the New Science.* San Francisco: Berrett-Kohler, 1992.

Information on Best Practices and Cases

The Business Enterprise Trust publishes teaching cases on initiatives for social and environmental responsibility in the workplace, makes annual awards to cutting-edge companies, and produces other educational materials. 240 Junipero Serra Blvd., Stanford, CA 94305. 415-321-5100

The Council on Economic Priorities' monthly Research Reports likewise target exemplary companies (positive and negative) and explore trends. Annually, CEP offers an award for America's Corporate Conscience (spring) and exposes dangerous corporate practices with the

Campaign for Cleaner Corporations (fall). Computerized Corporate Environmental Profiles on many major companies may be ordered. 30 Irving Pl., 9th Floor, New York, NY 10003.

Business and Society Review (Management Reporters, Inc. 25-13 Old King's Highway North, Suite 107, Darien, CT 06820.) and *Business Ethics* (Mavis Publications, 52 S. 10th St., #110. Minneapolis, MN 55403-2001) magazines are excellent journals with details on business innovations and controversies covering organizational, social, and environmental ethics.

Global Village News (1381 Sutter St., Suite 1010., San Francisco, CA 94109), a joint publication of Businesses for Social Responsibility and the Social Venture Network, contains a monthly column on best practices in areas from management to community service to environmental protection.

The Environmental Exchange publishes *What Works,* a newsletter on transportation alternatives and other methods for promoting environmental sustainability at a community level. The editors have also put together two reports: *Air Pollution Solutions* (May 1992) and *Local Solutions to Toxic Pollution* (1993). Order from: Public Interest Publications, P.O. Box 229, Arlington, VA 22210 (800) 537-9359.

Innovation Network is a nonprofit organization that offers contract research and consulting for nonprofits on models and strategy. InnoNet also offers an evaluation program and materials for organizations wanting to take a systematic look at what's working for them. 1001 Connecticut Ave., N.W., Suite 900, Washington, D.C. 20036. (202) 728-0727.

Annual *Guide to Management and Leadership Resources for Nonprofits* is prepared by the Applied Research and Development Institute, 1805 S. Bellaire St., Suite 219, Denver, CO 80222. (303) 691-6076; fax (303) 691-6077.

Ecology and Sustainable Development

Basta, Nicholas J. *The Environmental Careers Guide.* New York: Wiley, 1991.
    Environmental Careers for Scientists and Engineers. New York: Wiley, 1992.

Bennett, Steven J. *Ecopreneuring: The Complete Guide to Small Business Opportunities from the Environmental Revolution.* New York: Wiley, 1991.

Cohn, Susan. *Green at Work: Finding a Business Career that Works for the Environment.* Washington, D.C.: Island Press, 1992.

Earth Work magazine, a publication of the Student Conservation Association, Box 550, Charlestown, New Hampshire 03603-0550.

Environmental Careers Organization. *The Complete Guide to Environmental Careers.* Washington, D.C.: Island Press, 1993.

Hawken, Paul. *The Ecology of Commerce.* San Francisco: Harper, 1993.

Henderson, Hazel. *Paradigms in Progress.* San Francisco: Bessett-Kohler, 1995.

In Business, "The Magazine of Environmental Entrepreneuring," from J. G. Press, Inc., 419 State Ave., Emmaus, PA 18049.

Mander, Jerry. *In the Absence of the Sacred: The Failure of Technology and the Survival of the Indian Nations.* San Francisco: Sierra Club Books, 1992.

Meadows, Donella, Dennis Meadows, and Jorgen Randers. *Beyond the Limits: Confronting Global Collapse, Envisioning a Sustainable Future.* Post Mills, VT: Chelsea Green Publishers, 1992.

Saunders, Tedd, and Loretta McGovern. *The Bottom Line of Green Is Black.* San Francisco: Harper, 1994.

Schmidheiny, Stephan. *Changing Course: A Global Business Perspective on Development and the Environment.* Cambridge: MIT Press, 1992.

Warner, David J. *Environmental Careers: A Practical Guide to Opportunities in the '90s* (1992). Lewis Publishers, 2000 Corporate Blvd., N.W., Boca Raton, FL 33431. (407) 994-0555.

Whole Terrain: A Journal of Reflective Environmental Practice. Published annually by Antioch New England Graduate School, Roxbury St., Keene, NH 03431. (603) 357-3122. $5.00 per year.

"Work and the Environment: A Bibliography," Work and Environment Initiative, Cornell University School of Industrial and Labor Relations, Ithaca, NY 14853-3901.

Notes

Introduction

1. Eleanor M. LeCain, "Green Business Is Booming," *Positive Alternatives*, Center for Economic Conversion (Summer 1993).

2. Interfaith Center for Corporate Responsibility (NY: Diane Bratcher, personal interview).

3. David Eisenberg, "Unconventional Medicine in the U.S.: Prevalence, Costs, and Patterns of Use," *New England Journal of Medicine* 328, no. 4 (Jan. 28, 1993).

4. Julia Kagan, "Survey: Success—Not What It Used to Be," *Working Woman* (Nov. 1993): 54.

5. Research by Challenger, Gray and Christmas, Chicago outplacement firm.

6. Margaret Wheatley, "The Motivating Power of Ethics in Times of Corporate Confusion," in *Papers on the Ethics of Administration*, ed. N. Dale Wright (Provo, UT: Brigham Young University, 1988).

7. Henry Dreher, "The Healing Power of Confession," *East/West Natural Health* (Aug. 1993).

8. Robert Bellah et al., *Habits of the Heart: Individualism and Commitment in American Society* (Berkeley: University of California Press, 1985), 65.

9. Sarah Conn, "Protest and Thrive: The Relationship Between Global Responsibility and Personal Empowerment," *New England Journal of Public Policy* (Fall 1993).

10. Thanks to Joe Maizlish for his interview of Howard Newman.

Work Beyond Jobs

1. William Bridges, *JobShift* (New York: Addison-Wesley, 1994).

2. Quoted by Galen Rowell, commencement address, University of California at Berkeley, College of Natural Resources, 1991.

3. Stephan Schmidheiny and the Business Council for Sustainable Development, *Changing Course: A Global Business Perspective on Development and Environment* (Cambridge: MIT Press, 1992).

4. Albert Gore, *Earth in the Balance* (Boston: Houghton Mifflin, 1992).

5. Paul Hawken, speech to the Commonwealth Club, San Francisco, 1994.

6. Cliff Hakim, *We Are All Self-Employed* (San Francisco: Berrett-Kohler, 1994).

7. John Warcham, *New Secrets of a Corporate Headhunter* (NY: Harper Business, 1994).

8. Thanks to career counselor and psychologist Michael O'Brien for emphasizing this point in an interview.

9. George T. Silvestri, "Occupational Employment: Wide Variations in Growth," *Monthly Labor Review,* U.S. Department of Labor (Nov. 1993): 58–86.

10. Environmental Business International, Inc.

11. Environmental Careers Organization, *The New Complete Guide to Environmental Careers* (Washington, D.C.: Island Press, 1992).

12. Donald Snow, *Inside the Environmental Movement: Meeting the Leadership Challenge* (Washington, D.C.: Island Press, 1991).

13. Julian Wolpert, "The Structure of Generosity in America." Aspen Institute Nonprofit Sector Research Fund Working Paper, 1994.

14. Albert Gore, *Creating a Government That Works Better and Costs Less: Report of the National Performance Reviews* (NY: New American Library, 1993).

Making a Living and a Difference Internationally

1. William Irwin Thompson, "The Feasibility of Thinking Globally and Acting Locally." *Annals of Earth* 9, no. 1 (1991): 6–13.

2. Wendell Berry, "Get Out of Your Car, Get on Your Horse," *Harper's* (Sept. 1990).

3. Deborah Leipziger, "The Transnational Corporation: Global Influence, Global Responsibility," *Research Report,* Council on Economic Priorities (Oct. 1993).

4. Hazel Henderson, *Paradigms in Progress* (Indianapolis, IN: Knowledge Systems, Inc., 1991), 77–78.

5. Former Pratt & Whitney executive Robert Carlson, quoted by Paul Hofheinz, "Rising in Russia," *Fortune* (Jan. 24, 1994): 92–97.

6. "Trade and Investment Mission to South Africa: Johannesburg, Cape Town, Durban, November 26–December 2, 1993," report, U.S. Department of Commerce.

Step 1

1. *Peterson's Job Opportunities in Business* (Princeton, NJ: Peterson's Guides, 1993).

2. O. W. Markley and Willis W. Harman, *Changing Images of Man* (Oxford: Pergamon Press, 1982).

3. Mihaly Csiksentmihalyi, *Flow* (New York: HarperCollins, 1991).

4. Sharon Connelly, *Workspirit,* dissertation, Doctor of Business Administration, George Washington University, 1984.

5. Sam Deep and Lyle Sussman. *What to Ask When You Don't Know What to Say: Seven Hundred Twenty Powerful Questions to Use for Getting Your Way at Work* (New York: Addison-Wesley, 1993).

6. Fran Peavey, "Strategic Questioning," in Peter Woodrow and Tova Green with Fran Peavey, *Insight and Action: How to Discover and Support a Life of Integrity and Commitment to Change* (Philadelphia: New Society Publishers, 1994).

7. Martin Seligman, *Learned Optimism* (New York: Random House, 1990).

8. Thanks to storyteller David Sharpe for this myth.

9. Thomas Berry, *The Dream of the Earth* (San Francisco: Sierra Club Books, 1989).

10. Peter Senge, *The Fifth Discipline: The Art and Practice of the Learning Organization* (New York: Doubleday Currency, 1992).

11. Joanna Macy, interviewed in *Interhelp: A Networking Newsletter* (Fall 1993), P.O. Box 1618, Brattleboro, VT 05301.

12. Robbe DiPietro, "Collecting and Marketing Mixed Office Paper," *In Business* (Nov./Dec. 1991).

13. Daniel Goleman, *Vital Lies, Simple Truths: The Psychology of Collective Self-Deception* (New York: Simon & Schuster, 1985).

14. Mark Braverman, "Violence: The Newest Worry on the Job," *NY Times,* Dec. 12, 1993.

15. James Hillman and Michael Ventura, *We've Had a Hundred Years of Psychotherapy and the World Is Getting Worse* (San Francisco: HarperCollins, 1992).

16. James Autry, *Love and Profit: The Art of Caring Leadership* (New York: Avon, 1991).

17. Quoted by Laurent Daloz in *Effective Teaching and Mentoring* (San Francisco: Jossey-Bass, 1986).

18. Duane Elgin, *Voluntary Simplicity* (New York: William Morrow, 1981).

19. Colman McCarthy, "In Search of Solitude," *New Age Journal* (May/June 1987).

20. Danaan Parry, *Warriors of the Heart* (Cooperstown, NY: Sunstone Publications, 1989).

Step 2

1. Deborah Baldwin, "As Busy as We Wanna Be," *Utne Reader* (Jan./Feb. 1994): 52.

2. Kathleen Riehle, *What Smart People Do When Losing Their Jobs* (New York: Wiley, 1991).

3. Dennis Jaffe and Cynthia Scott, *Take This Job and Love It* (New York: Simon & Schuster, 1991).

4. *Kennedy's Career Strategist,* newsletter, 1150 Wilmette Ave., Wilmette, IL 60091.

5. Joe Dominguez and Vicki Robin, *Your Money or Your Life?* (New York: Penguin, 1992).

6. Jay C. Levinson, *555 Ways to Earn Extra Money* (New York: Henry Holt, 1992).

7. Amy Dacyczyn, *Tightwad Gazette: Promoting Thrift as a Viable Alternative Lifestyle* (New York: Random House, 1993).

8. Thanks to psychologist Neil Wollman of Manchester College for these insights on stress and burnout.

9. David Gershon and Robert Gilman, *Household Eco-Teams Workbook,* Global Action Plan, 1991.

Step 3

1. James F. Turner, "Hitting Rock Bottom After Reaching the Top," in David Asman and Adam Myers, eds., *The Wall Street Journal on Management* (New York: New American Library, 1985).

2. Thanks to Fran Peavey for stressing this point in presentations and writings.

3. Carolyn R. Shaffer and Kristin Anundsen, *Creating Community Anywhere* (Los Angeles: Tarcher/Perigee, 1993).

4. Robbie Miller Kaplan, *The Whole Career Sourcebook* (New York: AMACOM, 1991).

5. Jeff Reid, "Networking Overtime," *Utne Reader* (Sept./Oct. 1993).

6. What I call a personal focus group is derived from the "Clearness" process, originally developed by the Society of Friends, described in Tova Green and Peter Woodrow, with Fran Peavey, *Insight and Action* (Philadelphia: New Society Publishers, 1994).

7. Michael Lerner, *Surplus Powerlessness* (Atlantic Highlands, NJ: Humanities Press, 1991).

8. Contact *Utne* Neighborhood Salon Association, 1624 Harmon Place, Minneapolis, MN 55403.

9. Bruce Allen, "Businesses Blooming," *Positive Alternatives,* Center for Economic Conversation, Mountain View, CA (Spring 1994).

Step 4

1. Richard Saul Wurman, *Information Anxiety: What to Do When Information Doesn't Tell You What You Need to Know* (New York: Bantam, 1990).

2. Joseph Pereira, "Stride Rite: Good Deeds vs. Good Jobs," *Wall Street Journal* (May 28, 1993).

3. Maria Shao, "Ben & Jerry's Grows Up," *Boston Globe,* July 3, 1994.

4. Scott Allen. "State, E.P.A. Agree on $20 Million Fine," Boston *Globe,* September 11, 1994.

5. Bruce Livesey, "The Politics of Greenpeace," *Canadian Dimension,* August/September, 1994.

6. Orrin Klapp, *Overload and Boredom: Essays on the Quality of Life in the Information Society* (Westport, CT: Greenwood Press, 1986).

7. Ann Heanue, ed., *Less Access to Less Information by and about the U.S. Government.* Washington, D.C.: American Library Association, semiannual report series.

8. Bill Walker, "Green Like Me," *Greenpeace* magazine, May/June, 1991.

9. Edwin Nevis, *Organizational Consulting: A Gestalt Approach* (Cleveland, OH: Gestalt Institute of Cleveland Press, 1987).

10. Joyce Lain Kennedy and Thomas J. Morrow, *Electronic Job Search Revolution* (New York: Wiley, 1994).

11. *Encyclopedia of Associations.* Gale Research, Inc., Detroit Annual.

12. Dawn Marie Driscoll and Carol Goldberg, *Members of the Club* (Boston: Beacon Press, 1993).

13. *Public Interest Profiles,* Foundation for Public Affairs, 1019 19th St., N.W., Suite 200, Washington, D.C. 20036. (202) 872-1750.

14. Thanks to Matt Nicodemus for organizing this information.

15. Steven Covey, *The Seven Habits of Highly Effective People* (New York: Simon & Schuster, 1989).

16. Thanks to Sanford Lewis, director of the Good Neighbor Project for Sustainable Industries, and to reference librarian Fred Friedman, of the U.S. Environmental Protection Agency, for assistance with this section.

Step 5

1. Blanche Wiesen Cook, *Eleanor Roosevelt, Vol. I: 1884–1932* (New York: Viking Penguin, 1993).

2. Donella Meadows Lecture, Harvard Medical School, fall 1992.

3. John McPhee, *The Curve of Binding Energy* (New York: Farrar, Straus & Giroux, 1974).

4. Charles Handy, *The Age of Unreason* (Cambridge, MA: Harvard University Press, 1989).

5. Joseph Campbell with Bill Moyers, *The Power of Myth* (New York: Doubleday, 1988).

6. Sidney Simon, *In Search of Values: 31 Strategies for Finding Out What Really Matters Most to You* (New York: Warner, 1993).

7. I had been using these exercises in workshops for a year or so when I came upon questions similar to the first two in Barbara Sher's excellent new book, *I Could Do Anything If I Only Knew What It Was* (New York: Delacorte, 1994).

8. This exercise was inspired by the self-assessment process of Boston career counselor William Burns of Career and Financial Services.

9. Presentation by Cliff Hakim at International Association of Career Management Professionals, Boston, September 1994.

10. For more discussion of these principles:
Watkins, Mary. *Invisible Guests: The Development of Imaginal Dialogues* (Hillsdale, NJ: The Analytic Press, 1986).
Blasi, Augusto, and Robert Oresick. "Self-Consistency and the Development of the Self," in Polly Young-Eisendrath and James Hall, *The Book of the Self* (New York: New York University Press, 1987).

11. Donald Marrs, *Executive in Passage* (Los Angeles: Barrington Sky Publishing, 1992).

12. Molly Young Brown, *Growing Whole: Self-Realization on an Endangered Planet* (San Francisco: HarperCollins, 1994).

13. Inventories of skills and accomplishments were fine-tuned with help from Sally Crocker of Pathfinder Career Counseling, Barrington, RI.

14. The Johnson O'Connor Human Engineering Laboratory offers a standard battery of aptitude tests and follow-up counseling in eleven major cities. Contact their headquarters at 11 E. 62nd St., New York, NY 10021, for a list of locations and a brochure.

15. Wendell Berry, "To Think of the Life of a Man," *Collected Poems* (San Francisco: North Point Press, 1985).

16. Jerry Mander, *In the Absence of the Sacred: The Failure of Technology and the Survival of the Indian Nations* (San Francisco: Sierra Club Books, 1991).

17. David McClelland, *The Achieving Society* (New York: Free Press, 1967).

18. Michael Maccoby, *Why Work? Leading the New Generation* (New York: Simon & Schuster, 1988).

19. Robert Frager, *Who Am I? Personality Types for Self-Discovery* (New York: Tarcher/Putnam, 1994).

20. Kathleen Hurley and Theodore Dobson, *My Best Self* (New York: HarperCollins, 1993).

21. Carol Pearson and Sharon Seivert, *Heroes at Work,* Workbook available by mail order from Mt. Vernon Institute on Women and Work, Mt. Vernon College; Carol Pearson, *Awakening the Heroes Within* (San Francisco: HarperCollins, 1991); Carol Pearson, *Magic at Work* (New York: Doubleday, 1995).

22. Richard Saul Wurman, op. cit.

23. All the exercises in the remainder of this chapter are inspired by the work of Joanna Macy in helping people enhance their sense of connectedness and responsibility in the world. See her *Despair and Personal Power in the Nuclear Age* (Philadelphia: New Society Publishers, 1983) or *World as Lover, World as Self* (San Francisco: Parallax Press, 1992).

24. The lifeline exercise is also used by Charles Handy in *The Age of Unreason,* and modified as the "Nature Line" by psychologist Gerald Bailey of North Easton, Mass.

Step 6

1. Rick Jarow, "The Anti-Career Workshop," presentation at Interface Institute, Cambridge, MA, 1994.

2. Richard N. Bolles, *What Color Is Your Parachute?,* appendix, "How to Find Your Mission in Life."

3. Dominguez and Robin, *Your Money or Your Life?*

4. Mary Scott and Howard Rothman, *Companies with a Conscience* (New York: Birch Lane Press, 1992).

5. Gene Dalton and Paul Thompson, *Novations: Strategies for Career Management,* self-published in Provo, UT, 1993.

6. Thanks to Matt Nicodemus for developing this exercise.

Step 7

1. Natalie Goldberg, *Long Quiet Highway: Waking Up in America* (New York: Bantam, 1993).

2. Quoted by Mark Sommer in *Living in Freedom: The Exhilaration and Anguish of Prague's Second Spring* (San Francisco: Mercury House, 1992), 236.

3. Marsha Sinetar, *Do What You Love, The Money Will Follow* (New York: Dell, 1987), 15.

Step 8

1. Max DePree, *Leadership Is an Art* (New York: Doubleday Currency, 1989).

2. Natalie Goldberg, *Long Quiet Highway,* op. cit.

3. Jim Forrest, "Merton and Joy," in Gerald Twomey, ed., *Thomas Merton: Prophet in the Belly of a Paradox* (Boston: Paulist Press, 1978).

Step 9

1. Natalie Goldberg, *Long Quiet Highway,* op. cit.

2. "Women Composing Their Careers," presentation at Harvard Graduate School of Education Seminar, 1992.

Step 10

1. Thanks to futurist Barbara Marx Hubbard for helping to popularize the term "cocreation."

2. "Workplace Flexibility: A Research Report." Work/Family Directions, Boston, 1993.

3. Bob Baker, "Hire Power," *Los Angeles Times Magazine* (April 26, 1992): 8.

4. S. Joseph Hagermayer, "For a Glass Factory, an Unusual Ally," *Philadelphia Inquirer,* Aug. 6, 1989.

5. Julia Lieblich, "Managing a Manic-Depressive," *Harvard Business Review* (May–June 1994): 20–32.

6. Daniel Levinson, *The Seasons of a Man's Life* (New York: Ballantine, 1986).

7. Tedd Saunders and Loretta McGovern, *The Bottom Line of Green Is Black* (San Francisco: Harper, 1994).

8. Nonprofit Academic Centers Council research reported in *Eagle Connector* (1994, no. 1).

9. Joel Makower, ed., *Green Business Letter* (Feb. 1994), Tilden Press, Washington, D.C.

10. Marlise Simons, "Belgians Turn 'Madness' of Consumer Waste to Profit," *International Herald Tribune* (Jan. 5, 1994).

11. For details contact: New Society Publishers, 4527 Springfield Ave., Philadelphia, PA 19143.

12. Associated Press, "Be Kind to Others," *The China News* (Nov. 7, 1993).

13. Lawrence Otis Graham, *The Best Companies for Minorities* (New York: Plume, 1993).

14. Geoffrey Bellman, *Getting Things Done When You Are Not in Charge* (San Francisco: Berrett-Kohler, 1993).

15. Gareth Morgan, *Images of Organization* (Newbury Park, CA: Sage Publications, 1986).

16. Peter Block, *The Empowered Manager* (San Francisco: Jossey-Bass, 1987).

17. Francis Wilkinson, "Power to the People: Hazel O'Leary Rewires the Department of Energy," *Rolling Stone.* March 24, 1994, New York.

18. Gifford Pinchot, *Intrapreneuring* (New York: Harper & Row, 1985).

19. Donald Soeken and Karen Soeken, "A Survey of Whistleblowers: Their Stressors and Coping Mechanisms" (March 1987), self-published report available from 15702 Tasa Place, Laurel, MD 20707. See also Donald Soeken, "J'Accuse," *Psychology Today* (Aug. 1986).

20. Jim Morris, "Clamp Down: The Silencing of Nuclear Industry Workers," *Houston Chronicle,* special edition (December 1993).

21. *Courage Without Martyrdom: A Survival Guide for Whistleblowers,* Government Accountability Project, 810 First Street, N.W., Suite 630, Washington, D.C. 20002.

22. Jeff Goldberg, "Truth and Consequences," *Omni* (Nov. 1990).

23. An eye-opener on this subject is Donald L. Barlett and James B. Steele's *America: What Went Wrong?* (Kansas City, KA: Andrews and McMeel, 1992).

24. Paul Hawken, *The Ecology of Commerce* (San Francisco: Harper-Business, 1993).

25. "Americans Are Willing to Sacrifice to Reduce Pollution, They Say," *Wall Street Journal* (April 20, 1990).

26. Eban B. Goodstein, *Jobs and the Environment: The Myth of a National Trade-Off* (Washington, D.C.: Economic Policy Institute, 1994).

27. Christopher Flavin for Worldwatch Institute, *Saving the Planet,* N.Y.: Norton, 1991.

28. Dan Lacey, *Your Rights in the Workplace* (Berkeley: Nolo Press, 1992).

29. "Mexican Firings Violate NAFTA, Unions Charge," *Solidarity,* United Auto Workers' magazine (Mar. 1994).

30. Edward O. Welles, "It's Not the Same America," *Inc.* (May 1994).

31. Dave Johnson and Adrienne Burke, "Red Flags Are Popping Up," *Industrial Safety and Hygiene News* (May 1994).

32. "Paying to Lose Our Jobs" (New York: National Labor Committee in Support of Worker and Human Rights in Central America, 1992).

33. Len Krimerman, *Grassroots Economic Organizing* newsletter (Sept. 1993).

34. Dave Elsila, "A Child's Crusade Against Sweater Sweatshops," *Solidarity* (September 1994).

Acknowledgments

One otherwise forgettable day in 1990, the phone rang. On the line was Matt Nicodemus, an activist with an idea, looking for a writer. Matt had been involved in spearheading an innovative campaign called the Graduation Pledge of Social and Environmental Responsibility in Job Decisions. The Pledge is a ceremony of commitment which had by then been integrated into commencements at over two dozen campuses. Wherever the Pledge was planted, students responded, "Of course we want to make this commitment. But how do we know which employers are really compatible with our values?"

Matt launched the project that became this book. For two years, he played a major role in research and project management and attracted countless volunteer assistants with his singular charisma. Finally, Matt heeded the call of his own "work in the world." He took a leap and landed in Asia as an English teacher and consultant on corporate social responsibility.

Joe Maizlish, a therapist in Los Angeles, was also part of the original team. Thanks to Joe for his stubborn, creative nonviolence, and for his fine interview with engineer Howard Newman.

David Albert gave us invaluable early feedback on the idea and, through his writing on Gandhian economics, challenged us with a high standard of integrity.

Miranda Ring, a longtime friend and respected counselor, was generous with both time and resources as my guide into the world of career counseling.

Phyllis Stein at Radcliffe Career Services offered crucial support by sponsoring an early support group. Numerous career counselors on campuses and in professional career centers let me develop this material by offering talks and workshops to their clients.

Fred Friedman, Sanford Lewis, and Charles Nicodemus were supportive guides in the process of investigating employers, as were Alice Tepper Marlin and the staff at the Council on Economic Priorities.

Thanks for capable research assistance go to Louise Brewster and the rest of "Matt's Gang" in Arcata; Avery Kamilla, Marie Favorini, and Michelle Decker; and Ross Donald of Renewable News Network for resources and friendship.

During this four-year project, I interviewed well over a hundred people about their work histories, the dilemmas they faced, and the resources that had helped them. Some of their stories are included explicitly in the book; all of them have shaped my thinking and have been alive in my mind during the writing. The same is true for many resource people who have shared their expertise on workplace trends and social change. Thanks to each of you for your time, openness, and thoughtful wrestling with hard questions.

Without the feedback of numerous reviewers, this book would have contained some stunning gaffes and omissions. Thanks to the friends and strangers who accepted my lunch invitations and listened to my monologue. Special gratitude to Deborah Knox, Sue Wolff, Michele Vitti-Lawton, Damon Reed, Sally Crocker, Sarah Conn, Kit Hayes, Malachy Shaw-Jones, and Nancy Costikyan for their feedback on the content; to Madeleine Schwab, Chris Lyons, Janet Levin, and John Goodrich for trying out many of the exercises; and to Dalya Massachi, a talented journalist, for her editorial assistance. Julia Lieblich urged me not to "dumb it down." I hope I took that advice to heart.

While the exercises in this book were being developed, I was supported financially by grants from several foundations and individual donors. These include the Foundation for Deep Ecology, the Jack and Pauline Freeman Foundation, the Sisters of Notre Dame, and the Sisters of St. Joseph. Heartfelt thanks to you all and especially to Lucius Walker and Ellen Bernstein at the Interreligious Foundation for Community Organization for their sponsorship.

Leslie Meredith and Brian Tart, at Bantam, are an editorial team I've been proud to work with. They prove that sharp minds and good humor do coexist. Tim Seldes and Jenny Dunham at Russell & Volkening have been supportive advocates at every stage.

Friends and family put up with the usual writer stuff with more than the usual grace. To them, and to my tireless, loyal, feisty, creative, schmoozy, glorious writers' group, much love.

Index

T

ABOUT THE AUTHOR

Melissa Everett is a writer, speaker, and workshop leader who works to inspire and assist people as they build careers that reflect their highest social and environmental values. Ms. Everett has built an extensive resource collection on emerging career fields as well as social and environmental ethics in the private and public sectors. These resources and methods are the basis for this book. Her previous books are *Breaking Ranks* (Philadelphia: New Society Publishers, 1989) and *Bearing Witness, Building Bridges* (Philadelphia: New Society Publishers, 1986).